Frontline Dram

Adapting Classics

Emma by Michael Fry, ~~~~~~~~~~~~~ **Fanny Hill** by April De Angelis, **Great Expectations** by John Clifford, **The Mill on the Floss** by Helen Edmundson

Frontline Drama 4 is part of an anthology series of the most original, exciting drama and new writing on theatre in the nineties.

Emma
'Michael Fry has dramatised a classic novel to show how the gloriously eclectic medium of theatre can lend its own particular charm and insight into the work of a famous writer . . . Jane Austen herself would surely applaud.'
Time Out

Fanny Hill
'April De Angelis has taken John Cleland's scandalous 18th-century novel and given it flesh, blood and a dramatic life of its own.' *Guardian*

Great Expectations
'John Clifford's script shows his customary arresting dialogue, his command of emotional climax and his sense of tension . . . few adaptations can have so proclaimed, vaunted and exulted in sheer theatricality.' *Scotsman*

The Mill on the Floss
'With rare theatrical vibrancy, Helen Edmundson's free adaptation distils the essence of George Eliot's feminist novel.' *Evening Standard*

Frontline Drama 4
Adapting Classics

Jane Austen's *Emma*
Michael Fry

John Cleland's *The Life and Times of Fanny Hill*
April De Angelis

Charles Dickens's *Great Expectations*
John Clifford

George Eliot's *The Mill on the Floss*
Helen Edmundson

Introduced by Michael Fry

Methuen Drama

First published in Great Britain in 1996
by Methuen Drama
an imprint of Reed International Books Ltd
Michelin House, 81 Fulham Road, London SW3 6RB
and distributed in the United States of America
by Heinemann, a division of Reed Elsevier Inc.
361 Hanover Street, Portsmouth, New Hampshire NH 03801 3959

ISBN: 0 413 70490 4

A CIP catalogue record for this book is available at the British Library

Typeset by Wilmaset Ltd, Birkenhead, Wirral
Printed by Cox & Wyman Ltd, Reading, Berkshire

Caution
All rights whatsoever in these plays are strictly reserved. Application for
performance etc. should be addressed to:
Emma, Micheline Steinberg Playwrights' Agent, Suite 409, Triumph House, 191
Regent Street, London W1R 7WF.
The Life and Times of Fanny Hill, Casarotto Ramsay Ltd, National House, 60–66
Wardour Street, London W1V 4ND.
Great Expectations: amateurs in English throughout the world (except in North
America): Nick Hern Books, 14 Larden Road, London W3 7ST; professionals in any
medium and in any language throughout the world (and by stock and amateur
companies in North America): Alan Brodie Representation, 211 Piccadilly, London
W1V 9LD.
The Mill on the Floss: amateurs in English throughout the world (except in North
America): Nick Hern Books, 14 Larden Road, London W3 7ST; stock and amateur
performance in the United States of America and Canada: The Dramatic Publishing
Company, PO Box 129, Woodstock, Illinois 60098; professionals in any medium and
in any language throughout the world (excluding stock performance in North
America): The Agency, 24 Pottery Lane, Holland Park, London W11 4LZ.
Applications should be made before rehearsals begin. No performance may be given
unless a licence has been obtained.

Contents

Publisher's Note

Frontline Drama 4 is a continuation of a series of three new-play volumes previously published by Methuen under the title *Frontline Intelligence*. Upcoming volumes of *Frontline Drama* will continue to focus on new, original plays as well as broadening the series brief to encompass adaptations and foreign plays in English-language translations. However, we also intend to alternate these new-play volumes from time to time with polemical ones which look at themes and issues affecting the British theatre today.

As a publisher, Methuen Drama prides itself on encompassing all drama from classical to contemporary, so this edition of *Frontline Drama 4*, on the theme 'Adapting Classics', could not be a better way to chart the new direction of this series.

Michael Earley
Publisher
Methuen Drama

Introduction

Upstart Crows

Adaptation is hardly a recent phenomenon. Drama predates the novel by a good many centuries and it could be claimed that Greek tragedy, consisting, as it did, largely of a new perspective on a pre-existing story or myth, was a precursory form of stage adaptation. In today's more source-aware climate, *Othello* would probably be billed as 'by Giraldi Cinthio, adapted for the stage by William Shakespeare' (Cinthio's collection of tales, *Hecatommithi*, having been published some forty years earlier). In fact, Shakespeare's nefarious title of 'upstart crow', given by his contemporary, Robert Greene, for 'beautifying feathers not his own' refers precisely to Shakespeare's garnering of other writers' work for his own plays, although he was hardly unique amongst Elizabethan and Jacobean playwrights in so doing. The 'upstart crow's' alterations are usually so radical, and so superior to their source, that adaptation is rather a tame word for his accomplishments, but it sometimes helps to stay the denigrating forces when they are reminded that the first great adaptor was the Bard.

Adaptations were immensely popular, but less great, during the Victorian period. The theatrical revival, resulting from a rapid growth in the population and improvements in public transport, meant that the new, rather dull, dramatists were forced to churn out plays to an impossibly tight schedule and they found it easier (as Vincent Crummles reminds us in *Nicholas Nickleby*) to translate a French melodrama or adapt a recent novel. There were consequently over 200 different adaptations of Dickens's novels alone during this period, a quarter of which were *Nicholas Nickleby*. The copyright laws of the time prevented Dickens from taking action against the many unauthorised versions, and the plays were often staged only five or six days after publication or – worse – before the novel had even finished its serialisation. This so enraged Dickens that he started to develop a narrative method (such as the first-person tense or complex time schemes) to circumvent any potential adaptation. He even changed the ending of *The Old Curiosity Shop*, to spite the hack adaptors who thought they had predicted it.

It is possible that this plethora of poor, nineteenth-century adaptations is partly to blame for the prejudice in some quarters (frequently journalistic) about adaptation on today's stages. The same intolerance seems not to occur in film, where more than half of all screenplays are adapted from other fictional sources, and nor does it pertain to opera, where contemporary librettists are often as reliant on earlier root material as their more bruited predecessors.

A recent survey of the annual repertory reports from British theatres (the same statistics do not, as yet, apply to their American counterparts) shows how, over the last few years, the number of new and classical plays presented has decreased, in favour of a huge profusion of adaptations. The reasons for this seem pretty self-evident. With the steady erosion of their grant-aid, and hence a reduction in their number of actor weeks (the number of actors that can be employed over the year) the theatres are able to offer less and less of the classical repertoire, there being a limit to the amount of smart doubling that can be achieved on a conspicuously large stage. New plays ought to fare better, since most contemporary playwrights are realistic enough to write for diminutive casts, but new plays are considered to be (and sometimes proven to be) risky box-office – unknown titles by unknown writers failing to woo large enough chunks of equivocal, cash-starved audiences.

So the theatre managements have come to rely on adaptations, together with the annual Christmas attraction, to balance their books. They can satisfy the audience's desire for something known and classical (the known-er the better) and they can satisfy their consciences by commissioning living playwrights to draft them. Some fairly illustrious playwrights, novelists and poets have all essayed the genre (among them David Edgar, Christopher Hampton, Fay Weldon and Liz Lochhead) and whilst there may be more kudos for the callow playwright in having an original play produced over a four-week run at the Bush or the Royal Court, s/he may find it ultimately more lucrative to have an adaptation produced at five or six of the larger repertory theatres.

Performers, as well as audiences have, additionally, become rather partial to adaptation. The Victorian novelists, in particular, created an inimitable pageant of characters to play, wrote glorious dialogue and told mesmerising stories. The actors usually play more than one part, and the play can be written to order, to suit length, budget, cast number, male-female ratio (there is a happy bias towards female characters in much of Victorian fiction), gender irregularities (always fun) and the directors and designers, composers and choreographers can all vaunt their resourcefulness and brilliance. For some playwrights, books are excellent raw material to work from, because so much of the groundwork is already in place and he or she can focus on developing an innovative style and approach.

This introduction, whilst partial, makes no overall plea for or against the art of adaptation – except to surmise that it *is* an art-form. Instead, it will try to argue that when adaptations are dashed off ingenuously for purely commercial reasons, they tend to lack dramatic merit and motives are questionable. However, when a novel is adapted (and produced) affectionately and imaginatively by a writer who has equal regard for his or her source material as for the dramatic medium, the ensuing play often celebrates the theatrical spirit at its most resplendent, and transcends any criticism of a parasitic nature.

*

The adaptations selected for this volume are all taken from novels generally considered to be 'classics' of their kind – mostly Victorian classics. François Truffaut once suggested that 'a masterpiece is something that has already found its perfection of form, its definitive form' and whilst a study of these four plays may not entirely discredit his remark, it is to be hoped that, in their own right, they show a sense of animation which both reflects and broadens the original material. (Actually, it is to be hoped that they *do* discredit his remark.)

There are two basic hurdles facing the would-be adaptor: does he stick closely to the original novel and risk an over-literary, reverential and possibly protracted play, or does he adapt it more liberally and risk changing its emphasis, rewriting some of the text and attracting the critical ire of the audience that knows and loves the book. Unless the adaptor has the luxury of [David Edgar's] *Nicholas Nickleby*'s eight and a half hour time-frame, he is unlikely to be able to reproduce every detail and character from the original and in any case a reader's response to a book is inescapably subjective, so whatever the adaptor does is going to displease someone. If the novelist suggests that the heroine is tall, with long, dark hair, then it would be silly, and provocative, to cast a short, curly-haired blonde, but on the whole, since the playwright is never going to be able to produce a facsimile of the book on the stage, he may as well aim for what he, himself, considers its most salient points. (He might, at the same time, do well to consider which of the three main types of adaptive audience he is writing for: those who know the book well (and probably adore it); those who haven't read it, but might afterwards; and those who haven't read it, are unlikely ever to read it, but are prepared to have a pleasant night out all the same.)

Criticism of adaptations, whether favourable or adverse, frequently centres on their 'fidelity' to the original novel. But fidelity is itself a rather arbitrary word in this context. Does fidelity occur only when the adaptation uses the same characters, contexts, motivations, events and perspectives as the novel? Does fidelity exist only when the author's words, and no others, are used? (Is the playwright able to mimic the novelist's style and write a kind of pastiche Austen or Dickens when necessary, and does that count?) Is the purpose of the adaptation to give the audience an experience analogous to a reading of the novel, with the audience going on a similar journey as the reader, or can it recreate judiciously selected aspects of it? How much, in short, should the novel be simply the raw material for the play? How much, in short(er), should it be *adaptive*, and how much can it be *interpretative*?

There is a danger in the adaptor making an overly personal statement, or taking too firm a stance, in his play, in case he starts to distort the basic tone and premise of the original, or, worse still, starts to challenge the entire thesis on which the novel is based. Whatever the adaptor chooses to leave in, or to omit, will tell us his response to the book, and he should be careful not to be over-partisan in his selectivity. Adaptations seem to date faster than novels or plays precisely because what are considered the most relevant aspects of the story for one generation, will be very different for the next. Perspectives change and so does the nature of theatre itself. Two chairs and a backdrop are a perfectly acceptable setting for today's productions, but would have been impossible a hundred, fifty or even thirty years back. Thomas Hardy's own adaptation of *Tess of the d'Urbervilles*, for example, seems inadequate today, partly because he was not an especially gifted dramatist (though a jolly good poet and novelist), but also because the Victorian theatre required authentic scenery, a box-set, sentimentality and no doubling of parts. Hardy had, therefore, to limit his number of characters, omitting some fairly crucial ones, confine himself to just four scenes (all interior) and hence devalue much of the story.

The ability of an audience to accept direct narrative, which would have helped Hardy, and others, has only surfaced in recent years, partly thanks to the pioneering work of Shared Experience during the late seventies. Earlier adaptors had to fatally reallocate important thoughts and outlines into the mouths of their characters. In a 1940s, American, version of *Emma*, some of Jane Austen's most sardonic prose is transferred, unsuccessfully, into the mouth of the title character: 'Why is it so much worse that Harriet should be in love with Mr Knightley than with Mr Churchill? Oh, no, good heavens! No it cannot be! It hits me with the speed of an arrow! I am in love with Mr Knightley myself!'

The novel and the drama have similarities, but they are

manifestly different literary forms. The Oxford English
Dictionary uses the words 'action' and 'story' in its definitions
of both of them, and both are concerned with a plot, carried
on by characters who convey information partly, or entirely,
through dialogue. They both require exposition in a way that
poetry, for example, does not, and both aim, on the whole, to
give a semblance – or the delusion – of real life. Conrad, in his
preface to the unfortunately-titled, *The Nigger of Narcissus*,
writes: 'My task which I am trying to achieve, is by the power
of the written word, to make you hear, to make you feel, above
all, to make you *see*.' And few novelists, or dramatists, would
disagree with the metaphorical implications of that
explanation.

The differences between the novel and the play are more
numerous. The novel is a private experience, read by one
person in a location and at a time of his or her own choosing. It
can be read in one sitting (or lying), or it can take a few days,
weeks and even months. The reader can refer back to earlier
chapters if he so wishes. He can skip a few pages if he finds
them unilluminating. He can tell how long the novel is going
to be and can also, as Jane Austen points out in a narrative
aside at the end of *Northanger Abbey*, see the 'tell-tale
compression of the pages before [him]'. The reader makes his
own interpretation of events and conjures up his own image of
the characters and the settings.

The audience member has a very different responding
effect during his two to three hours traffic of the stage. He is
involved in a communal experience – an event – generally in
darkness. The audience tends to react simultaneously,
laughing or jumping or applauding together. (People
reading alone tend not to laugh hysterically.) There is a fixed
starting and finishing time and sometimes an interval. There
are no chapter breaks (obviously), although there may be
scenic equivalents. Whilst the audience members may be
allowed to draw their own conclusions about a character's
behaviour, the choices are less arbitrary than they would be
on the page, as they are watching real people (real actors)
doing actual things.

Novels tend to be written in the past tense, plays in the

present. It is inevitably 'now' on stage, and the passing of time has to be handled very prudently by the playwright. 'It was a bright autumn Sunday, sixteen years after Silas Marner had found his new treasure on the hearth' is something that is not easily transferrable to the stage.] The novel tells the story; in the play the story has to tell itself. Description and depiction are not the same thing (even though they sound similar). Aristotle's definition of *mimesis* and *diegesis* – showing and telling – is rather crucial to an understanding of how adaptations differ from novels. A novelist can describe the background details, the characters' motivations, jump from location to location, whereas the dramatist has to let the actions speak for themselves, and to ensure, with the director, that the audience doesn't miss anything (miss a trick, one could say about *Fanny Hill*). We are told – we can 'see' – in a novel what we could not possibly know in a real situation. In a play we are sometimes cognizant of what certain characters are *not* (dramatic irony), but we can only know what a character is really thinking if he breaks into soliloquy.

The advantage that the stage *does* have over the novel is simultaneity. The drama may not skip as easily from one location to another, but it can present two or more different occurrences at the same time. Drama also communicates faster than fiction, so we save a lot of time, and pages, not having to be told how a character looked – we can see it for ourselves; and an actor's face can be propitiously expressive.

The American critic, Brander Matthews, suggested that the adaptor should never read the novel itself, but simply be told the story and handle the situations afresh. This seems slightly nonsensical since one of the major challenges facing the would-be dramatist is that the classical works of fiction are not simply about telling a *story* (anyone can tell a story), it is about the *telling* of the story – in other words, about the author's style and authorial voice. (Aristotle: 'For it is not enough to know *what* we ought to say, we must say it *as* we ought'.) Flaubert considered that the novelist should be like 'God in creation' – felt but not seen; other novelists, such as Fielding or Thackeray, thought just the opposite and frequently intrude upon their story to tell you what they think

– sometimes taking whole chapters in which to do so. Austen,
Dickens and Eliot are harder to construe, since their
narrative is singularly sophisticated and works on
innumerable levels. (E.M. Forster speaks of George Eliot's
'massiveness – she has no nicety of style'.)

What all novelists *do* have is a point of view, usually
expressed in some form or other by the narrator figure, and
before the adaptor can begin work on his play, he must try to
establish what the narrative line is: Who is speaking to the
reader? A character, an author, a presence? From what
perspective are they telling the story? How reliable, or ironic,
is the narrative? How judgmental? Is the narrator a first-
person narrator? If so, how involved in the story is/was he?
How aware is he that he is telling a story? The handling of
narration is one of the most important decisions the adaptor
has to make and once he has verified the source novelist's
approach, there are further questions which he has to ask
himself: 'Am I going to retain the first-person narrator figure
in my play [if there is one]? If yes, how much a part of the
action will he or she be? If no, who is going to take over the
narrator's function? Another character? The entire cast? Will
they all take turns to play him? (In Giles Havergal's very
witty adaptation of *Travels with My Aunt*, the three main
actors take it in turns to play the first-person narrator figure of
Henry Pulling.) Or will he dispense with narration
altogether, judging that there is no place for it in drama?

Fleeting acknowledgements should be made to the
contributions of the actors and the production team in the
genesis of an adaptation. One further difference between the
novel and the play is that the latter is a highly collaborative
affair, and the audience will be guided by the performers, as
well as the dramaturgy, in their reactions to the piece. In
drama, what is *not* said is as important as what *is* said and the
inner feelings and thoughts of the characters in the novel can
often be successfully conveyed through the obvious
subtextual reaction of the actor.

*

The four adaptations selected by Methuen for this volume were all initially produced by small to mid-scale touring companies. Three of them have since been revived by various repertory theatres for fixed runs with large(r) production budgets, but the flexibility necessitated by their original, pliable stagings undoubtedly affected their composition and resourcefulness. Each of them offers useful examples of the concepts referred to above.

April De Angelis' version of *Fanny Hill*, whilst the most freely adapted of the four novels in terms of language and tone, is, paradoxically, the most faithful to the basic storyline of the original. Hardly any details of the narrative are excluded (there are, admittedly, far less intricasies of plot in Cleland's writing than in that of Austen, Dickens or Eliot) although a new character called Swallow (!) is introduced.

Like the adaptation of *Emma*, this *Fanny Hill* is a kind of meta-theatre – it draws attention to its own theatricality. Instead of two, longish letters to an unidentified 'Madam', as in the novel, Fanny's story is here played out by two young prostitutes and a client, with an older, shrewder Fanny offering stage directions and acting the mature roles. This Fanny seems not to have been granted the improbably happy ending which the novel's Fanny is, accentuating the contemporary viewpoint. Whereas Cleland seems, at times, almost to celebrate the working life of a prostitute and ignores its sleazier sides, De Angelis introduces the notions of smallpox, the pox and the necessity of eliminating unwanted children by murdering them.

The sexual acts obviously cannot be as explicit as they are in the novel, which was censored for two hundred years (although Fanny's name is made more obvious), so other dramatic metaphors and gestural displays are used. The modern vernacular and the device of the onstage cellist developing into an active participant, constantly remind the audience that they are watching, not a re-enactment of the novel, but a highly subjective, contemporary synopsis.

John Clifford's adaptation of *Great Expectations*, using, almost exclusively, Dickens's own words, tells the story of Pip's moral development and, like the novel, tells it from a cognizant and reflective perspective, through the character of the first-person narrator himself. Clifford even accentuates the retrospective tone, by introducing all of the other characters (some dead) during the opening scene, and allowing them a smattering of their later lines. He initially adds Estella as co-narrator (she is the only other member of the cast to play just one character) but it remains Pip's story, and he is on stage almost throughout.

The adaptation is very succinct and trenchant, the stage directions are simple and clear and Dickens's language is pared down to a point where it becomes, at times, almost poetic. The flavour and the wit adroitly retain the atmosphere of a Dickensian novel, and whilst certain characters and plot details are omitted, the main thrust of Pip's haunted tale is preserved. Clifford puts a slightly different emphasis on the ending of the story, reverting to Dickens's less ambiguous, original last chapter.

Helen Edmundson's realisation of *The Mill on the Floss* retains much of George Eliot's dialogue (the accents and the spelling especially) but contains none of the narrative – the story is told entirely scenically. It is a particularly subjective adaptation, but remains unquestionably true to the spirit and premise of the novel, even clarifying some of the story – the opening ducking of the witch, for example, giving added poignancy to the ending.

The splitting of the protagonist into three works in a different way from Giles Havergal's analogous division in *Travels with My Aunt*. Instead of spasmodically changing the actor playing the part, Maggie is here divided very specifically and chronologically into First Maggie, Second Maggie and Third Maggie, metamorphosing, in front of us, from one to the other at key moments in the novel. Bringing back earlier Maggies, so that sometimes all three are on stage together, fighting and debating, is an ingenious way of transferring Maggie's inner turmoil *diegesis* into stage *mimesis*. The other characters are dealt with diversely: as in the novel, Philip, Lucy and Stephen are treated objectively (Stephen Guest in the flesh becomes especially credible) but gentle fun is poked at Mrs Tulliver and the aunts and uncles become even more caricatured (the first production exaggerating this further still).

All of these adaptations call for inventive direction, but *The Mill on the Floss* requires a particular use of the theatrical medium to generate its impact: the use of lighting and sound to create environment, most crucially of an aquatic kind; and the services of a movement director to conceive the stylised games, gestures and balletic ending.

My own adaptation of *Emma* does not so much require theatricality, as draw attention to it. Jane Austen, of all novelists, seems particularly suited to the page rather than the stage. Dialogue constitutes only about a half of her words, and it is usually what is *not* said by the characters that contributes to her style and genius.

In searching for a dramatic structure which could retain the tone, and some of the narrative, of the novel, it struck me that theatre was, in fact, very much a part of the life of middle-class Georgian England, and particularly, by all accounts, the Austen family. Jane Austen's letters speak of many visits to the theatre and 'private theatricals', which play such a significant part in *Mansfield Park*, were performed with great regularity by the Austen family itself, in the rectory dining-room or the barn.

Sarah's 'Emma' After Jane, as the adaptation was originally called, takes its lead from just this sort of activity. Five young people, in Georgian attire, decide to stage, rather than simply read, a version of *Emma*. They strangely manifest similar traits to some of the characters in the novel and there is a great deal of rivalry and in-fighting, particularly for the playing of certain roles. The narrative is shared between them and carefully assigned to Sarah (who plays Emma and provides the commentary which is supposedly Emma describing herself), Jane (who gently mocks some of Emma's lack of self-insight) and Elizabeth (who provides the more brutally insightful observations which are generally recognisable as the author's own). The dramatic method is intended to provide an ironic distance from the story at all times and the actors are either the characters in the novel, or the young people in the room, or occasionally both.

*

Anthony Burgess thought that 'brilliant adaptations are nearly always of fiction of the second or third class'. Since it will, presumably, be hard to dispute the first-class nature of the four novels chosen here, it remains for the dear reader, (or the lovely actor), to assess the impact, fidelity and 'brilliance' of the adaptations that follow.

Michael Fry, 1996

Emma

**adapted from Jane Austen
by Michael Fry**

Some Notes on the Staging

Everything that is needed for the presentation of the play-within-the-play should be found in the cupboards and boxes in the attic-room in which the play is set. In the original production the designer developed the idea of a wardrobe which, when turned around, was found to be backless and very suitable for the inside of a carriage or the entrance to the Bates' more modest home. Most of the other acting areas were created with chairs and tables, although a slightly raised upstage area usefully doubled as exteriors. Props were sought, with varying degrees of success, when called for, and (minimal) costume accessories in the shape of bonnets, shawls, jackets and dog collars were found hanging on rails and coat-stands.

Despite the fairly extensive doubling and the nature of the play, the characterisation should rarely border on the caricature, and whilst there are sundry, jocular interventions, for the most part the scenes themselves are taken seriously by the actors, and played relatively straight. All five actors are obviously on stage throughout, either sitting at the side, watching, or enthusiastically moving their 'scenery'.

M.F.

Emma was first performed, in a version entitled *Sarah's 'Emma' After Jane*, by Great Eastern Stage. It opened at the Trinity Arts Centre, Gainsborough, on 17 September 1990 prior to a national tour and a run at the Battersea Arts Centre, London. The cast was as follows:

Sarah	Fiona McAlpine
Jane	Katherine Fry
Elizabeth	Sally Mortemore
William	Dominic Gray
Robert	Michael Gould

Directed by Michael Fry
Designed by Caroline Elliott
Costumes by Arabella White
Music by Matthew Scott
Choreography by Sheila Irwin
Lighting by Graham McCluskey

Characters

Sarah, *whose house they are in*
Jane, *her best friend*
Elizabeth, *not quite such a good friend*
William, *Sarah's brother*
Robert, *his friend*

Characters in the story they perform:
Sarah *plays* **Emma**
Jane *plays* **Harriet Smith**, **Miss Bates**, **Isabella** *and* **Mrs Elton**
Elizabeth *plays* **Jane Fairfax**, **Mrs Weston** *and* **Mr Woodhouse**
William *plays* **Frank Churchill**, **Mr Elton**, **Mr John Knightley** *and* **Mr Martin**
Robert *plays* **Mr Knightley**, **Mr Weston** *and* **Mrs Bates**

Setting

An upstairs room in Sarah's parents' house – a sort of box-room or attic, used on occasions, as here, for 'private theatricals'. The furniture, costumes and props are all found (or made do with) in the room, in boxes, wardrobes etc.

Prologue

A piano sonata is heard in the distance. It increases in volume. The curtain rises.

A dusty attic.

Sarah *enters and looks around, enthralled. She sits down at the piano and accompanies the sonata.* **Jane** *enters and takes* **Sarah***'s place at the piano.* **Sarah** *moves away to investigate the contents of a wardrobe. She might blow the dust off a shawl or a bonnet.* **Elizabeth** *enters and moves over to the piano as* **Jane** *gets up to look inside a chest. The sonata comes to an end just as* **Elizabeth** *sits down to play. She looks surprised.*

Sarah   You see! This is the very place for it. It will suit our purposes admirably.

Jane   But where is the stage?

Sarah   We have no need of a *stage*. Look! All the scenery is already here!

Jane   We must have a curtain! There is very little sense in a play without a curtain. Robert and William will snigger at us.

Elizabeth   We haven't *selected* a play yet.

Sarah (*opening a large chest*)   Here you are!

She takes out a few books, and hands them around.

There are plenty to choose from!

Jane   We are rather limited in number. Even with Robert and William.

Elizabeth   That is, if Robert deigns to join us, after all.

Sarah   We shan't give him house-room unless he joins us.

Jane   I do hope I get to play a love scene with him.

Elizabeth   You're not responsible enough to play a love scene.

Sarah   I think *I'll* play the love scene with him. You can have William.

Jane   I don't want William. *You* do the love scene with William!

Sarah   I'm not doing a love scene with my brother! Mamma wouldn't like that at all!

This seems incontrovertible.

Elizabeth (*looking at the first book*)   *The Tragedy of Matilda*, by Thomas Franklin.

Sarah   I've never heard of it!

Jane (*picking up another copy*)   *The Rivals!* That's awfully amusing. I saw that in town last year. (*Significantly.*) Robert's family took me.

Sarah   *Lovers Vows*! They perform that in *Mansfield Park*. I could be Amelia.

Elizabeth   It's not a very seemly piece. We played it last year – at Robert's house! We had to grasp one another around the waist!

Jane (*taking **Sarah***'s *copy*)   Well, I'm not playing anyone called Agatha Fribourg!

Sarah (*reading another play*)   *The Wonder*, by Susannah Centlivre. 'Don Lopez!' 'How d'ye, Frederick? I hope Antonio's out of danger. Your son, Felix, is safe, I hope.' Who *are* all these people?

Elizabeth   They're all men!

Jane   It sounds far too confusing!

Elizabeth   *Sir Charles Grandison*, a play, by Jane Austen. Oh! That might be of interest. (*She reads.*) 'Sir Harcourt: "I wish women were not quite so delicate, with all their fits and faints!".' No, I don't think so.

She throws it back in the chest.

Sarah (*picking up another book*)   *Emma*!

Jane   Emma who?

Sarah   Jane Austen's *Emma*!

Elizabeth   It's not a play.

Sarah   It could be. And it's better than *Sir Charles Grandison*.

Jane   Well, who would play Emma then?

Elizabeth   I think I'd make an exceptional Emma!

Jane   You're too tall. I'd be a very sympathetic Emma.

Sarah   Too short.

Jane *and* **Elizabeth**   Who does that leave then?

Sarah (*inarguably*)   My idea. My house. My Emma.

Jane *and* **Elizabeth**   Naturally . . .

They each pick up a copy.

Act One

Sarah (*reading*)   Emma Woodhouse, handsome, clever and rich, with a comfortable home and happy disposition, seemed to unite some of the best blessings of existence and had lived nearly twenty-one years in the world with very little to distress or vex her.

Jane   She was the youngest of the two daughters of a most affectionate, indulgent father, and had, in consequence of her sister, Isabella's, marriage, been mistress of his house from a very early period. Her mother had died too long ago for her to have more than an indistinct remembrance of her caresses, and her place had been supplied by an excellent woman as governess, who had fallen little short of a mother in affection.

Sarah   Sixteen years had Miss Taylor been in Mr Woodhouse's family, less as a governess than as a friend, very fond of both daughters, but *particularly* of Emma.

Jane   Even before Miss Taylor had ceased to hold the nominal office of governess, the mildness of her temper had hardly allowed her to impose any restraint; and the shadow of authority being long passed away, they had been living together as friend and friend, very mutually attached, and Emma doing just what she liked; highly esteeming Miss Taylor's judgement, but directed chiefly by her own . . .

Elizabeth   The *real* evils indeed of Emma's situation were the power of having *rather* too much of her own way, and a disposition to think a *little too well* of herself.

Sarah   Sorrow came.

Jane   A gentle sorrow – but not at all in the shape of any disagreeable consciousness –

Elizabeth   Miss Taylor married.

Jane It was Miss Taylor's loss which first brought grief. It was on the wedding day of this beloved friend that Emma first sat, with her father . . .

Jane *and* **Sarah** (*staring pointedly at* **Elizabeth**) With her father . . .

Elizabeth *grudgingly puts on a blanket to play* **Mr Woodhouse** *and sits down opposite* **Sarah**'*s* **Emma**.

Jane With her father . . . in mournful thought of any continuance.

Elizabeth (*fractiously*) Poor Miss Taylor! I wish she were here again. What a pity it is that Mr Weston ever thought of her!

Emma (*fulsomely*) I *cannot* agree with you, Papa, you know I cannot. Mr Weston is such a good-humoured, agreeable man that he thoroughly deserves a good wife – and you would not have had Miss Taylor live with us for ever and bear all my odd humours, when she might have a house of her own?

Mr Woodhouse (*getting more into the spirit*) A house of her own! But where is the advantage of a house of her own? This is three times as large. And you never have any odd humours, my dear.

Emma How often we shall be going to see them, and they coming to see us! We shall be always meeting! *We* must begin, we must go and pay our wedding-visit very soon.

Mr Woodhouse My dear, how am I to get so far? Randalls is such a distance. I could not walk half so far.

Emma No, Papa, nobody thought of your walking. We must go in the carriage to be sure.

Mr Woodhouse The carriage! But James will not like to put the horses to for such a little way – and where are the poor horses to be while we are paying our visit?

Emma They are to be put into Mr Weston's stable, Papa. You know we have settled that already. We talked it all over with Mr Weston last night.

Jane   Mr Knightley . . .

William *and* **Robert** *enter the room at an opportune moment, the first enthusiastic, the other more diffident. It is, however,* **Robert** *who is handed a copy of the text and pressured into playing* **Mr Knightley**. *He listens to his character description.*

Jane   Mr Knightley, a sensible man about seven or eight and thirty, was not only a very old and intimate friend of the family, but particularly concerned with it as the elder brother of Isabella's husband. He lived about a mile from Highbury, was a frequent visitor and always welcome.

Mr Woodhouse   It is very kind of you, Mr Knightley, to come out at this late hour to call upon us. I am afraid you must have had a shocking walk.

Mr Knightley   Not at all, sir. It is a beautiful, moonlit night and so mild that I must draw back from your great fire.

He looks round for the fire, finds it and does a little drawing-back manoeuvre.

Mr Woodhouse   But you must have found it very damp and dirty. I wish you may not catch cold.

Mr Knightley   Dirty, sir! Look at my shoes. Not a speck on them.

Mr Woodhouse   Well! That is quite surprising for we have had a vast deal of rain here. I wanted them to put off the wedding.

Mr Knightley   By the bye, I have not wished you joy. Being pretty well aware of what sort of joy you must both be feeling, I have been in no hurry with my congratulations. But I hope it all went off tolerably well. How did you all behave? Who cried most?

Mr Woodhouse   Ah, poor Miss Taylor! It is a sad business.

Mr Knightley   Poor Mr and Miss Woodhouse, if you please. But I cannot possibly say 'poor Miss Taylor'. I have a great regard for you and Emma, but when it comes to the question of dependence or independence . . . At any rate, it must be better to have only one to please, than two.

Emma   Especially if one of those two is such a fanciful, troublesome creature! That is what you have in your head, I know – and what you would certainly say if my father were not by.

Mr Woodhouse   I believe it is very true, my dear, indeed. I am afraid I am sometimes very fanciful and troublesome.

Emma   My dearest Papa! I meant only myself! Mr Knightley loves to find fault with me you know. We always say what we like to one another.

Mr Woodhouse   Dear Emma bears everything so well. But Mr Knightley, she is really very sorry to lose Miss Taylor, and I am sure she will miss her more than she thinks.

Mr Knightley   It is impossible that Emma should not miss such a companion. But she knows how very acceptable it must be at Miss Taylor's time of life to be settled in a home of her own. Every friend of Miss Taylor must be glad to have her so happily married.

Emma   And you have forgotten one matter of joy to me, and a very considerable one – that I made the match myself. I made the match, you know, four years ago, and when success has blessed me in this instance, dear Papa, you cannot think that I shall leave off match-making.

Mr Knightley   I do not understand what you mean by 'success'. Success supposes endeavour. You make a lucky guess and that is all that can be said in this instance.

Emma   And have you never known the pleasure and the triumph of a lucky guess? If *I* had not promoted Mr Weston's visits here and given many little encouragements, and smoothed many little matters, it might not have come to anything after all.

Mr Knightley   A straightforward, open-hearted man like Weston and a rational, unaffected woman like Miss Taylor, may be safely left to manage their own concerns. You are more likely to have done harm to yourself, than good to them, by interference.

Mr Woodhouse (*slightly confused by the way the conversation is going*)   Emma never thinks of herself if she can do good to others. But my dear, pray do not make any more matches. They are silly things and break up one's family circle grievously.

Emma   Only one more, Papa, only for Mr Elton. Poor Mr Elton! There is nobody in Highbury who deserves him, and he has been here a whole year! I thought when he was joining their hands today, he looked so very much as if he would like to have the same kind office done for him!

Mr Woodhouse   Mr Elton is a very pretty young man to be sure, and a very good young man and I have a great regard for him. But if you want to show him any attention, my dear, ask him to come and dine with us some day. That will be a much better thing. Perhaps Mr Knightley would be so kind as to meet him.

Mr Knightley   With a great deal of pleasure, sir, at any time, and I agree with you entirely that it will be a much better thing. Invite him to dinner, Emma, and help him to the best of the fish and the chicken, but leave him to choose his own wife. Depend upon it, a man of six and twenty can take care of himself.

Jane *starts to play the piano.* **Elizabeth** *flings off her blanket.*

Sarah   As Emma sat, the following morning, quietly contemplating the long days ahead and wondering how best to occupy herself, a note arrived from Mrs Goddard, the mistress of the Boarding School, requesting – in most respectful terms – to be allowed to bring Miss Smith with her.

Jane *and* **Elizabeth** *fight over who is to play* **Harriet Smith**. **Jane** *wins, and gets to wear the curly, blonde wig.*

Sarah   This was a most welcome request for Miss Smith was a girl of seventeen whom Emma knew very well by sight and had long felt an interest in on account of her beauty.

Jane *beams*.

Elizabeth (*malevolently*)   Harriet Smith was the natural daughter of 'somebody'. 'Somebody' had placed her, several years back, at Mrs Goddard's school, and 'somebody' had lately raised her from the condition of scholar to that of parlour-boarder. She was a very pretty girl, and her beauty happened to be of a sort which Emma particularly admired. She was *short, plump*, with a fine bloom, blue eyes and a look of *great sweetness*.

Harriet *is being interrogated by* **Emma**.

Emma   And how long have you resided at Mrs Goddard's, Harriet?

Harriet   Oh, a long time, Miss Woodhouse. At least ten . . . or twelve years.

Emma   And your background? Your parentage? Where were you brought up?

Harriet   I couldn't tell you, Miss Woodhouse. Mrs Goddard says that I was 'dropped' at her door and that I now belong to her and the school.

She giggles nervously.

Emma   Well, then where do you spend your holidays? At the school?

Harriet   Oh no, not always. Last summer I was fortunate enough to be asked to spend some weeks with the Martin family of Abbey-Mill Farm. Mrs Martin was most insistent that of all the girls *I* should be asked to stay with them and help with the fruit picking and the curing. And both the Miss Martins were so eager to make me feel part of the family. And such a large house! Mrs Martin has *two* parlours, two very good parlours indeed. One of them quite as large as Mrs Goddard's drawing-room! (*She giggles again.*) And I was allowed, sometimes, to help with the milking. The Martins have eight cows, two of them Alderneys and one a little Welsh cow, a very pretty Welsh cow, indeed, and Mrs

Martin was kind enough to say that, seeing as I was so fond of it, it should be called *my* cow.

Emma   Well, Harriet, what an exciting summer you must have had with all those Martin women. And what –

Harriet   Oh no, Miss Woodhouse! It's not just Mrs and Miss Martin.

Emma   It isn't?

Harriet (*blushing*)   No, *Mr* Martin was also very considerate and courteous towards me.

Emma   Mr Martin, the husband of Mrs Martin?

Harriet   No. Mrs Martin is unfortunately a widow. Mr Martin is her son, who runs the farm.

Emma   And what does the younger Mrs Martin do?

Harriet (*blushing deeper*)   There *is* no younger Mrs Martin, Miss Woodhouse. Mr Martin is, at present, unmarried.

Emma   I see.

Harriet   He would always join in all our evening games and encourage me to walk with him sometimes when it was dark. He once went three miles round in order to bring me some walnuts because I happened to mention how fond I am of walnuts. And he got his shepherd's son into the parlour one night to sing for me.

Emma   Was that the large parlour, or the smaller one?

Harriet   The larger one. Mr Martin sings a little himself. He appears very accomplished in everything he does. Once, when I was with him, he was bid more for his wool than anybody in the country! I believe that everybody speaks well of him. Mrs Martin told me once that it was impossible for anybody to be a better son, and that she was sure whenever he married he would make a good husband. Not that she was in any hurry for him to marry, of course.

Emma   Of course.

She considers.

What sort of looking man is Mr Martin?

Harriet   Oh, not handsome! Not at all handsome. I
thought him very plain at first, but I do not think him so
plain now. One does not, you know, after a time. But did you
never see him? He is in Highbury every now and then, and he
is sure to ride through every week on his way to Kingston.

Emma   That may be, and I may have seen him fifty times,
but without having any idea of his name. A young farmer,
whether on horseback or on foot is the very last sort of person
to raise my curiosity. The yeomanry are precisely the order
of people with whom I feel I can have nothing to do.

Harriet   Oh yes, Miss Woodhouse. Mrs Martin said that
she hoped his wife would be –

Emma   I wish you may not get into a scrape, Harriet,
whenever he does marry. I mean as to being acquainted with
his wife. There can be no doubt of your being a gentleman's
daughter and you must support your claim to that station by
everything within your own power, or there will be plenty of
people who would take pleasure in degrading you.

Harriet   Yes, to be sure, I suppose there are. But while I
visit at Hartfield and you are so kind to me, Miss
Woodhouse, I am not afraid of what anybody can do . . .

Sarah   Harriet Smith's intimacy at Hartfield was soon a
settled thing.

Jane   Quick and decided in her ways, Emma lost no time in
inviting, encouraging and telling her to come very often, and
as their acquaintance increased, so did their satisfaction in
each other.

Elizabeth   As a walking companion Emma had very early
foreseen how *useful* she might find her. Harriet certainly was
not clever, but she had a sweet, docile, *grateful* disposition.

Sarah   Her early attachment to herself was very amiable
and her inclination for good company, and power of
appreciating what was elegant and clever, showed that there

was no want of taste, though strength of understanding must not be expected.

Jane   They met Mr Martin the very next week, as they were walking on the Donwell road.

William *jumps up eagerly*.

Jane   He was on foot and after looking very respectfully at Emma, looked with most unfeigned satisfaction at her companion.

William *overdoes his unfeigned satisfaction*.

Sarah   His appearance was very neat and he looked like a sensible young man, but his person had no other advantage.

William *sulks*.

Elizabeth   They remained but a few minutes together as Miss Woodhouse must not be kept waiting. He touched his cap very gracefully, and passed on.

Harriet (*excitedly*)   Only think of our happening to meet him! How very odd! It was quite a chance, he said, that he had not gone round by Randalls.

Pause.

Well, Miss Woodhouse, is he like what you expected? What do you think of him? Do you think him so very plain?

Emma   He *is* very plain, undoubtedly. Remarkably plain. But that is nothing compared with his entire want of gentility. I had no right to expect much, and I did not expect much, but I had no idea that he could be so very clownish, so totally without air. I had imagined him, I confess, a degree or two nearer gentility.

Harriet (*quietly*)   To be sure, he is not so genteel as a real gentleman. He is not like Mr Knightley. He has not such a fine air and way of walking.

Emma   Mr Knightley's air is so remarkably good, that it is not fair to compare Mr Martin with him. You might not see one in a hundred with gentleman so plainly written as in Mr Knightley. But what say you to Mr Weston – or Mr Elton?

Compare Mr Martin with either of them. You must see the difference.

Harriet   I do . . .

Emma   In one respect, perhaps, Mr Elton's manners are superior to Mr Knightley's or Mr Weston's. They have more gentleness. I think a young man might be very safely recommended to take Mr Elton as a model. He seems to me to be grown particularly gentle of late . . .

Elizabeth   Mr Elton was, of course, the very person fixed on by Emma for driving the young farmer out of Harriet's head.

Jane   She thought it would be an excellent match and only too palpably desirable, natural and probable for her to have much merit in planning it. She feared it was what everybody else must think of and predict.

Sarah   Mr Elton was reckoned to be very handsome, though not by her, there being a want of elegance of feature which she could not dispense with – but the girl who could be gratified by a Robert Martin's riding about the country to get walnuts for her might very well be conquered by Mr Elton.

Harriet *smiles at her. She smiles back.*

Mr Knightley   I do not know what your opinion may be, Mrs Weston, of this great intimacy between Emma and Harriet Smith, but I think it a bad thing.

Mrs Weston   A bad thing! Why so?

Mr Knightley   I think they will neither of them do the other any good.

Mrs Weston   You surprise me! Emma must do Harriet good and by supplying her with a new object of interest, Harriet may be said to do Emma good. She may not be the superior young woman which Emma's friend ought to be. But on the other hand, as Emma wants to see her better informed, it will be an inducement to her to read more herself. They will read together.

Mr Knightley   Emma has been meaning to read more
ever since she was twelve years old. I have seen a great many
lists of her drawing up at various times of books that she
meant to read regularly through – and very good lists they
were – very well chosen and very neatly arranged –
sometimes alphabetically and sometimes by some other rule.
The list she drew up when only fourteen – I remember
thinking it did her judgement so much credit that I preserved
it some time. But I have done with expecting any course of
steady reading from Emma. She will never submit to
anything requiring industry and patience. Where Miss
Taylor failed to stimulate, I may safely affirm that Harriet
Smith will do nothing. You could never persuade her to read
half so much as you wished – you know you could not.

Mrs Weston (*smiling*)   I dare say that I thought so then,
but since we have parted, I can never remember Emma's
omitting to do anything that I wished.

Mr Knightley   There is hardly any desiring to refresh such
a memory as that. (*Pause.*) But I, who have had no such
charm thrown over my senses, must still see, hear and
remember. Emma is spoiled by being the cleverest of her
family. At ten years old she had the misfortune of being able
to answer questions which puzzled her sister at seventeen.
And ever since she was twelve, Emma has been mistress of the
house and of you all. In her mother she lost the only person
able to cope with her. But Harriet Smith – I have not half
done with Harriet Smith. I think her the very worst
companion that Emma could possibly have. She knows
nothing herself and looks upon Emma as knowing
everything. Her ignorance is hourly flattery. How can
Emma imagine she has anything to learn herself while
Harriet is presenting such delightful inferiority?

Mrs Weston   I either depend more upon Emma's good
sense than you do, or I am more anxious for her present
comfort, for I cannot lament the acquaintance. How well she
looked last night!

Mr Knightley   Oh, you would rather talk of her person than her mind, would you? Very well, I shall not attempt to deny Emma's being pretty. I confess I have seldom seen a face or figure more pleasing to me than hers. But I am a partial old friend. I have a very sincere interest in Emma. There is an anxiety, a curiosity in what one feels for Emma. I wonder what will become of her.

Mrs Weston   So do I. Very much.

Beat.

Mr Knightley   She always declares she will never marry, which of course means just nothing at all. But I have an idea that she has never yet seen a man she cared for. It would not be a bad thing for her to be very much in love with a proper object. I should like to see Emma in love, and in some doubt of a return. It would do her good. But there is nobody hereabouts to attach her, and she goes so seldom from home.

Mrs Weston   There does indeed seem as little to tempt her to break her resolution at present, but Mr Weston and myself were talking . . .

Mr Knightley   Talking? (*pause.*) Of the harvest? Of the weather? What does Weston think of the weather? Shall we have rain? . . .

Emma *is teaching* **Harriet** *to play the piano (a somewhat lost cause).* **Mr Elton** *watches admiringly, trying to ignore the wrong notes.*

Harriet *leaves the room, smiling fetchingly.*

Mr Elton   You have given Miss Smith all that she required. You have made her graceful and easy. She was a beautiful creature when she came to you, but in my opinion, the attractions you have added are infinitely superior to what she received from nature.

Emma   I am glad you think I have been useful to her, Mr Elton, but Harriet only wanted drawing out and receiving a few, very few hints. She had all the natural grace of sweetness of temper and artlessness in herself. I have done very little.

Mr Elton   Well, if it might be possible to contradict *a lady* . . .

Harriet *passes across the stage.*

Emma   What an exquisite possession a good picture of her would be! I almost long to attempt her likeness myself. You do not know it I dare say, but two or three years ago I had a great passion for taking likenesses and was thought to have quite a tolerable eye. Really, I could almost be persuaded to venture again, if Harriet would sit to me. It would be a delight to have her picture!

Mr Elton   Let *me* entreat you! It would indeed be a delight! Let *me* entreat you, Miss Woodhouse, to exercise so charming a talent in favour of your friend. I know what your drawings are. How could you suppose me ignorant? Is not this room rich in specimens of your landscapes and flowers and has not Mrs Weston some inimitable figure-pieces in her drawing-room at Randalls?

Emma   But I am afraid, Mr Elton, that Harriet will not like to sit. She thinks so little of her own beauty.

Harriet *crosses back.*

Emma   Harriet, we have decided that you should have your likeness taken.

Mr Elton   And we are to be honoured, deeply honoured, by Miss Woodhouse, herself, agreeing to once more set pen to paper and undertake the task herself!

Harriet   Oh, no! Oh, Miss Woodhouse –

Emma   Nonsense, Harriet. It is all decided.

She fetches her portfolio.

Mr Elton   I am certain, Miss Smith, that you will not deny us the pleasure of Miss Woodhouse's dexterous fingers . . .

Emma (*displaying her wears*)   No great variety of faces for you. I had only my own family to study from. There is my father . . . another of my father. Mrs Weston again, and again, and again, you see. Dear Mrs Weston! Always my kindest friend on every occasion. There is my sister, Isabella. Then come all my attempts at her children. All five of them. (*She passes them to* **Mr Elton**, *who acclaims each in turn*.) Then here is my last – my last and best –

Mr Elton Your father –

Emma My brother, Mr John Knightley. And yet, after all my pains, and when I had really made a very good likeness of him (Mrs Weston and myself were quite agreed in thinking it very like), after all this came my sister's cold approbation of 'Yes, it was a little like, but to be sure it did not do him justice'.

Mr Elton *tuts*.

Emma I did then forswear, as I said, ever drawing anybody again, but for Harriet's sake, or rather for my own, and as there are no husbands and wives in the case at present, I will break my resolution now.

Mr Elton (*applauding and laughing knowingly*) Yes, indeed! No husbands and wives in the case *at present*, indeed, as you observe. Exactly so. No husbands and wives . . .

He stands over her shoulder. **Emma** *draws a vertical line*.

Oh excellent, Miss Woodhouse. The celerity with which you work. Such application. Such industry. Truly remarkable. You catch her eyes perfectly.

Emma *continues*.

Mr Elton Miss Smith's proportions to the 'T'. Yes, the nose is just like that. So clever, so skilful. (*Pause*.) So masterful –

Emma (*patiently*) Perhaps you would be so good as to read to us, Mr Elton. That would be a kindness indeed. It will amuse away the difficulties of my painting and help Harriet to concentrate.

Mr Elton With whatever assistance I can offer, Miss Woodhouse, I shall endeavour to encourage the swift completion of this worthy enterprise.

He picks up a book and beams at **Harriet**.

Once upon a time . . .

The lights dim slightly. When they brighten, he is still reading, but the 'likeness' is nearing completion. **Mr Knightley** *and* **Mrs Weston** *have arrived to admire it.*

Mrs Weston   You must sign it, Emma. Put your name, just in the bottom corner there, in your best style. (*To* **Mr Elton**, *who is enthusiastically miming* The Three Little Pigs.) Miss Woodhouse has given her friend the only beauty she wanted. The expression of the eye is most correct, but Miss Smith has not those eyebrows and eyelashes. It is the fault of the fact that she has them not.

Mr Elton (*staring at the painting and then at* **Harriet**)   Do you think so? I cannot agree with you. It appears to me a most perfect resemblance in every feature. I never saw such a likeness in my life. We must allow for the effect of shade, you know.

Mr Knightley   You have made her too tall, Emma.

Sarah   Emma knew that she had, but would not admit it.

Mr Elton   Oh no! Certainly not too tall. Consider, she is sitting down – which naturally presents a different – which in short gives exactly the idea – and the proportions must be preserved, you know. Proportions, fore-shortenings.

Emma (*good-humouredly*)   I'm sure my father will be concerned at Harriet's sitting out of doors in the likeness without a shawl on. Won't you, Papa?

They all look round, discover nobody is available to play **Mr Woodhouse** *and substitute a broom for him.*

Won't you, Papa?

The broom nods.

Mr Elton   You, sir, may say anything, but I must confess that I regard it as a most happy thought, the placing of Miss Smith out of doors – and the tree is touched with such inimitable spirit! Any other situation would have been much less in character. The naivety of Miss Smith's manners – and altogether – oh, it is most admirable! I cannot keep my eyes from it. I never saw such a likeness.

Emma   We must have it framed for you, Harriet.

Harriet   Oh no, please, Miss Woodhouse, I wouldn't want –

Mr Elton   Naturally it must be framed. And I volunteer myself, to travel to London to dispatch it – that is, if I might be entrusted with the commission. What infinite pleasure would I have in executing this task. It is impossible to say how much I should be gratified by being employed on such an errand.

Emma   You are kindness itself, Mr Elton, but we couldn't possibly put you to so much trouble, could we, Harriet?

Harriet   Oh –

Emma   We wouldn't put you to such a troublesome office for the world, would we, Harriet?

Harriet   Oh, well –

Mr Elton   Please, Miss Woodhouse . . . please, Miss Smith, these entreaties are vainless. It is determined. I am unbending. It must be my responsibility to get this excellent likeness framed.

He takes the painting.

What a precious deposit!

He exits.

Sarah (*alone*)   This man is almost too gallant to be in love, thought Emma. But he is of an excellent character, and will suit Harriet exactly. He does sigh and lament, and study for compliments rather than I could endure as a principal. I come in for a pretty good share as a second. But it is his gratitude on Harriet's account.

Harriet *rushes across the stage carrying a letter.*

Harriet (*breathlessly*)   Miss Woodhouse! Miss Woodhouse!

Emma   Harriet?

Harriet   He has written me a letter!

Emma   Already?

Harriet   It is a proposal of marriage, Miss Woodhouse!

Emma (*delighted*)   Oh, Harriet!

Harriet   From Mr Martin! Who would have thought it?

Emma (*disappointed*)   Who would have thought it?

Harriet   Will you read the letter? Pray do. I'd rather you would.

Sarah   Emma was not sorry to be pressed. She read and was surprised.

Elizabeth   The style of the letter was much above her expectation. There were not merely no grammatical errors, but as a composition it would not have disgraced a gentleman.

Sarah   It was short, but expressed good sense, warm attachment, even delicacy of feeling.

Harriet   Well, Miss Woodhouse? What do you think? Is it a good letter, or is it too short?

Emma (*confused*)   Yes, indeed, a very good letter. So good a letter, Harriet, that everything considered, I think that one of his sisters must have helped him. No doubt he is a sensible man, and I suppose may have a natural talent for . . . thinks strongly and clearly . . . A better written letter, Harriet, than I had expected.

She hands it back.

Harriet   Well . . . Well, and . . . and what shall I do?

Emma   What shall you do! You mean with regard to this letter?

Harriet   Yes.

Emma   But what are you in doubt of? You must answer it, of course – and speedily.

Harriet   Yes, but what shall I say? Dear Miss Woodhouse, do advise me.

Emma   Oh, no, no! The letter had much better be all your own. You will express yourself very properly, I am sure. There is no danger of your not being intelligible, which is the first thing. Your meaning must be unequivocal. No doubts and no demurs. And such expression of gratitude and concern for the pain you are inflicting as propriety requires, will present themselves unbidden to your mind, I am persuaded.

Harriet (*looking down*)   You think I ought to refuse him, then.

Emma   Ought to refuse him! My dear Harriet, what do you mean? I thought – but I beg your pardon, perhaps I have been under some mistake. I had imagined you were consulting me only as to the wording of your reply. (*Pause.*) You mean to return a favourable answer, I collect.

Harriet   No, I do not. That is – I do not mean – What would you advise me to do? Pray, dear Miss Woodhouse, tell me what I ought to do?

Emma   I shall not give you any advice, Harriet. I will have nothing to do with it. This is a point which you must settle with your own feelings.

Harriet (*staring at the letter*)   I had no idea that he liked me so much.

Elizabeth   For a little while Emma persevered in her silence. But beginning to apprehend the bewitching flattery of that letter might be too powerful, she thought it best to say:

Emma   I lay it down as a general rule, Harriet, that if a woman doubts as to whether she should accept a man or not, she certainly ought to refuse him. If she can hesitate as to 'Yes' she ought to say 'No' directly. I thought it my duty as a friend, and older than yourself, to say thus much to you. But do not imagine that I want to influence you.

Harriet Oh no, I am sure you are a great deal too kind to –
Do you think I had better say 'No'?

Emma (*smiling*)   Not for the world would I advise you
either way. You must be the best judge of your own
happiness. If you prefer Mr Martin to every other person . . .
You blush, Harriet. Does anybody else occur to you under
such a definition? At this moment whom are you thinking of?

Harriet *turns away, confused, twisting and turning the letter*.

Sarah   The symptoms were favourable.

Harriet   Miss Woodhouse, as you will not give me your
opinion, I must do as well as I can by myself. And I have now
quite determined, and really almost made up my mind – to
refuse Mr Martin. Do you think I am right?

Emma   Perfectly, perfectly right, my dearest Harriet. You
are doing just what you ought. While you were at all in
suspense I kept my feelings to myself, but now that you are so
completely decided I have no hesitation in approving. We
will not be parted. A woman is not to marry a man merely
because she is asked, or because he is attached to her and can
write a tolerable letter.

Harriet   Oh no, and it is but a short letter too!

Emma   Very true.

Harriet   I think Mrs Goddard would be very much
surprised if she knew what had happened. I am sure Miss
Nash would – for Miss Nash thinks her own sister very well
married, and it is only a linen-draper!

Elizabeth   Harriet slept at Hartfield that night.

Sarah   Emma judged it best in every respect, safest and
kindest, to keep her with them for a while.

Jane   Though not all of the time, of course . . .

Enter **Mr Knightley**.

Mr Knightley   And where is your friend, Miss Smith, this
morning?

Emma She has gone to fetch something from Mrs Goddard's. I expect her at any moment. She is always eager to return to Hartfield.

Mr Knightley Yes. I cannot rate her beauty as you do, Emma, but she is a pretty little creature, and I am inclined to think well of her disposition. Her character depends upon those she is with, but in good hands she will turn out a valuable woman.

Emma I am glad you thinks so, and the good hands, I hope, may not be wanting.

Mr Knightley You are expecting her again, you say, this morning?

Emma Almost every moment. She has been gone longer than she intended.

Mr Knightley I have reason to think that Harriet Smith will soon have an offer of marriage, and from a most unexceptionable quarter.

Emma (*beaming*) Indeed? Has Mr El

Mr Knightley Robert Martin is the man. (**Emma** *stops beaming*.) Her visit to Abbey-Mill this summer seems to have done his business. He is desperately in love and means to marry her.

Emma He is very obliging, but is he sure that Harriet means to marry him?

Mr Knightley Well, well, means to make her an offer then. Will that do? He came to the Abbey two evenings ago on purpose to consult me about it. Now, as we may fairly suppose he would not allow much time to pass before he spoke to the lady, and as he does not appear to have spoken yesterday, it is not unlikely that he should be at Mrs Goddard's today, and that she may be detained by a visitor.

Emma (*smiling*) Pray, Mr Knightley, how do you know that Mr Martin did not speak yesterday?

Mr Knightley Certainly, I do not absolutely know it. But it may be inferred. Was she not the whole day with you?

Emma   Come, I will tell you something, in return for what you have told me. He did speak yesterday – that is he wrote, and was refused.

Mr Knightley   I beg your pardon?

Emma   Mr Martin wrote, and he was refused.

Mr Knightley (*standing up*)   Then she is a greater simpleton than I ever believed her! What is the foolish girl about?

Emma   Oh, to be sure, it is always incomprehensible to a man that a woman should ever refuse an offer of marriage. A man always imagines a woman to be ready for anybody who asks her!

Mr Knightley   Nonsense, a man does not imagine any such thing! But what is the meaning of this? Harriet Smith refuse Robert Martin? Madness if it is so, but I hope you are mistaken.

Emma   I saw her answer. Nothing could be clearer.

Mr Knightley   You saw her answer! You wrote her answer too. Emma, you persuaded her to refuse him.

Emma   And if I did (which I am far from allowing) I should not feel that I had done wrong. Mr Martin is a very respectable young man, but I cannot admit him to be Harriet's equal, and am rather surprised that he should have ventured to address her.

Mr Knightley (*loudly*)   Not Harriet's equal! No, he is not her equal indeed, for he is as much her superior in sense as in station. Emma, your infatuation about that girl blinds you. What are Harriet Smith's claims, either of birth, nature or education, to any connection higher than Robert Martin? She is the natural daughter of nobody knows whom, with probably no settled provision at all, and certainly no respectable relations. She is known only as parlour-boarder at a common school. She is not a sensible girl, nor a girl of any information. She is pretty and she is good-tempered and that is all. Even *your* satisfaction I was sure of. I remember saying to myself, 'Even Emma, with all her partiality for Harriet will think this a good match.'

Emma   I cannot help wondering at your knowing so little of Harriet as to say any such thing. What! Think a farmer a good match for my intimate friend! Not regret her leaving Highbury for the sake of marrying a man whom I could never admit as an acquaintance of my own! The sphere in which she moves is much above his – it would be degradation!

Mr Knightley   A degradation to illegitimacy and ignorance to be married to a respectable, intelligent gentleman-farmer! Till you chose to turn her into a friend, her mind had not distaste for her own set, nor any ambition beyond it. She was as happy as possible with the Martins in the summer. And Robert Martin would never have proceeded so far if he had not felt persuaded of her not being disinclined to him. I know him well. Depend upon it, he had encouragement.

Elizabeth   It was most convenient to Emma not to make a direct reply to this assertion.

Silence. **Emma** *tries to think of something to say.*

Mr Knightley   Robert Martin has no great loss – if he can but think so. Your views for Harriet are best known to yourself. But as you make no secret of your love of matchmaking, it is fair to suppose what views and plans and projects you have – and as a friend I shall just hint to you that if Elton is the man, I think it will be all labour in vain.

Emma (*laughing*)   Thank you, Mr Knightley, but I certainly have no intention of matching Harriet up with Mr Elton. (*Pause.*) Mr Elton, indeed!

Mr Knightley   Depend upon it, Elton will not do. Elton is a very good sort of man, and a very respectable vicar of Highbury, but not at all likely to make an imprudent match.

Emma   I am very much obliged to you. If I had set my heart on Mr Elton's marrying Harriet, it would have been very kind to open my eyes, but at present I only want to keep

Harriet to myself. I have done with matchmaking indeed. I could never hope to equal my own doings at Randalls. I shall leave off while I am well.

Mr Knightley (*coldly*)   Good morning to you.

He exits.

Mr Elton (*joining* **Emma** *and* **Harriet**)
My first doth affliction denote,
Which my second is destin'd to feel
And my whole is the best antidote
That affliction to soften and heal.

Emma *and* **Harriet** *applaud. The (framed) picture is hanging up.*

Emma   That will do splendidly, Mr Elton. Your collection is certainly mounting up, Harriet.

Mr Elton   A collection of riddles! What a delightful pastime. Miss Smith is fortunate in having her friend to assist with the assignment.

Emma   Oh, everyone has been most obliging with their contributions.

Harriet   Mrs Nash's collection numbers three hundred, and she has let me use a great many of them.

Mr Elton   Three hundred! Goodness me!

Emma   You will have to offer us more than just one riddle, Mr Elton.

Mr Elton   But I don't know any others, Miss Woodhouse. My knowledge of puzzles is extremely limited.

Emma   Then why will not you write one for us yourself? That is the only security for its freshness, and nothing could be easier to you.

Mr Elton   Oh no, my dear Miss Woodhouse. I have never written, hardly ever, anything of the kind in my life. I am the stupidest fellow! I'm afraid that not even Miss Woodhouse . . . or Miss Smith . . . could inspire me to it.

Pause.

However . . .

He takes a piece of paper from his pocket.

I happen to have on me a charade which a 'friend' of mine
has recently written to a young lady, the object of his
admiration.

He looks significantly at **Emma**, *who smiles back, knowingly, at
him.*

I do not offer it for Miss Smith's collection. Being my friend's,
I have no right to expose it in any degree to the public eye,
but perhaps you may not dislike looking at it.

He hands it to **Emma**, *bows and leaves.*

Emma (*holding it out to* **Harriet**)   Take it. It is for you.
Take your own.

Harriet   Oh, Miss Woodhouse. I'm almost afraid to touch
it. You read it for me.

Emma (*unravelling it*)   Oh well, as you think best, Harriet.

My first displays the wealth and pomp of kings,
Lords of the earth! their luxury and ease.
Another view of man, my second brings,
Behold him there, the monarch of the seas!

But ah! united, what reverse we have!
Man's boasted power and freedom, all are flown;
Lord of the earth and sea, he bends a slave,
And woman, lovely woman, reigns alone.

Thy ready wit . . . the word will soon supply,
May its approval beam in that soft eye!

She stares at it, considers it and passes it to **Harriet** *who starts to
puzzle over it confusedly.*

Emma (*away from* **Harriet**)   Very well, Mr Elton, very
well indeed. I have read worse charades. 'Courtship' – a very
good hint. I give you credit for it. This is feeling your way.
This is saying very plainly – 'Pray, Miss Smith, give me leave
to pay my addresses to you. Approve my charade and my
intentions in the same glance'. 'May its approval beam in

that soft eye!' Harriet exactly. Soft is the very word for her eye – of all epithets the justest that could be given. 'Thy ready wit the word will soon supply'. Well . . . A man must be very much in love indeed to describe her so. Things must come to a crisis soon now.

Harriet *is still puzzling over the charade.*

Emma   A very proper compliment, Harriet. There can be no doubt of its being written for you and to you. The state of his mind is as clear and decided as my wishes on the subject have been ever since I knew you. I congratulate you, my dear Harriet, with all my heart. This is a connection which offers nothing but good. It will fix you in the centre of all your real friends, close to Hartfield and to me, and confirm our intimacy for ever.

Harriet (*embracing her*)   Oh, dear Miss Woodhouse. Dear, dear Miss Woodhouse. Mr Elton who might marry anybody! It is so much beyond anything I deserve.

Jane   Mr Elton must now be left to himself. It was no longer in Emma's power to superintend his happiness or quicken his measures. The coming of her sister's family was near at hand and it became, therefore, the primary object of all her attentions to prepare the house and quieten her father's anxieties about their journey.

Elizabeth   His alarms, as usual, were needless and Mr and Mrs John Knightley, their five children . . . (*Four dolls, of various shapes and sizes, and a furry animal are found and presented.*) . . . and a competent number of nursemaids . . . (*They decide not to look for the nursemaids.*) all reached Hartfield in safety.

The **John Knightleys** *arrive.*

Isabella   My dear Father –

They search for the broom, realise **Elizabeth** *is available and throw it aside.*

My dear Father . . . (*She embraces him.*) Both you and Emma are looking remarkably well (*Sympathetically.*) considering . . .

Mr Woodhouse Ah, poor Miss Taylor – it is a grievous business.

Isabella But Mr Weston is surely an excellent man. I believe he is one of the best tempered men that ever existed. (*To her husband.*) Excepting yourself and your brother, I do not know his equal for temper. I shall never forget his flying little Henry's kite for him that very windy day last Easter.

Mr John Knightley Where is the son? Did he make an appearance at the wedding?

Emma He has not been here yet. There was a strong expectation of his coming soon after the marriage, but it ended in nothing and I have not heard him mentioned lately.

Mr Woodhouse But you should tell them of the letter, my dear. Mr Churchill wrote a letter to poor Mrs Weston to congratulate her, and a very proper, handsome letter it was.

Isabella How very pleasing and proper of him. But how sad it is that he should not live at home with his father! There is something so shocking in a child's being taken away from his parents and natural home! I never can comprehend how Mr Weston could part with him . . .

Elizabeth Mr Frank Churchill was one of the boasts of Highbury. Twenty-four years earlier, Captain Weston had married Miss Churchill, of a great Yorkshire family, and nobody was surprised except her brother and his wife –

Jane Who were full of pride and importance –

Elizabeth And who threw her off with due decorum.

Jane It was an unsuitable connection and did not produce much happiness. Captain Weston, who had been considered, especially by the Churchills, as making an amazing match, was proved to have much the worst of the bargain, for when his wife died after a three years' marriage, he was rather a poorer man than at first, and with a child to maintain.

Elizabeth Mr and Mrs Churchill, having no children of their own, offered to take the whole charge of little Frank and so the child was given up to their care and their wealth and Highbury had never seen him since.

Sarah   Now it so happened, that in spite of Emma's resolution of never marrying, there was something in the name, in the idea of Mr Frank Churchill, which always interested her. She had frequently thought – especially since his father's marriage with Miss Taylor, that if she *were* to marry, he was the very person to suit her in age, character and condition. She had a great curiosity to see him, a decided intention of finding him pleasant and a sort of pleasure in the idea of their being coupled in their friends' imagination.

Jane   All of these thoughts were kept, at present, to herself, of course, although she was pretty sure that Mr and Mrs Weston were harbouring similar ones.

A carol.

Elizabeth   Christmas arrived and the whole family were invited to dine with the Westons on Christmas Eve. Harriet, Mr Knightley and Mr Elton were the only persons invited to meet them.

Jane   Circumstances unfortunately intervened in striking down poor Harriet with a dreadful cold in the head, and Mrs Goddard would, on no account, hear of her leaving the school.

Dinner at the **Westons**. **Mr Weston** *standing up and toasting his son*. **Mr Elton** *seated next to* **Emma**.

Mr Elton   Are you perfectly warm, Miss Woodhouse?

Emma   Perfectly warm, thank you, Mr Elton.

Mr Elton   And your father? Do you think that he is warm enough? Might I ask Mrs Weston whether or not she has a blanket for him?

Emma   He too looks warm enough.

Mr Elton   Mrs Weston is truly a most remarkable woman. She entertains so charmingly, and always so solicitous of the needs of others. Her beneficence has, I have no doubt, passed on to her former pupil.

Emma   Very possibly.

She tries to turn away to listen to **Mr Weston** *discourse on his son.*

Mr Elton   I was fortunate enough this evening, to be able to view, once more, your unexceptionable drawing of Miss Smith. Your hand has captured her every feature with truly remarkable skill. The thickness of the pen around her hair, is, for me, particularly admirable and –

Emma   I am so sorry, Papa. I did not quite catch what you said.

Mr Woodhouse, *who has said nothing, looks confused.* (*He could, of course, still be a broom.*)

Mr Weston   We only want two more to be just the right number. I should like to see two more here – your pretty little friend, Miss Smith, and my son. Frank is expected any day now. I had a letter from him this morning, and he will be with us within a fortnight.

Emma   What a very great pleasure it will be to you, Mr Weston! And Mrs Weston (**Elizabeth** *metamorphoses into* **Mrs Weston**.) is so anxious to be acquainted with him, that she must be almost as happy as yourself.

Mr Weston   Yes, she would be, but that she thinks there will be another put-off. She does not depend upon his coming so much as I do.

Mrs Weston   Indeed, I am very much afraid that it will all end in nothing. It depends entirely upon his aunt's spirits and pleasure – in short, upon her temper. Mrs Churchill rules at Enscombe and his coming now depends upon her being willing to spare him.

Mr Elton (*who has started to drink a little*)   I do entreat you, my dear Miss Woodhouse, to promise me not to venture as far as Mrs Goddard's until I have seen Mr Perry and learnt his opinion of poor Miss Smith's illness.

Emma   Yes, thank you, Mr Elton.

Mr Elton (*tapping the table*)   No, you must absolutely
promise! It would sadden me beyond measure if you too were
subject to an influenza in this treacherous weather.

Emma   If Harriet is in need of my attention and affections
then –

Mr Elton   Ah, so scrupulous for others, and yet so careless
for herself! She wanted me to nurse my cold by staying at
home today, and yet will not promise to avoid the danger of
catching an ulcerated sore throat herself! Is this fair, Mrs
Weston? Judge between us. I am sure of your kind support
and aid.

Mrs Weston *looks surprised.*

Mr Weston (*looking out of the window, gleefully*)   I very much
fear that the snow storm has increased so dramatically that
there seems no possibility of your getting back to Hartfield
tonight.

Mr Woodhouse *and* **Isabella** *look alarmed.*

Mr Weston   I will have to keep you all at Randalls for
another few days at least.

Mr Woodhouse *and* **Isabella** *look even more alarmed.*

Mr Weston   But accommodation might be found for
everyone, don't you agree, my dear?

He looks round for his wife, but she has become **Mr Woodhouse**.

Mr Woodhouse   What is to be done, my dear Emma,
what is to be done?

Isabella   The children, John, the children! We must return
directly!

Emma   There is not the smallest difficulty in any of our
getting home. The coachmen both agree that there is
nothing to apprehend if we leave within the hour.

Mr Woodhouse *and* **Isabella**   Well, then, we had better
leave at once.

Mr Elton (*now very drunk*)   Shall I ring the bell? In my
opinion –

Emma Yes, do.

Jane The carriages came. Mr Woodhouse, always the first object on such occasions, was carefully attended to his own by Mr Knightley and Mr Weston.

Elizabeth Isabella stepped as quickly as she could after her father. John Knightley, forgetting that he did not belong to their party, stepped in after his wife very naturally.

Sarah And Emma found, on being escorted and followed into the second carriage by Mr Elton, that the door was to be lawfully shut on them, and that they were to have a tête-à-tête drive.

Emma *and* **Mr Elton** *in the carriage.*

Mr Elton (*immediately seizing her hand*) My dearest Miss Woodhouse, what an opportunity for us! I beg your very undivided attention to listen to those sentiments which are doubtless already well-known to you. I must avail myself of this precious opportunity to tell you how ardently, how devotedly I love you and beg your hand. I hope . . . I fear . . . oh, how I adore you! I must die if you refuse me – although I rather flatter myself that my ardent attachment and unexampled passion cannot fail to have some effect on so benevolent a mind as your own. In short, I am resolved to be accepted as soon as possible. There can be no delay! No diffidence! Tell me that you are mine!

Emma I am very much astonished, Mr Elton! This to me! You forget yourself – you take me for your friend – any message for Miss Smith I shall be happy to deliver, but no more of this to me, if you please.

Mr Elton Miss Smith! Message to Miss Smith! What can you mean? Of course I take you for my friend! Have you not been my friend these past six weeks?

Emma Mr Elton, this is the most extraordinary conduct. After such behaviour, as I have witnessed during the last month, to Miss Smith – such attentions as I have been in the daily habit of observing – to be addressing me in this manner – this is an unsteadiness of character, indeed, which I had not supposed possible! Believe me, sir, I am very far, *very* far from gratified in being the object of such professions.

Mr Elton   Good heavens! What can be the meaning of this? Miss Smith?! I never thought of Miss Smith in the whole course of my existence – never paid her any attentions, but as your friend – never cared whether she were dead or alive, but as your friend. If she has fancied otherwise, her own wishes have misled her, and I am very sorry – extremely sorry – But Miss Smith indeed! Who can think of Miss Smith when Miss Woodhouse is near!

Emma *is speechless.* **Mr Elton** *tries once more to take her hand.*

Mr Elton   Charming Miss Woodhouse! Allow me to interpret this interesting silence. It confesses you have long understood me.

Emma   No, sir, it confesses no such thing! Your pursuit of Miss Smith (pursuit it appeared) gave me great pleasure, but had I supposed that she were *not* your attraction to Hartfield, I should certainly have thought you judged ill in making your visits so frequent.

Mr Elton   I think seriously of Miss Smith? Miss Smith is a very good sort of girl and I should be happy to see her respectably settled, I wish her extremely well, and no doubt there *are* men who might not object to – everybody has their level – but as for myself, I am not, I think, quite so much at a loss. No, madam, my visits to Hartfield and the encouragement I received –

Emma   Encouragement! I give you encouragement! Sir, you have been entirely mistaken in supposing it. I have seen you only as the admirer of my friend. In no other light could you have been more to me than a common acquaintance. I am exceedingly sorry, but it is as well that the mistake ends where it does. I have no thoughts of matrimony at present. Good night, Mr Elton.

Mr Elton (*icily*)   Good night . . . Miss Woodhouse!

He leaves the carriage. **Emma** *is left with her thoughts.*

Jane It was a wretched business, indeed! Such an overthrow of everything she had been wishing for! Such a blow for Harriet!

Emma   Oh, if only I had not persuaded Harriet into liking the man, I could have borne anything. But poor Harriet!

Elizabeth   Perhaps it was not fair to expect him to feel how very much he was her inferior in talent, and all the elegancies of mind. But he must know that in fortune and consequence she was greatly his superior.

Jane   However, after raving a little about the seeming incongruity of gentle manners and a conceited head, Emma was obliged, on common honesty, to stop and admit that her own behaviour to him had been so complaisant and obliging as might warrant a man of ordinary observation like Mr Elton in fancying himself a very decided favourite.

Emma   Here have I, actually talked poor Harriet into being very much attracted to this man. She might never have thought of him with hope, if I had not assured her of his attachment. Oh, that I had been satisfied with persuading her not to accept young Martin! There I was quite right. That was well done of me, but there I should have stopped and left the rest to chance.

Jane   The distressing explanation she would have to make to Harriet, and all that poor Harriet would be suffering, were enough to occupy her in most unmirthful reflections some time longer, and she went to bed at last with nothing settled but the conviction of her having blundered most dreadfully!

Piano.

Act Two

Mr Knightley *and* **Emma**.

Mr Knightley   So, Mr Frank Churchill is not to come, after all.

Emma   No. Mrs Weston is exceedingly disappointed. Mr and Mrs Churchill seem determined to keep him away for as long as they can.

Mr Knightley (*coolly*)   The Churchills are very likely in fault, but I dare say he might come if he would.

Emma   I do not know why you should say so. He wished exceedingly to come, but his uncle and aunt will not spare him.

Mr Knightley   I cannot believe that he has not the power of coming, if he made a point of it. A man at his age – what is he? – three or four and twenty – cannot be without the means of doing as much as that.

Emma   That's easily said, and easily felt by you, who have always been your own master. You do not know what it is to have tempers to manage.

Mr Knightley   A little while ago he was at Weymouth. This proves he can leave the Churchills.

Emma   Yes, sometimes he can.

Mr Knightley   There is one thing, Emma, which a man can always do, if he chooses, and that is his duty. It is Frank Churchill's duty to pay this attention to his father. He knows it to be so, by his promises and messages, and if he wished to do it, it might be done. He can sit down and write a fine, flourishing letter, full of professions and falsehoods, and persuade himself that he has hit upon the very best method in the world of preserving peace at home and preventing his father's having any right to complain. His letters disgust me.

Emma   You seem determined to think ill of him.

Mr Knightley (*shortly*) Not at all! I do not want to think ill of him. I should be as ready to acknowledge his merits as any other man, but I hear of none, except what are merely personal – that he is well grown and good-looking, with smooth, plausible manners.

Emma Well, if he have nothing else to recommend him, he will be a treasure at Highbury. We do not often look upon fine young men, well-bred and agreeable. We must not be nice and ask for virtues into the bargain.

Mr Knightley You will excuse my being so much overpowered. If I find him conversible, I shall be glad of his acquaintance, but if he is only a chattering coxcomb, he will not occupy much of my time or thoughts.

Emma We are both prejudiced; you against, I for him.

Mr Knightley Prejudiced! I am not prejudiced.

Emma But I am very much, and without being at all ashamed of it. My love for Mr and Mrs Weston gives me a decided prejudice in his favour.

Mr Knightley He is a person I never think of from one month's end to another.

He leaves. **Emma** *stares after him.*

Elizabeth Emma and Harriet had been walking together one morning, and in Emma's opinion, been talking enough of Mr Elton for that day. She could not think that Harriet's solace or her own sins required more.

Sarah They were just approaching the house where lived Mrs and Miss Bates and Emma determined to call on them and seek safety in numbers.

Jane Mrs Bates, the widow of a former vicar of Highbury, was a very old lady, almost past everything but tea and quadrille.

Robert *is forced to cover himself with a shawl and become* **Mrs Bates**.

Jane   She lived with her single daughter in a very small
way and was considered with all the regard which a harmless
old lady, under such untoward circumstances, can excite.

Elizabeth   Her daughter enjoyed a most uncommon
degree of popularity for a woman neither young, handsome,
rich nor married.

Jane (*becoming* **Miss Bates**)   And yet she was a happy
woman, and a woman whom no one named without
goodwill. She loved everybody, was interested in
everybody's happiness and thought herself a most fortunate
creature.

Sarah   A short visit would be most opportune. There was
always sufficient reason for such an attention; Mrs and Miss
Bates loved to be called on.

Robert (*removing his shawl*)   And Emma knew she was
considered by the very few who presumed ever to see
imperfection in her, as rather negligent in that respect.

The **Bates'** *parlour.* **Robert** *and* **Jane** *put on identical pairs of
glasses.* **Emma** *arrives, dragging a large rag doll – a miniature
Harriet, with the same colour dress and perhaps the same wig.*

Miss Bates   So kind of you to call, Miss Woodhouse. And
how is your dear father? How is Miss Smith? (*She takes the doll
and puts her on a chair.*) How are your shoes? Have you walked
a great distance? I took my mother out this morning and she
walked right to the end of the road. And back. May I offer
you some cake. Mrs Perry was good enough to bring it for us
yesterday. And Mrs Cole has just been with us – just called in
for ten minutes and was so good as to sit an hour with us, and
she took a piece of cake and was kind enough to say she liked it
very much. Mrs Cole began inquiring after Jane as soon as
she came in. Whenever she is with us, Mrs Cole does not
know how to show her kindness enough, and I must say that
Jane deserves it as much as anybody can. And so she began
inquiring after her directly, saying 'I know you cannot have
heard from Jane lately, because it is not her time for writing'
and I immediately said 'But indeed we *have*, we had a letter

this very morning.' I do not know that I *ever* saw anybody more surprised. 'Have you, upon your honour!' said she, 'Well, that is *quite* unexpected. Do let me hear what she says.'

Emma Oh, have you heard from Miss Fairfax so lately. I am extremely happy. I hope she is well?

Miss Bates (*hunting for the letter*) Thank you. You are so kind! Oh, here it is. I was sure it could not be far off. But I had put my huswife upon it, you see, without being aware, and so it was quite hid, but I had it in my hand so very lately that I was almost sure it must be on the table. I was reading it to Mrs Cole, and since she went away, I was reading it again to my mother, for it is such a pleasure to her – a letter from Jane – that she can *never* hear it often enough; so I knew it could not be far off, and here it is, only just under my huswife – and since you are so kind as to wish to hear what she says – but first of all, I really must, in justice to Jane, apologise for her writing so short a letter – only two pages, you see – hardly two – and in general she fills the whole paper and crosses half. My mother often wonders that I can make it out so well. She often says, when the letter is first opened, 'Well, Hetty, now I think you will be put to it to make out all that chequer-work' – don't you ma'am? – and I tell her, I am sure she would contrive to make it out herself, if she had nobody to do it for her – I am sure she would pore over every word.

Emma Miss Fairfax has a most beautiful handwriting.

Miss Bates You are extremely kind. You who are such a judge and write so beautifully yourself. My mother does not hear, she is a little deaf, you know. Ma'am, do you hear what Miss Woodhouse is so obliging to say about Jane's handwriting?

Mrs Bates (*with earphone*) Eh?

Miss Bates (*shouting*) Miss Woodhouse is kind enough to say that Jane has a most beautiful handwriting.

Mrs Bates (*shouting*) A beautiful what?

Miss Bates   A most beautiful handwriting. Was that what you said, Miss Woodhouse? My mother always hears Jane better than she does me. And I think that Jane will not find her grandmamma at all deafer than she was two years ago. It really is full two years, you know, since she was here.

Emma   Are you expecting Miss Fairfax here soon?

Miss Bates   Oh yes, next week. My mother is so delighted, for she is to be three months with us at least. The case is that the Campbells are going to Ireland, you see . . .

William   Jane Fairfax was an orphan, the only child of Mrs Bates' youngest daughter. By birth she belonged to Highbury, and when at three years old she was unfortunate enough to lose both her parents, she became the charge and the consolation of the grandmother and aunt, there seemed every possibility of her being permanently fixed there.

Jane   But the compassionate feelings of a friend of her father gave a change to her destiny. This was Colonel Campbell, himself possessed of a girl, about Jane's age, who took charge of her education and Jane had thereafter lived with them entirely, only visiting her grandmother from time to time.

Elizabeth   They continued together till the marriage of Miss Campbell, who by that luck which so often defies anticipation in matrimonial affairs, giving attraction to what is moderate rather than to what is superior, engaged the affections of Mr Dixon, a young man, rich and agreeable, almost as soon as they were acquainted, and was eligibly and happily settled, while Jane Fairfax had yet her bread to earn.

Elizabeth *becomes* **Jane Fairfax**.

Emma (*politely*)   How do you do, Miss Fairfax. I was sorry to hear that you had been unwell recently.

Jane Fairfax (*equally politely*)   Thank you, Miss Woodhouse, I am now fully recovered, I hope.

Emma   I trust that Mr and Mrs Dixon are happily settled in Ireland. You spent the summer in Weymouth with them, I believe.

Jane Fairfax   Yes.

Pause.

Emma   Is Mr Dixon a handsome man?

Jane Fairfax   I'm told that he is generally considered to be so.

Emma   Is he generally considered a good match for Miss Campbell?

Jane Fairfax   I believe so.

Emma   You must have been at Weymouth at the same time as Mr Weston's son, Mr Frank Churchill.

Jane Fairfax   I believe I was.

Emma   Did you see him very often?

Jane Fairfax   Not very often, no.

Emma   Tell us all, is *he* a handsome man?

Jane Fairfax   I believe he is reckoned to be a very fine young man.

Emma   And is he agreeable?

Jane Fairfax   He is generally thought so.

Emma (*more frustrated*)   Did he appear a sensible young man? A man of much information?

Jane Fairfax   At a watering place, or in a common acquaintance, it is difficult to decide on such points. Manners were all that I could safely judge. I believe everybody finds his manners pleasing. That is all I can really tell you.

Sarah   Emma could not forgive her.

Jane   Mr Frank Churchill, himself, however, was once again expected at Highbury and a day had actually been settled upon for his arrival.

Sarah   Emma was therfore startled to enter the parlour the day before the impending visit to see two gentlemen sitting with her father – Mr Weston and his son.

Mr Weston (*getting up*)   And here is Miss Woodhouse, herself, about whom you cannot have heard too much, Frank. (*To* **Emma** *and* **Mr Woodhouse**.) You see – I told you all that he would be here before the time named. I remember what I used to do myself. One cannot *creep* upon a journey, one cannot help getting on faster than one has planned and the pleasure of coming in on one's friends before the look-out begins, is worth a great deal more than any little exertion it needs.

Frank   It is a great pleasure where one can indulge it, although there are not many houses that I should presume on so far. But in coming *home* I felt I might do anything.

Mr Weston *beams at him*.

Emma   And how do you find Randalls, Mr Churchill? Is it everything you imagined it to be?

Frank   It is superior to all expectation, Miss Woodhouse. Beautifully situated – so near to Hartfield, after all – admirably sized and delightfully furnished. I could not have wished for anything better.

Emma   Well, if you have similar compliments to pay for Highbury itself, I'm sure that you will not want for friends before the day is out.

Frank   It is an exquisite village. I have always felt an interest in Surrey which none but one's *own* country gives, and my curiosity to visit has been much aroused by my father's correspondence.

Emma   It is a pity that your curiosity should not have been satisfied up until this moment.

Frank   Ah, yes. And are you a horsewoman, Miss Woodhouse? Are there pleasant rides? And balls? Do you have regular balls? Is Highbury a musical society? Is it a large neighbourhood?

Emma (*laughing*)   I am sure that the answer will be yes to all those questions. We are immensely proud of our village and you will be able to say nothing against it.

Mr Weston (*moving over to them*)   Well, I must be taking my leave of you, Emma. I have business at the Crown about my hay, and a great many errands for Mrs Weston at Ford's. But I certainly do not need to hurry anybody else . . .

Frank (*standing up*)   As you are going further on business, sir, I will take the opportunity of paying a visit, which must be paid some day or other, and therefore may as well be paid now. (*He turns to* **Emma**.) I have the honour of being acquainted with a neighbour of yours, a lady residing in or near Highbury. A family of the name of Barnes, or Bates. Do you know any family of that name?

Mr Weston   To be sure we do! Mrs Bates – we passed her house – I saw Miss Bates at the window. True, true, you are acquainted with Miss Fairfax. I remember you knew her at Weymouth, and a fine girl she is. Call upon her, by all means.

Frank   There is no necessity for my calling this morning. Another day would do as well. But there was that degree of acquaintance at Weymouth which –

Mr Weston   Oh, go today, go today! Do not defer it! What is right to be done cannot be done too soon. And besides, I must give you a hint, Frank; any want of attention to her here should be carefully avoided. You saw her with the Campbells when she was the equal of everybody she mixed with, but here she is with a poor old grandmother, who has barely enough to live on. If you do not call early it will be a slight.

Frank   I submit to your advice, sir.

Emma   I have heard her speak of the acquaintance. (**Frank** *turns to her*.) She is a very elegant young woman.

Frank   Indeed.

Emma   Did you often see her at Weymouth? Were you in the same society?

Frank It is always the lady's right to decide on the degree of acquaintance.

Emma Upon my word you answer as discreetly as she could do herself, she is so very reserved, so unwilling to give the least information about anybody, that I really think you may say what you like of your acquaintance with her.

Frank May I indeed? Then I will speak the truth, and nothing suits me so well. I met her frequently at Weymouth. I had known the Campbells a little in town; and at Weymouth we were very much in the same set. Colonel Campbell is a very agreeable man, and Mrs Campbell a friendly, warm-hearted woman. I like them all.

Emma You know Miss Fairfax's situation in life, I conclude; her destiny as a governess?

Frank (*hesitating*) Yes – I believe I do. Did you ever hear Miss Fairfax play? Her musical skills were much talked of in Weymouth.

Emma Ever hear her! I have heard her play every year of our lives since we both began. She plays charmingly.

Frank I wanted the opinion of someone who could really judge. She appeared to *me* to play well, that is, with considerable taste, but I know nothing of the matter myself. I remember one proof of her being thought to play well: a man, a very musical man, and in love with another woman – engaged to her, in fact – would yet never ask that other woman to sit down to the instrument, if the lady in question could sit down instead – never seemed like to hear one if he could hear the other. That I thought, in a man of known musical talent was some proof.

Emma Proof indeed! Mr Dixon is very musical, is he? We shall know more about them all, in half an hour from you, than Miss Fairfax would have vouchsafed in half a year.

Frank Yes, Mr Dixon and Miss Campbell were the persons, and I thought it a very strong proof.

Emma   Poor Mrs Dixon! I am glad she is gone to settle in Ireland.

Frank   You are right. It was not very flattering to Miss Campbell; but she really did not seem to feel it.

Emma   So much the better – or so much the worse: I do not know which. But Miss Fairfax must have felt the improper and dangerous distinction.

Frank (*quickly*)   There appeared such a perfectly good understanding between them . . . (*He stops.*) But I am, in this, as so many other things, in complete agreement with you, Miss Woodhouse.

She smiles graciously at him.

Jane   Emma's very good opinion of Frank Churchill was a little shaken the following day, by hearing that he was gone off to London, merely to have his hair cut.

Sarah   There was certainly no harm in his travelling sixteen miles twice over on such an errand, but there was an air of foppery and nonsense about it which she could not approve.

Elizabeth   And nor could Mr Knightley.

Mr Knightley   Sixteen miles just to have his hair cut? Just the silly, trifling fellow I took him for!

Emma   Well, I suppose young men must be allowed their little whims.

Mr Knightley   Emma, I have a piece of news for you. You like news – and I heard an article on my way hither that I think will interest you.

Emma   News? Oh yes, I always like news. What is it? Why do you smile so?

Enter, rapidly, **Miss Bates** *and* **Jane Fairfax**.

Miss Bates   Oh, my dear friends, how are you this morning. My dear Miss Woodhouse – I come quite overpowered. My thanks to you and your father for such a

beautiful hindquarter of pork! We are so indebted to you!
Have you heard the news? Mr Elton is to be married!

Mr Knightley   There is my news. I thought it would
interest you.

Miss Bates   But where could you hear it? Where could you
possibly hear it, Mr Knightley? For it is not five minutes since
I received Mrs Cole's note – no it cannot be more than five –
or at least ten – for I had got my bonnet and spencer on, just
ready to come out – I was only gone down to speak to Patty
again about the pork – Jane was standing in the passage,
were you not, Jane? – for my mother was so afraid that we
had not any salting-pan large enough. And then came the
note. A Miss Hawkins – that's all I know. A Miss Hawkins of
Bath. My mother is so pleased! She says she cannot bear to
have the poor old vicarage without a mistress. Jane, you have
never seen Mr Elton.

Jane Fairfax (*indifferently*)   No – I have never seen Mr
Elton. Is he . . . is he a tall man?

Miss Bates   And he has been gone such a short time. A
Miss Hawkins. Well, I had always rather fancied it would be
some young lady hereabouts; not that I ever – Mrs Cole once
whispered something to me – but I immediately said, 'No,
Mr Elton is a most worthy young man, but –' At the same
time, nobody could wonder if Mr Elton should have aspired
. . . Miss Woodhouse lets me chatter on, so good-
humouredly. She knows I would not offend for the world.
How does Miss Smith do? Have you heard from Mrs John
Knightley lately? And all the little Knightleys? Jane, do you
know I always fancy Mr Dixon like Mr John Knightley? I
mean in person – tall, and with that sort of look – and not
very talkative.

Jane Fairfax   Quite wrong, my dear aunt. There is no
likeness at all.

Miss Bates   Very odd! One takes up a notion and runs
away with it. Mr Dixon, you say, is not, strictly speaking,
handsome.

Jane Fairfax   Handsome! Oh no, far from it. Certianly plain. I told you he was plain.

Miss Bates   My dear, you said that Miss Campbell would not allow him to be plain, and that you yourself –

Jane Fairfax   Oh, as for me, my judgement is worth nothing. But I gave what I believed the general opinion when I called him plain. (*She turns to* **Emma**.) Are you looking forward to the Coles' party, Miss Woodhouse?

The Coles' party. A march playing distantly. **Miss Bates** *is talking to* **Emma** *and* **Mrs Weston**.

Miss Bates   And then this morning, out of the blue, it was suddenly delivered! A pianoforte. A very elegant pianoforte. Not a grand, of course, but a large-sized, square one. It arrived from Broadwood's to all astonishments, but particularly to Jane's. Jane was the most astonished of the three of us. She was quite at a loss, quite confused as to who could possibly have ordered it. We can only think it must have come from Colonel Campbell. But Jane had a letter from them very lately and not a word was said about it.

Emma *turns, to see* **Frank** *standing next to her*.

Emma   Why do you smile?

Frank   Nay, why do you?

Emma   Me? I smile for pleasure at Colonel Campbell's being so rich and liberal. It is a handsome present.

Frank   Very.

Emma   I rather wonder why it was never made before.

Frank   Perhaps Miss Fairfax had never been staying here so long before.

Emma   You may say what you choose, but your countenance testifies that your thoughts on the subject are very much like mine.

Frank   Not at all. I smile because you smile, and shall probably suspect what you suspect. But if Colonel Campbell is not the person, who can be?

Emma   What do you say to Mr Dixon?

Frank   Mr Dixon. Very well. Yes, I immediately perceive that it must be the joint present of Mr and Mrs Dixon. We were speaking the other day, you know, of his being a warm admirer of her performance.

Emma   Yes, and what you told me on that head, confirmed an idea which I had entertained before. I do not mean to reflect upon the good intentions of either Mr Dixon or Miss Fairfax, but I cannot help suspecting either that, after making his proposals to her friend, he had the misfortune to fall in love with her, or that he became conscious of a little attachment on her side. One might guess twenty things without guessing exactly the right, but I am sure there must be a particular cause for her choosing to come to Highbury instead of going with the Campbells to Ireland.

Frank   And upon my word, your suspicions have an air of great probability. Mr Dixon's preference of her music to her friend's, I can answer for being very decided.

He looks intently in the direction of **Jane Fairfax**.

Emma (*after a moment*)   What is the matter?

Frank (*turning back*)   Thank you for rousing me. I believe I have been very rude, but really Miss Fairfax has done her hair in so odd a way – so very odd a way, that I cannot keep my eyes from her. I never saw anything so *outrée*. Those curls! This must be a fancy of her own. I see nobody else looking like her! I must go and ask her whether it is an Irish fashion. Shall I? Yes, I will. I declare I will – and you shall see how she takes it – whether she colours.

He goes over to the other side of the room. **Mrs Weston** *joins* **Emma** *and looks after him.*

Mrs Weston   Frank is over halfway through his visit. His father and I will be very sorry to see him go.

Emma   Perhaps this time it will not be so long before we see him again.

Mrs Weston   Perhaps. My dear Emma, I am longing to talk to you. I have been making discoveries and forming plans, just like yourself. Do you know how Miss Bates and her niece came here?

Emma   How? They were invited, were they not?

Mrs Weston   Oh yes, but how they were conveyed hither? The manner of their coming?

Emma   They walked, I conclude. How else could they come?

Mrs Weston   Mr Knightley's carriage brought them, and is to take them home again.

Emma   Very likely. I know no man more likely than Mr Knightley to do anything really good-natured or considerate. He is not a gallant man, but he is a very humane one; and this, considering Jane Fairfax's ill health, would appear a case of humanity to him.

Mrs Weston   Well, you give him credit for more simple benevolence in this instance than I do. For while Miss Bates was telling me of his kindness, a suspicion darted into my head, and I have never been able to get it out again. In short, I have made a match between Mr Knightley and Jane Fairfax. See the consequence of keeping you company!

Emma (*indignantly*)   Mr Knightley and Jane Fairfax! Dear Mrs Weston, how could you think of such a thing? Mr Knightley! Mr Knightley must not marry! You would not have little Henry cut out from Donwell? Oh, no, no, Henry must have Donwell. I cannot consent at all to Mr Knightley's marrying. And Jane Fairfax too, of all women!

Mrs Weston   Nay, she has always been a first favourite with him, as you very well know.

Emma   But the imprudence of such a match.

Mrs Weston   I am not speaking of its prudence; merely its probability.

Emma   But Mr Knightley does not want to marry. Do not put it into his head! He is as happy as possible by himself, with his farm, and his sheep, and his library and all the parish to manage. You take up an idea and run away with it, Mrs Weston.

Frank (*returning*)   Come, you must play for us, Miss Woodhouse. Mrs Cole has requested, most insistently, that you begin the musical entertainment.

After much false modesty, and eager cries from the party guests, **Emma** *sits down at the piano and* **Frank** *sings. Afterwards there are cries for* **Jane Fairfax** *to take her turn.* **Frank** *accompanies her in a duet.*

Mr Knightley (*as she finishes*)   That will do. You have had quite enough for one evening, in your present, delicate state.

Frank   Come, come. I think you could manage another without effort, Miss Fairfax. The first part of this song is so very trifling. The strength of it falls on the second.

Mr Knightley (*loudly*)   This fellow thinks of nothing but showing off his own voice. This must not be! Miss Bates, are you mad, to let your niece sing herself hoarse in this manner? Go and interfere! They have no mercy on her.

Emma *looks carefully at him.*

William   Frank Churchill had danced once at Highbury, and was now determined to host a ball of his own.

Sarah   Emma was naturally very willing to assist and advise in the preparations.

Jane   But two days of joyful security were immediately followed by the overthrow of everything. A letter arrived from Mr Churchill to urge his nephew's instant return. Mrs Churchill was unwell – far too unwell to do without him, and he must set off for Enscombe without delay.

Hartfield.

Frank (*to* **Emma**)   Of all horrid things, leave-taking is the worst.

Emma   But you will come again. This will not be your only visit to Randalls.

Frank (*shaking his head*)   Ah, the uncertainty of when I may be able to return!

Emma   Our poor ball must be quite given up.

Frank   Ah, that ball! Why did we wait for anything? How often is happiness destroyed by preparation, foolish preparation! You told us it would be so. Oh, Miss Woodhouse, why are you always so right?

Emma   Indeed, I am very sorry to be right in this instance. I would much rather have been merry than wise.

Frank   Such a fortnight as it has been! Every day more precious and delightful than the day before. Happy those who can remain at Highbury!

Emma   As you do us such ample justice now, I will venture to ask whether you did not come a little doubtingly at first? You would not have been so long in coming if you had had a pleasant idea of Highbury.

He laughs, rather self-consciously.

And you must be off this very morning?

Frank   Yes, my father is to join me here and I must be off immediately. I am almost afraid that every moment will bring him.

Emma   Not five minutes to spare even for your friends Miss Fairfax and Miss Bates? How unlucky. Miss Bates' powerful, argumentative mind might have strengthened yours.

Frank   Yes, I *have* called there; passing by the door, I thought it better. I went in for three minutes, and was detained by Miss Bates' being absent. She is a woman that one may, that one must laugh at; but that one would not wish to slight. It was better to pay my visit, then . . .

He gets up and looks out of the window.

In short, perhaps, Miss Woodhouse – I think you can hardly be quite without suspicion . . .

He looks at her.

Emma (*uncertain of his meaning*)   You were quite in the right; it was most natural to pay your visit then . . .

He sighs.

Frank   It was something to feel that all the rest of my time might be given to Hartfield. My regard for Hartfield is most warm . . .

He looks at her again. She looks back, equally uncertain.

Goodbye, Miss Woodhouse.

He leaves the stage.

Emma   He is in love with me! He is far more in love with me than I had supposed! He almost told me he loved me! How am I to bear the change? I must be in love with him. I should be the oddest creature in the world if I were not in love. What a strange feeling!

A bell rings offstage.

William (*entering*)   Mama has tea ready downstairs!

General excitement and babble. Piano.

Exit.

Act Three

The theatricals resume after tea. Everyone in a very jolly mood.

Sarah Mrs Elton was first seen at church; but though devotion might be interrupted, curiosity could not be satisfied by a bride in a pew, and it must be left for the visits in form which were then to be paid, to settle whether she were very pretty indeed –

Jane Or only rather pretty –

Elizabeth Or not pretty at all.

Sarah Emma had feelings, less of curiosity than of pride or propriety, to make her resolve on not being the last to pay her respects.

Robert And bride and groom returned the visit shortly afterwards.

Mrs Elton What a delightful home you have, Miss Woodhouse. It reminds me exactly of my brother, Mr Suckling's seat. Hartfield is exactly like Maple Grove! Very like Maple Grove indeed. The modernity of the house and the expansiveness of the garden. I am quite struck by the likeness! This room is the very shape and size of the morning-room at Maple Grove – my sister's favourite room. (*To* **Mr Elton**.) Did the likeness not strike you, Mr E? Is it not astonishingly like? I could really almost fancy myself at Maple Grove. (*A sentimental little sigh.*) Whenever you are transplanted, like me, Miss Woodhouse, you will understand how very delightful it is to meet with anything at all like what one has left behind. I always say this is quite one of the evils of matrimony.

Emma Indeed.

Mrs Elton My brother and sister will be enchanted with this place. The laurels at Maple Grove are in the same profusion as here, and stand very much in the same way.

Emma　When you have seen more of this country, I am afraid you will think you have overrated Hartfield. Surrey is full of beauties.

Mrs Elton　Oh, yes, I am quite aware of that. It is the garden of England, you know. Surrey is the garden of England.

Emma　Yes, but we must not rest our claims on that distinction. Many counties, I believe, are called the garden of England, as well as Surrey.

Mrs Elton　No, I fancy not. I never heard any county but Surrey called so.

Emma *is silenced.*

Mrs Elton　My brother and sister have promised us a visit in the spring, or summer at the farthest, and that will be our time for exploring. While they are with us, we shall explore a great deal, I dare say. They will have their *barouche-landau*, of course, which holds four perfectly; and therfore, without saying anything of *our* carriage, we should be able to explore the different beauties extremely well. They would hardly come in their *chaise*, I think, at that season of the year. Mr Suckling is extremely fond of exploring. We explored to King's-Western twice last summer, in that way, just after their first having the *barouche-landau*. You have many parties of that kind here, I suppose, Miss Woodhouse, every summer?

Emma　No, not immediately here. We are a very quiet set of people, I believe, more disposed to stay at home than engage in schemes of pleasure.

Mrs Elton　Ah, there is nothing like staying at home, for real comfort. Nobody can be more devoted to home than I am. I was quite a proverb for it at Maple Grove. Many a time has Selina said, when she has been going to Bristol, 'I cannot get this girl to move from the house. I absolutely must go in by myself, though I hate being stuck in the *barouche-landau* without a companion.' And yet I am no advocate for entire seclusion. I think, on the contrary, when people shut themselves up entirely from society, it is a very bad thing.

Emma I dare say.

Mrs Elton We have been calling at Randalls, and found them both at home; and very pleasant people they seem to be. I like them extremely. Mr Weston seems an excellent creature – quite a first-rate favourite with me already, I assure you. And *she* appears so truly good – there is something so motherly and kind-hearted about her, that it wins upon one directly. She was your governess, I think?

Emma *opens her mouth, then closes it again.*

Mrs Elton Having understood as much, I was rather astonished to find her so very ladylike! But she is really quite the gentlewoman.

Emma Mrs Weston's manners were always particularly good.

Mrs Elton And *who* do you think came in while we were there? Who do you think, Miss Woodhouse?

Emma (*wondering*) Who?

Mrs Elton Knightley! Knightley himself! Was it not lucky – for not being within when he called the other day, I had never seen him before; and of course, as so *particular* a friend of Mr E's, I had a great curiosity. 'My friend, Knightley' has been so often mentioned, that I was really impatient to see him; and I must do my *caro sposo* the justice to say that he need not be ashamed of his friend. Knightley is quite the gentleman.

Mr Elton *stands.*

Mrs Elton Ah, and so we leave you, dear Miss Woodhouse. So happy to have seen your delightful house. I will write to Selina as soon as I get home to tell her of the remarkable likeness.

They exit.

Emma   Insufferable woman! Worse than I had supposed.
Absolutely insufferable! Knightley! – I could not have
believed it. Knightley! Never seen him in her life before, and
call him Knightley! – and to *discover* that he is a gentleman! I
doubt whether he will return the compliment and discover
her to be a lady. I could not have believed it! Oh, what would
Frank Churchill say to her, if he were here. How angry and
diverted he would be! Ah, there I am – thinking of him
directly. Always the first person to be thought of! How I
catch myself out! Frank Churchill comes as regularly into my
mind . . .

Mrs Elton   I see how it is! I see what a life I am to lead
among you. Upon my word we shall be absolutely dissipated.
We really seem quite the fashion. If this is living in the
country, it is nothing very formidable. From Monday to
Saturday next, I assure you we have not a disengaged day!

Dinner at Hartfield.

Mr Weston   I hope you enjoyed your walk this morning,
Miss Fairfax, and did not venture far, or I am sure you must
have been wet. We scarcely got home in time. I hope you
turned directly.

Jane Fairfax   I went only to the post office, and reached
home before the rain was much. It is my daily errand. I
always fetch the letters when I am here. It saves trouble, and
is a something to get me out. A walk before breakfast does me
good.

Mr Weston   Not a walk in the rain, I should imagine.

Jane Fairfax   No, but it did not absolutely rain when I set
out.

Mrs Elton   My dear Jane, what is this I hear? Going to the
post office in the rain! You sad girl, how could you do such a
thing? It is a sign I was not there to take care of you.

Jane Fairfax   I assure you, Mrs Elton, I have not suffered
in the least from a few drops of rain.

Mrs Elton   Oh, do not tell me! You really are a very sad girl, and do not know how to take care of yourself. To the post office indeed! I never heard the like! There must be some arrangement made, there must indeed. I shall speak to Mr E. The man who fetches our letters every morning (one of our men, I forget his name) shall inquire for yours too and bring them to you.

Jane Fairfax (*earnestly*)   Excuse me, I cannot by any means consent to such an arrangement, so needlessly troublesome to your servant. If the errand were not a pleasure to me, it could be done, as it always is when I am not here, by my grandmamma's.

Mrs Elton   Oh, my dear, but so much as Patty has to do! And it is a kindness to employ our men.

Jane Fairfax (*to* **Mrs Weston**)   The post office is a wonderful establishment! The regularity and dispatch of it! If one thinks of all that it has to do, and all that it does so well, it is really astonishing!

Mr Weston   Quite astonishing.

Jane Fairfax   And when one considers the variety of hands, and of bad hands too, that are to be deciphered, it increases the wonder!

Mrs Elton (*left out*)   April is the season for rain, you know. Here is April come already, Jane. I get quite anxious about you. June will soon be here. We really must find you a suitable situation before the summer comes.

Jane Fairfax   Thank you, but I do not wish to make any inquiries yet. I –

Mrs Elton   Oh, my dear, we cannot begin too early. You are not aware of the difficulty in procuring exactly the desirable thing.

Jane Fairfax   I was not aware? Dear Mrs Elton, who can have thought of it as *I* have done?

Mrs Elton   But you do not know how many candidates there *are* for the first situations. I saw a vast deal of that in the neighbourhood round Maple Grove. A cousin of Mr Suckling, Mrs Bragge, had such an infinity of applications; everybody was anxious to be in her family for she moves in the first circle. Wax-candles in the schoolroom! You may imagine how desirable! Of all houses in the kingdom, Mrs Bragge's is the one I would most wish to see you in. I shall write to Mrs Partridge in a day or two and give her a strict charge to be on the look-out for anything eligible.

Jane Fairfax Excuse me, ma'am, but this is by no means my intention. I make no enquiry myself, and should be sorry to have any made by my friends. There are places in town, offices, where inquiry would soon produce something, offices for the sale – not quite of human flesh – but of human intellect.

Mrs Elton Oh, my dear, human flesh! You quite shock me. If you mean a fling at the slave-trade, I assure you Mr Suckling was always rather a friend to the abolition.

Jane Fairfax I was not thinking of the slave-trade. Governess-trade, I assure, was all that I had in view.

Mrs Elton Well, we shall see, we shall see. We will work on her, shan't we, Miss Woodhouse?

Emma *smiles*.

Sarah Emma was more preoccupied by the news that Frank Churchill was soon to be once more amongst them, and for a considerable length of time.

William Mrs Churchill had decided that, Yorkshire being rather chilly in the spring, a spell down South would bring her enormous benefits and so they had taken a house in Richmond for the season.

Sarah A very little quiet reflection was enough to satisfy Emma as to the nature of her agitation on hearing this news. She was soon convinced that it was not for herself she was feeling apprehensive or embarrassed; it was for him. Her own attachment had really subsided into a mere nothing. But if *he*, who had undoubtedly been always so much the most in love of the two, were to be returning with the same warmth of sentiment which he had taken away, it would be very distressing and she wished she might be able to keep him from an absolute declaration.

Music starts.

Robert   Mr Weston was determined that no misfortune occur again to prevent the ball and the room at the Crown was once again taken, the day after Frank's arrival at Highbury.

The ball is in place.

Frank   I have a great curiosity to see Mrs Elton. I have heard so much of her. It cannot be long, I think, before she comes. And she is bringing Miss Bates and Miss Fairfax, I believe.

Emma   Mrs Elton is extremely solicitous towards Miss Fairfax.

Frank   Yes. (*Hearing something.*) Ah, this must be they. (*He moves away, then wanders back.*) I am forgetting that I am not acquainted with Mrs Elton. I have no business to put myself forward.

Mrs Elton *is escorted in by* **Mr Weston**.

Mrs Elton   Good evening, my dear Mr Weston, I hope that we are not too early. It is never done to –

Mr Weston   But Miss Bates and Miss Fairfax! We thought you were to bring them.

Jane   The mistake had been slight. The carriage was sent back for them.

Mrs Elton (*to* **Mr Weston**)   They will be with us in no time, I am sure. Our coachman and horses are so extremely expeditious! I believe we drive faster than anybody. What a pleasure it is to send one's carriage for a friend! By the by, Mr Weston, your son is a very fine young man indeed. You know I candidly told you I would form my own opinion and I am happy to say that I am extremely pleased with him. You may believe me. I never compliment. And he is to be with us for quite a while, I believe.

Mr Weston   Yes, Mrs Churchill has taken it into her head
that Enscombe is too cold for her. The fact is, I suppose, that
she is tired of Enscombe. She has now been a longer time
stationary there, than she ever was before, and she begins to
want change.

Mrs Elton   Dear me, yes, I quite understand. Selina is just
the same. She also –

Mr Weston (*pensively*)   You cannot be ignorant, Mrs
Elton, of my connection with the family, nor of the treatment
I have met with. *She* was the instigator. Frank's mother
would never have been slighted as she was but for her. Mr
Churchill has pride, but his pride is nothing to his wife's. And
what inclines one less to bear, she has no fair pretence of
family or blood. She was nobody when he married her,
barely the daughter of a gentleman. But ever since her being
turned into a Churchill she has out-Churchilled them all in
high and mighty claims. In herself, I assure you, she is an
upstart.

Mrs Elton   Only think! Well, that must be infinitely
provoking! I have quite a horror of upstarts. Maple Grove
has given me a thorough disgust for people of that sort. For
there is a family in that neighbourhood who are such an
annoyance to my brother and sister from the airs they give
themselves! Your description of Mrs Churchill made me
think of them directly. People of the name of Tupman, very
lately settled there, and encumbered with many low
connections, but giving themselves immense airs, and
expecting to be on a footing with the old, established
families. How they have got their fortune nobody knows.
They came from Birmingham, which is not a place to
promise much, you know, Mr Weston. One has not great
hopes from Birmingham. I always say there is something
direful in the sound.

Emma (*to* **Frank**)   How do you like Mrs Elton?

Frank   Not at all.

Emma   You are ungrateful.

Frank   Ungrateful! What do you mean? (*He smiles.*) No, do
not tell me. I do not want to know what you mean. Where is
my father? When are we to begin dancing?

The first dance.

Elizabeth   The ball proceeded pleasantly.

Jane   The only distressing element, for Emma, was in Mr
Knightley's not dancing. There he was, among the standers-
by, where he ought not to be. His tall, firm, upright figure
among the bulky forms and stooping shoulders of the elderly
men. Whenever she caught his eye, she forced him to smile,
but in general he was looking very grave.

Emma *is left dancing on her own (with a pretend partner).*

Sarah   The last two dances before supper were begun, and
Harriet had no partner – the only lady sitting down – and so
equal had been hitherto the number of dancers – that how
there could be anyone disengaged was the wonder!

Robert   But Emma's wonder lessened soon afterwards, on
seeing Mr Elton sauntering about. *He* would not ask Harriet
to dance if it were possible to be avoided.

Mrs Weston (*standing up to move over to him*)   Do not you
dance, Mr Elton?

Mr Elton   Most readily, Mrs Weston, if you will dance
with me.

Mrs Weston   Me! Oh no, I would get you a better partner
than myself. I am no dancer.

Mr Elton   If Mrs Gilbert wishes to dance, I shall have
great pleasure, I am sure – for though beginning to feel
myself rather an old married man, and that my dancing days
are over, it would give me very great pleasure at any time to
stand up with an old friend like Mrs Gilbert.

Mrs Weston   Mrs Gilbert does not mean to dance, but
there is a young lady disengaged whom I should be very glad
to see dancing – Miss Smith.

Mr Elton   Miss Smith! Oh . . . I had not observed. You are extremely obliging . . . and if I were not an old married man . . . but my dancing days are over, Mrs Weston. You will excuse me. Anything else I should be most happy to do, at your command . . . but my dancing days are over . . .

Emma *is still dancing.*

Sarah   Emma was mortified for Harriet. She saw Mr Elton walk over to Mr Knightley and arrange himself for a settled conversation while smiles of high glee passed between him and his wife. She would not look again. Her heart was in a glow, and she feared her face might be as hot.

Emma *continues dancing.*

Sarah   In another moment a happier sight caught her. Mr Knightley leading Harriet to the set!

Mr Knightley *leads* **Harriet** *to the set.*

Sarah   Never had she been more surprised, seldom more delighted, than at that instant. His dancing proved to be just what she had believed it, extremely good, and Mr Elton retreated into the card-room, looking (Emma trusted) very foolish.

Emma *moves over to* **Mr Knightley** *as the dance finishes.*

Emma   I cannot thank you enough for your gallantry to Harriet.

Mr Knightley   Nonsense. What else could any sensible person have done. Unpardonable rudeness!

Emma   And her scorn and her smiles. Harriet is worth ten of her.

Mr Knightley   They aimed at wounding more than Harriet. Emma, why is it that they are your enemies? (*She does not reply. He smiles.*) She ought not to be angry with you, I suspect, whatever *he* may be. Confess, Emma, you did want him to marry Harriet.

Emma   I did, and they cannot forgive me.

Mr Knightley (*shaking his head*)   I shall not scold you. I leave you to your own reflections.

Emma   Can you trust me with such flatterers? Does my vain spirit ever tell me I am wrong?

Mr Knightley   Not your vain spirit, but your serious spirit. If one leads you wrong, I am sure the other tells you of it.

Emma   I do own myself to have been completely mistaken in Mr Elton. There is a littleness in him which you discovered and which I did not.

Mr Knightley   And in return for your acknowledging so much, I will do you the justice to say that you would have chosen for him better than he has chosen for himself. Harriet Smith has some first-rate qualities, which Mrs Elton is totally without. I found Harriet more conversible than I expected.

Another dance begins.

With whom are you going to dance?

Emma (*hesitating*)   With you, if you will ask me.

Mr Knightley (*offering his hand*)   Will you?

Emma   Indeed I will. You have shown that you can dance, and you know we are not really so much brother and sister as to make it at all improper.

Mr Knightley   Brother and sister! No indeed!

They dance.

Act Four

Sarah Emma wandered about the lawn the next morning in an extremely happy frame of mind. The impertinence of the Eltons, which for a few minutes had threatened to ruin the rest of her evening, had been the occasion of some of its highest satisfactions; and she looked forward to another happy result – the cure of Harriet's infatuation. Harriet rational, Frank Churchill not too much in love with herself, and Mr Knightley not wanting to quarrel with her, how very happy a summer must be before her!

Elizabeth Having arranged all these matters, looked them through and put them all to rights, the great iron sweepgate opened, and two persons entered whom she had never less expected to see together – Frank Churchill, with Harriet leaning on his arm – actually Harriet!

Enter **William** *and* **Jane**.

Sarah A moment sufficed to convince her that something extraordinary had happened. Harriet looked white and frightened (**Jane** *looks white and frightened.*) and he was trying to cheer her. (**William** *slaps* **Jane**'s *face. She slaps him back.*) As soon as they were all three in the hall, Harriet immediately sinking into a chair, fainted away.

Elizabeth A young lady who faints, must be recovered; questions must be answered, and surprises be explained.

Frank Miss Smith was walking with Miss Bickerton along the Richmond road, Miss Woodhouse. Half a mile out of Highbury they were unfortunate enough to wander upon a party of gipsies.

Emma Gipsies!

Frank Apparently so. Miss Bickerton became excessively fearful and ran up a steep bank. Poor Miss Smith was suffering from the cramp, after all her exertions at dancing last night and was unable to follow quickly enough. She was soon surrounded by the whole group.

Emma   The whole group!

Frank   By a most fortunate chance I happened to be walking by – to pick up my horses on another part of the road. (I borrowed a pair of scissors from Miss Bates last night and was obliged to stop at her door and go in for a few minutes on my way back to Richmond.) And a most propitious delay it was for I happened upon Miss Smith and her assailants at that very moment.

Emma   Assailants!

Frank   I naturally brought her straight to Hartfield. There could be no other place . . . But I dare stay no longer. These several delays, Miss Woodhouse, leave me not another minute to lose. I bid you good day.

He exits.

Sarah   Such an adventure as this – a fine young man and a lovely young woman thrown together in such a way, could hardly fail of suggesting ideas even to the coldest heart and the steadiest brain!

Elizabeth   So Emma thought, at least.

Sarah   And knowing, as she did, the favourable state of mind of each at this period, it struck her the more. *He* was wishing to get the better of his attachment to herself, *she* just recovering from her mania for Mr Elton. It seemed as if everything united to promise the most interesting consequences.

Harriet   (*the next day*)   Miss Woodhouse – if you are at leisure – I have something that I should like to tell you – a sort of confession to make – and then, you know, it will be over.

Emma   I am certainly at leisure, Harriet.

Harriet   It is my duty, and I am sure it is my wish, to have no reserves with you on this subject. I do not want to say more than is necessary, and I dare say you understand me.

Emma Yes, I hope I do.

Harriet (*warmly*) How I could so long a time be fancying myself . . . It seems like madness! I can see nothing extraordinary in him now. I do not care whether I meet him or not – except of the two I had rather not see him. To convince you that I have been speaking truth, I am now going to destroy what I ought to have destroyed long ago – what I ought never to have kept.

She reveals something from her bag.

Cannot you guess what this parcel holds?

Emma Not the least in the world. Did he ever give you anything?

Harriet No – I cannot call them gifts; but they are things that I have valued very much.

She hands the parcel to **Emma**.

Emma (*reading*) 'Most Precious Treasures.'

Harriet *unfolds the parcel. Well-wrapped in silver paper is a small box. Well-wrapped in cotton wool is a small plaster.*

Harriet Now, you must recollect.

Emma No, indeed I do not.

Harriet Dear me, I should not have thought it possible! Do not you remember his cutting his finger with your penknife, and your recommending court plaster? But as you had none about you and knew I had, you desired me to supply him; and so I took mine out and cut him a piece; but it was a great deal too large, and he cut it smaller, and kept playing some time with what was left, before he gave it back to me. And so then, in my nonsense, I could not help making a treasure of it – so I put it by never to be used, and looked at it now and then as a great treat.

Emma And so you actually put this piece of court plaster by for his sake?

Harriet (*returning to the box*) Here – here is something still more valuable, I mean that *has* been more valuable, because this is what really did belong to him, which the court plaster never did.

She brings out the end of an old pencil.

Emma   And what else?

Harriet   That's all. I have nothing more to show you, or to say – except that I am now going to throw them both behind the fire, and I wish you to see me do it.

Emma   But is it really necessary to burn the court plaster? I have not a word to say for the bit of old pencil, but the court plaster might be useful.

Harriet   I shall be happier to burn it. It has a disagreeable look to me. There it goes, and there is an end, thank heaven, of Mr Elton!

They both regard the fire solemnly.

(*Eventually.*)   I shall never marry.

Emma   Never marry! That is a new resolution.

Harriet   It is one that I will never change, however.

Emma   I hope it does not proceed from . . . I hope it is not in compliment to Mr Elton?

Harriet   Mr Elton indeed! Oh no! (*Under her breath.*) So superior to Mr Elton . . .

Emma (*looking at her thoughtfully*)   Harriet, I will not affect to be in doubt of your meaning. Your resolution or rather your expectation of never marrying, results from an idea that the person whom you might prefer, would be too greatly your superior in situation to think of you. Is it not so?

Harriet   Oh, Miss Woodhouse, believe me I have not the presumption to suppose . . . indeed I am not so mad . . . but it is a pleasure to me to admire him at a distance, and to think of his infinite superiority to all the rest of the world.

Emma   I am not at all surprised at you, Harriet. The service he rendered you was enough to warm your heart.

Harriet   Service! Oh it was such an inexpressible
obligation! The very recollection of it, and all that I felt at
the time – when I saw him coming – his noble look – and my
wretchedness before. Such a change! From perfect misery to
perfect happiness!

Emma   It is very natural. It is natural and it is honourable.
But that it will be a fortunate preference is more than I can
promise. We were wrong before; we will be cautious now. He
is your superior, no doubt, and there do seem objections and
obstacles of a very serious nature; and yet, Harriet, more
wonderful things have taken place, there have been matches
of greater disparity. But take care of yourself. Though
however it may end, be assured that your raising your
thoughts to him, is a mark of good taste which I shall always
know how to value.

Harriet *kisses her hand silently and gratefully*.

Piano into the next scene.

Elizabeth   In this state of schemes and hopes and
connivance, June opened upon Hartfield.

Jane   To Highbury in general it brought no material
change. The Eltons were still talking of a visit from the
Sucklings, and of the use to be made of their *barouche-landau*.

William   Jane Fairfax was still at her grandmother's, and
as the return of the Campbells from Ireland was again
delayed, she was likely to remain there full two months
longer.

Elizabeth   Provided at least she were able to defeat Mrs
Elton's activity in her service, and save herself from being
hurried into a delightful situation against her will.

An evening party at Hartfield. Piano ends. The **Harriet** *doll is
sitting at the table.*

Mr Woodhouse   Miss Bates, let Emma help you to a little
bit of tart – a very little bit. Ours are all apple tarts. You need
not be afraid of unwholesome preserves here. I do not advise

the custard. Mr Perry is most singular in his view of custards being very disagreeable to the system.

Frank (*to* **Mr Weston**)   By the bye, sir, what became of Mr Perry's plan of setting up his carriage?

Mr Weston (*surprised*)   I did not know that he ever had any such plan.

Frank   Nay, I had it from you. You wrote me word of it three months ago.

Mr Weston   Me? Impossible!

Frank   Indeed you did. I remember it perfectly. Mrs Perry had told somebody, and was extremely happy about it.

Mr Weston   Upon my word I never heard of it till this moment.

Frank   Never! Bless me! How could it be? Then I must have dreamt it – but I was completely persuaded . . . I am a great dreamer. I dream of everybody at Highbury when I am away, and when I have gone through my particular friends, then I begin dreaming of Mr and Mrs Perry. Miss Bates, can I help you to a little bit of tart?

Miss Bates   Why to own the truth, if I *must* speak on this subject, there is no denying that Mr Frank Churchill might have – I do not mean to say that he did not dream it – I am sure *I* have sometimes the oddest dreams in the world – but if I am questioned about it, I must acknowledge that there *was* such an idea last spring; for Mrs Perry herself mentioned it to my mother, and the Coles knew of it as well as ourselves – but it was quite a secret, known to nobody else, and only thought of about three days. Jane, don't you remember grandmamma's telling of it when we got home? I forget where we had been walking to – very likely to Randalls; yes I think it was to Randalls. Mrs Perry was always particularly fond of my mother – indeed I do not know who is not – and she had mentioned it to her in confidence; and from that day to this I never mentioned it to a soul that I knew of. At the same time, I will not positively answer for my having never dropped a hint, because I do sometimes pop out a thing

before I am aware. I am a talker, you know. I am rather a
talker; and now and then I have let a thing escape me which I
should not. I am not like Jane. I wish I were. I will answer for
it *she* never betrayed the least thing in the world. Where is
she? Oh, just behind . . .

Tea is taken.

Frank   Miss Woodhouse, have your nephews taken away
their alphabets – their box of letters? It used to stand here.
Where is it? We had great amusement with those letters one
morning. I want to puzzle you again.

Emma   A splendid idea, Mr Churchill. The letters are just
over there.

She fetches the box and she, **Frank** *and* **Jane Fairfax** *start playing
with the letters.*

Robert   Mr Knightley's eyes watched Frank Churchill's
carefully. He suspected in him the determination of catching
Jane's eyes. He placed a word before her. Frank was next to
Emma, Jane opposite them – and Mr Knightley so placed as
to see them all; and it was his object to see as much as he could
with as little apparent observation. (*He acts unobtrusive.*) The
word was discovered, and with a faint smile pushed away.
The word was 'blunder', and there was a blush on Jane's
cheek and it was proclaimed round the room. (*It is proclaimed
round the room.*) He feared there must be some decided
involvement. He saw a short word prepared for Emma, and
given to her with a look sly and demure. He saw that Emma
had made it out and found it highly entertaining, though it
was something which she judged proper to appear to censure
for she said:

Emma   Nonsense! For shame!

Frank (*glancing in* **Jane Fairfax***'s direction*)   I will give it to
her – shall I?

Emma (*laughing*)   No, no, you must not; you shall not
indeed.

He passes it to **Jane Fairfax**.

Robert   Mr Knightley's excessive curiosity to know what this word might be, made him seize every possible moment for darting his eye towards it and it was not long before he saw it to be 'Dixon'.

Jane Fairfax (*blushing and angrily pushing it away*)   I did not know that proper names were allowed.

She moves away. **Frank** *follows.*

Mr Knightley   Pray, Emma, may I ask in what lay the great amusement, the poignant sting of the last word given to you and Miss Fairfax? I saw the word and am curious to know how it could be so very entertaining to the one, and so very distressing to the other?

Emma (*embarrassed*)   Oh, it all meant nothing; a mere joke among ourselves.

Mr Knightley (*seriously*)   The joke seemed confined to you and Mr Churchill.

Silence.

My dear Emma, do you think you perfectly understand the degree of aquaintance between the gentleman and lady we have been speaking of?

Emma   Between Mr Frank Churchill and Miss Fairfax? Oh yes, perfectly. Why do you make a doubt of it?

Mr Knightley   Have you never at any time had reason to think that he admired her, or that she admired him?

Emma   Never, never! Never for the twentieth part of a moment did such an idea occur to me. And how could it possibly come into your head?

Mr Knightley   I have lately imagined that I saw symptoms of attachment between them – certain expressive looks, which I did not believe meant to be public.

Emma   Cowper, Mr Knightley! Pure Cowper! 'Myself creating what I saw', you know. I am delighted to find that you can vouchsafe to let your imagination wander – but it will not do – very sorry to check you in your first essay – but indeed it will not do.

Mr Knightley *leaves. Piano.*

William   It was now the middle of June and the weather fine, and the impending arrival of Mr and Mrs Suckling –

Jane   From Maple Grove –

William   Led to plans for a Highbury outing to Box Hill. Mrs Elton was impatient to name the day, when a lame carriage-horse threw everything into sad uncertainty.

Mrs Elton   Is not this most vexatious, Knightley? And such weather for exploring! The year will wear away at this rate, and nothing done. What are we to do?

Robert   Mr Knightley proposed their all exploring to Donwell to help pick his strawberries, a suggestion that was gratefully received by all.

Donwell Abbey.

William   It was a long time since Emma had been at the Abbey. She was glad to look around her, eager to refresh and correct her memory with more particular observation, of a house and grounds which must ever be so interesting to her and all her family.

Sarah   She felt all the honest pride and complacency which her alliance with the present and future proprietor could fairly warrant. Isabella had connected herself unexceptionably. She had given them neither men, nor names, nor places that could raise a blush.

William   The whole party were assembled, excepting Frank Churchill, who was expected any moment from Richmond.

Red ribbons – or something – are laid out to form strawberry beds. Everyone picking.

Mrs Elton   Strawberries are the best fruit in England, I do declare. Everybody's favourite! And to gather them for one's self is the only way of really enjoying them. I have picked twice as many as you already, Jane.

Jane Fairfax   Indeed you have, Mrs Elton.

Mrs Elton   Now, I have been saving the best news until now! I have been bursting to tell you all morning, but I said to Mr E, I will wait until Jane and I have picked at least one basket before telling her. The dear girl won't be able to pick for excitement after I have told her!

Jane Fairfax   What excitement have you in store for me?

Mrs Elton   A situation! I have found it! I said I would find you one before the summer and I have got a most desirable situation for you. I received notice of it this morning.

Jane Fairfax   I thank you for your trouble. However, as I said –

Mrs Elton   It is not quite with Mrs Suckling, and neither is it with Mrs Bragge, but in position and splendour it falls short only of them. It is with Mrs Smallridge – a cousin of Mrs Bragge, who moves in only the finest circles!

Jane Fairfax   I must assure you that I cannot, at present, as I told you, engage in anything. I am most grateful for your efforts, but I really am determined to remain in Highbury until the Campbells return to England.

Mrs Elton   But this will be a delightful surprise for the dear Campbells! Oh, I am wild to have the offer closed with immediately!

Jane Fairfax   Mr Knightley, will you not show us the gardens? We have not yet seen the Abbey fish-ponds. Miss Woodhouse, do you not think this an excellent time for a walk?

Sarah   Emma thought it an excellent time, but was herself obliged to sit a while indoors with her father, to relieve Mrs Weston of the task.

She moves across to another part of the stage and attends to the broom. She and the broom are then disturbed by **Jane Fairfax***, tying up her* *bonnet in preparation for leaving. She stops, startled, when she catches sight of* **Emma**.

Jane Fairfax   Oh, Miss Woodhouse, will you be so kind, when I am missed, as to say that I am gone home? I have said nothing about it to anybody. It would only be giving trouble and distress.

Emma   Certainly, if you wish it, but you are not going to walk to Highbury alone?

Jane Fairfax   Yes – what should hurt me? I walk fast. I shall be at home in twenty minutes.

Emma   But it is too far to be walking quite alone. Let my father's servant go with you. Let me order the carriage. You are fatigued already.

Jane Fairfax   I am fatigued, but it is not the sort of fatigue . . . quick walking will refresh me. Miss Woodhouse, we all know at times what it is to be wearied in spirits. Mine, I confess, are exhausted. The greatest kindness you can show me, will be to let me have my own way, and only say that I am gone when it is necessary.

Emma   Well, I will do so . . .

Jane Fairfax   Thank you. (*She starts to leave.*) Oh, Miss Woodhouse, the comfort of being sometimes alone!

She goes.

Emma (*looking after her*)   Such a home, indeed! Such an aunt! I do pity you. And the more sensibly you betray of their just horrors, the more I shall like you. (*She turns to the broom.*) Look, Papa! Look what Mr Knightley has left for you. Books, medals, corals, shells. What a kind thought! He has left out all his collections for you. Look, these are some drawings of St Mark's in Venice, and here are some pictures of Box Hill, where we are all to go tomorrow. And here –

Frank Churchill *enters the room, looking hot and flustered.*

Frank   I am sorry for my delay, Miss Woodhouse. Mrs Churchill unfortunately suffered a nervous seizure just as I was leaving. I had quite given up every thought of coming, till very late. And had I known how hot a ride I was to have, I believe I would not have come at all! Nothing kills me like the heat! Any degree of cold I can bear, but heat is intolerable.

He throws the broom off the chair, sits down and flicks, irritably, through one of the drawing books.

Emma   You will be cooler if you sit still.

Frank   As soon as I am cooler I will go back again. I could very ill be spared – but such a point had I made of my coming! You will all be going soon I suppose. I met *one* as I came – madness in such weather! Absolute madness!

Emma   Perhaps you should take some refreshment Mr Churchill. Food and drink will cool you down and restore your humour. (*Pointing.*) Everything is laid out in the dining-room.

Frank   No, I need nothing. I am not hungry. It would only make me hotter.

Sarah   I am glad I have done with being in love with him, thought Emma. I should not like a man who is so soon discomposed by a hot morning. Harriet's easy temper will not mind it.

Frank   As soon as my aunt gets well, I shall go abroad. I shall never be easy till I have seen some of these places. You will have my sketches some time or other to look at – or my tour to read – or my poem. I feel a strong persuasion, this morning, that I shall soon be abroad. I want a change. I am thwarted in everything material. I do not consider myself at all a fortunate person.

Emma   Tomorrow we are going to Box Hill. You must join us.

Frank   No – it will not be worthwhile. If I come, I shall be cross.

Emma   Then pray stay at Richmond.

Frank   But if I do, I shall be crosser still. I can never bear to think of you all there without me.

Emma   These are difficulties which you must settle for yourself. Choose your own degree of crossness. I shall press you no more.

Frank   Well, if you wish me to stay and join the party, I will.

He smiles at her. They get up to join the others outside.

Jane   They had a very fine day for Box Hill; and all the other outward circumstances of arrangement, accommodation and punctuality were in favour of a pleasant party.

Robert   Mr Weston directed the whole, officiating safely between Hartfield and the vicarage, and everybody was in good time.

Sarah   Nothing was wanting but to be happy when they got there.

Jane   And yet, on arrival and showing a burst of admiration, there was a languor, a want of spirit, a want of union, that could not be got over.

Sarah (*propping up the Harriet doll next to her*)   At first it was downright dullness to Emma. She had never seen Frank Churchill so silent and stupid. Whilst he was so dull, it was no wonder that Harriet should be dull likewise (*She pats the doll.*) and they were both insufferable.

Jane   When they all sat down it was better, for Frank Churchill grew talkative and gay, making her his first object

Sarah   To amuse her, and be agreeable in her eyes, seemed all that he cared for.

Frank   How much I am obliged to you for telling me to come today! If it had not been for you, I should certainly have lost all the happiness of this party. I had quite determined to go away again.

Emma   Yes, you were very cross; and I do not know what about, except that you were too late for the best strawberries. I was a kinder friend than you deserved. But you were humble. You begged hard to be commanded to come.

Frank   Don't say I was cross. I was fatigued. The heat overcame me.

Emma   It is hotter today.

Frank   Not to my feelings. I am perfectly comfortable today.

Emma   You are comfortable because you are under command.

Frank   Your command? Yes.

Emma   Perhaps I intended you to say so, but I meant self-command. You had, somehow or other, broken bounds yesterday, and run away from your own management.

Frank   It comes to the same thing. I can have no self-command without a motive. You order me, whether you speak or not.

Emma   Your gallantry is really unanswerable. (*She lowers her voice.*) But nobody speaks except ourselves, and it is rather too much to be talking nonsense for the entertainment of so many silent people.

Frank (*lowering his voice*)   Our companions are excessively stupid. What shall we do to rouse them? Any nonsense will serve. They shall talk. (*Louder.*) Ladies and gentlemen, I am ordered by Miss Woodhouse (who wherever she is presides) to say, that she desires to know what you are all thinking of.

Mr Weston   My thoughts are all focused on how to cool down. Very obvious, and hardly original.

He laughs.

Miss Bates   Oh dear, I'm sure I don't know what to tell Miss Woodhouse. My thoughts are all –

Frank (*to* **Emma**)   It will not do. They are most of them affronted. I will attack them with more address. Ladies and gentlemen, I am ordered by Miss Woodhouse to say that she waives her right of knowing exactly what you may all be thinking of, and only requires something very entertaining from each of you. She demands from each of you either one

thing very clever, be it prose or verse, or two things
moderately clever – or three things very dull indeed, and she
engages me to laugh heartily at them all.

Miss Bates   Oh, very well! Then I need not be uneasy.
Three things very dull indeed. That will just do for me, you
know. I shall be sure to say three dull things as soon as ever I
open my mouth, shan't I? (*She looks round at everybody.*) Do not
you all think I shall?

Emma (*mischievously*)   Ah, ma'am, but there may be a
difficulty. Pardon me – but you will be limited as to number –
only three at once?

Silence from the picnickers. The implication eventually hits **Miss
Bates**.

Miss Bates (*blushing*)   Ah . . . well, to be sure . . . Yes, I see
what she means . . . and I will try to hold my tongue. (*She
turns to* **Jane Fairfax**.) I must make myself very
disagreeable, or she would not have said such a thing to an
old friend.

Mr Weston   I like your plan. Agreed, agreed, I will do my
best. I am making a conundrum. How will a conundrum
reckon?

Frank   Low, I am afraid, sir, very low. But she shall be
indulgent – especially to anyone who leads the way.

Emma   No, it will not reckon low. A conundrum of Mr
Weston's shall clear him and his next neighbour. Come, sir,
pray let me hear it.

Mr Weston   I doubt its being very clever, myself. It is too
matter of fact, but here it is – What two letters of the alphabet
are there, that express perfection?

Frank   What two letters? Express perfection? I am sure I
do not know.

Mr Weston   Ah, you will never guess. (*To* **Emma**.) You, I
am certain, will never guess. I will tell you. 'M' and 'A'. Em –
ma. Do you understand?

Emma *and* **Frank** *laugh loudly, if a little forcibly.*

Frank (*passing round a dog-collar and a rather vulgar hat*)   Ah, there go the Eltons! Happy couple! How well they suit one another! Very lucky – marrying as they did, upon an acquaintance formed only in a public place! How many a man has committed himself on a short acquaintance, and rued it all the rest of his life!

Jane Fairfax   Such things do occur, undoubtedly –

Frank (*with a cough*)   You were saying?

Jane Fairfax (*calmly*)   I was only going to observe, that though such unfortunate circumstances do sometimes occur both to men and women, I cannot imagine them to be very frequent. A hasty and imprudent attachment may arise – but there is generally time to recover from it afterwards. It can be only weak, irresolute characters (whose happiness must be always at the mercy of chance) who will suffer an unfortunate acquaintance to be an inconvenience, an oppression for ever.

Frank Churchill *nods thoughtfully. Silence.*

Frank   Well, I have so little confidence in my own judgement, that whenever I marry, I hope somebody will choose my wife for me. (*To* **Emma**.) Will you? Will you choose a wife for me? I am sure I should like anybody fixed on by you. Find somebody for me. Adopt her, educate her.

Emma   And make her like myself.

Frank   By all means, if you can.

Emma   Very well, I undertake the commission. You shall have a charming wife.

Frank   She must be very lovely – and have hazel eyes. I care for nothing else. I shall go abroad for a couple of years, and when I return I shall come to you for my wife. Remember.

Jane Fairfax (*to* **Miss Bates**)   Now, ma'am, shall we join Mrs Elton.

Miss Bates   If you please, my dear. With all my heart. I am quite ready. I was ready to have gone with her, but this

will do just as well. We shall soon overtake her. There she is –
no, that's somebody else. That's one of the ladies in the Irish
car party, not at all like her. Well, I declare . . .

Sarah Emma was very much excited by the commission.
Would not Harriet be the very creature described by Frank
Churchill? Hazel eyes excepted, two years more might make
her all that he wished.

Jane Frank Churchill's spirits now rose to a pitch almost
unpleasant, however. Even Emma grew tired at last of
flattery and merriment, and wished herself rather walking
quietly about with any of the others.

Elizabeth The appearance of the servants looking out for
them to give notice of the carriages was a joyful sight, and
even the solicitude of Mrs Elton to have her carriage first,
was gladly endured. Such another scheme, composed of so
many ill-assorted people, she hoped never to be betrayed
again.

Sarah Whilst waiting for the carriage, she found Mr
Knightley by her side.

Mr Knightley Emma, I must once more speak to you as I
have been used to do. I cannot see you wrong-acting without
a remonstrance. How *could* you be so unfeeling to Miss Bates?
How could you be so insolent in your wit to a woman of her
character, age and situation? Emma, I had not thought it
possible.

Emma (*blushing, but trying to laugh it off*) Nay, how could I
help saying what I did? Nobody could have helped it. It was
not so very bad. I dare say she did not understand me.

Mr Knightley I assure you she did. She felt your full
meaning. She has talked of it since. I wish you could have
heard how she talked of it – with what candour and
generosity. I wish you could have heard her honouring your
forebearance, in being able to pay her such attentions, as she
was for ever receiving from yourself and your father, when
her society must be so irksome.

Emma   Oh, I know there is not a better creature in the world, but you must allow, that what is good and what is ridiculous are most unfortunately blended in her.

Mr Knightley   They *are* blended, I acknowledge; and, were she prosperous, I could allow much for the occasional prevalence of the ridiculous over the good. Were she a woman of fortune, I would leave every harmless absurdity to take its chance. Were she your equal in situation – but Emma, consider how far this is from being the case. She is poor; she has sunk from the comforts she was born to and if she live to old age, must probably sink more. Her *situation* should secure your compassion. It was badly done, indeed! You, whom she had known from an infant, whom she had seen grow up from a period when her notice was an honour, to have you now, in thoughtless spirits, and the pride of the moment, laugh at her, humble her – and before her niece too. This is not pleasant to you, Emma – and it is very far from a pleasure to me; but I must, I will – I *will* tell you truths while I can, satisfied with proving myself your friend by very faithful counsel, and trusting that you will some time or other do me greater justice than you can do now. Good day to you.

He hands her in to the carriage and leaves.

Sarah (*looking vainly after him*)   He had misinterpreted the feelings which had kept her face averted and her tongue motionless. They were combined only of anger against herself, mortification and deep concern.

Jane   Never had she felt so agitated, mortified, grieved, at any circumstance in her life.

Sarah   How could she have been so brutal, so unfeeling to Miss Bates!

Jane   How could she have exposed herself to such ill opinion in any one she valued!

Sarah   Time did not compose her. As she reflected more, she seemed but to feel it more.

Elizabeth   Emma felt the tears running down her cheeks almost all the way home, without being at any trouble to check them, extraordinary as they were.

Piano.

Robert   The wretchedness of the scheme to Box Hill was in Emma's thoughts the whole of the next day. She was surprised and a little distressed to receive a note from Mr Knightley informing her that he had gone to spend a few days with Mr and Mrs John Knightley.

Elizabeth   And more surprised, but less distressed, to hear from Mrs Weston that Jane Fairfax had agreed, after all, to accept the post of governess with Mrs Smallridge.

Jane   The following day however, brought news from Richmond to throw everything else into the background.

William   An express arrived at Randalls to announce the death of Mrs Churchill!

Gasps all round.

A sudden seizure of a different nature from anything foreboded by her general state, had carried her off after a short struggle.

Jane   The great Mrs Churchill was no more.

William   How it would affect Frank was among the earliest thoughts of the Westons.

Mr Weston (*to* **Emma**)   Can you come to Randalls at any time this morning? Do, if it be possible, Mrs Weston wants to see you. She must see you.

Emma   Is she unwell?

Mr Weston   No, no, not at all – but ask no more questions. You will know it all in time.

Randalls. **Mrs Weston** *sitting anxiously*.

Emma   What is it, my dear friend? Something of a very unpleasant nature, I find, has occurred. I hope it has nothing to do with Mr Frank Churchill?

Mrs Weston (*nervously*)   Yes, my dear Emma. It . . . does relate to Mr Churchill.

Emma   But –

Mrs Weston (*putting up a hand*)   He has been here this morning, on a most extraordinary errand. He came to speak to his father on a subject . . . to announce an attachment . . .

Emma   An attachment?! (*Pause.*) Harriet . . . ? (*Pause.*) Myself . . . ?

Mrs Weston (*more awkwardly*)   More than an attachment, in fact. An engagement . . . a positive engagement . . . What will you say, Emma – what will anybody say, when it is known that Frank Churchill and Jane Fairfax are engaged – nay, that they have been long engaged!

Emma (*horrified*)   Jane Fairfax! Good God! You are not serious? You do not mean it?

Mrs Weston (*avoiding her gaze*)   You may well be amazed. But it is even so. There has been a long engagement between them ever since October – formed at Weymouth, and kept a secret from everybody, not a creature knowing it except themselves.

Emma (*completely lost for words*)   What! Engaged to her all the winter . . . before either of them came to Highbury?

Mrs Weston   This has hurt me, Emma, very much. It has hurt his father equally. *Some* part of his conduct we cannot excuse.

Silence. **Emma** *frowns.*

Emma   I will not pretend not to understand you; and to give you all the relief in my power, be assured that no such effect has followed his attentions to me, as you are apprehensive of.

Mrs Weston *kisses her.*

Emma   But this does not acquit him, Mrs Weston; and I must say, that I think him greatly to blame. What right had he to come among us with affection and faith engaged, and

with manners so very disengaged? How could he tell what
mischief he might be doing? How could he tell that he might
not be making me in love with him?

Mrs Weston   From something that he said, my dear
Emma, I rather imagine –

Emma   And how could *she* bear such behaviour! To look
on, while repeated attentions were offering to another
woman, before her face, and not resent it!

Mrs Weston   There were misunderstandings between
them, Emma. He said so expressly. The present crisis,
indeed, seemed to be brought on by them.

Emma   Well, I suppose we shall gradually grow reconciled
to the idea, and I wish them happy. But I shall always think it
a very abominable sort of proceeding. They must take the
consequence, if they have heard each other spoken of in a
way not perfectly agreeable!

Mrs Weston   I am quite easy on that head. I am very sure
that I never said anything of either to the other, which both
might not have heard.

Emma   You are in luck. *I*, however . . . (*She sighs deeply.*)

Emma *alone*.

Harriet, poor Harriet! To be a second time the dupe of my
misconceptions and flattery. Mr Knightley told me I had
been no friend to Harriet. I suppose in this instance I am not
the sole author of the mischief. Harriet, herself
acknowledged her preference for Frank Churchill before I
even gave her a hint on the subject. But I ought to have
prevented them. Common sense ought to have directed me
to tell Harriet that she must not allow herself to think of him,
and that there were five hundred chances to one against his
ever caring for her.

Enter **Harriet**, *excitedly*.

Harriet   Well, Miss Woodhouse, is not this the oddest
news that ever was?

Emma   What do you mean, Harriet? What have you heard?

Harriet   About Jane Fairfax. Did you ever hear anything so strange? Mr Weston told me all about it. Fancy! Jane Fairfax and Mr Frank Churchill have been privately engaged to each other this long while.

Emma *looks at her, dumbfounded.*

Harriet   How very odd! Had you any idea of his being in love with her? (*She looks down.*) You, who can see into everybody's heart . . .

Emma   Upon my word, I begin to doubt my having any such talent. Can you seriously ask me, Harriet, whether I imagined him attached to another woman at the very time that I was encouraging you to give way to your own feelings? You may be sure that if I had, I should have cautioned you accordingly.

Harriet (*colouring deeply*)   Me! Why should you caution me? You do not think I care about Mr Frank Churchill.

Emma   I am delighted to hear you speak so stoutly on the subject, but do you mean to deny that there was a time – and not very distant either – when you gave me reason to understand that you did care about him?

Harriet   Him! Never, never. Dear Miss Woodhouse, how could you so mistake me?

She turns away, distressed.

Emma   Harriet . . . what do you mean? Good heavens, what do you mean? Mistake you! Am I to suppose then . . .

She sits down.

Harriet (*after a while*)   I should not have thought it possible that you could have misunderstood me! Mr Frank Churchill indeed! I hope I have a better taste than to think of Mr Frank Churchill, who is like nobody by his side.

Emma   Harriet! Let us understand each other now,
without the possibility of further mistake. Are you speaking
of . . . Mr Knightley?

Harriet   To be sure I am! I never could have an idea of
anybody else . . . and so I thought you knew. When we
talked about him, it was clear as possible.

Emma (*with forced calmness*)   Not quite. For all that you
then said, appeared to me to relate to a different person. I am
sure the service Mr Frank Churchill had rendered you, in
protecting you from the gipsies, was spoken of.

Harriet   Oh, Miss Woodhouse, how you do forget! I was
thinking of a much more precious circumstance – of Mr
Knightley's coming and asking me to dance, when Mr Elton
would not stand up with me. That was the service which
made me begin to feel how superior he was to every other
being upon earth.

Emma   Good God! This has been a most unfortunate –
most deplorable mistake! What is to be done?

Harriet (*slowly*)   You would not have encouraged me then,
if you had understood me.

Silence.

Remember your own words, Miss Woodhouse, that more
wonderful things had happened, matches of greater disparity
had taken place than between Mr Frank Churchill and me;
and therefore if Mr Knightley should really . . . if he does not
mind the disparity . . . I hope, dear Miss Woodhouse, you
will not set yourself against it, and try to put difficulties in the
way.

Emma   But have you any idea of Mr Knightley's returning
your affection?

Harriet (*modestly*)   Yes, I must say that I have.

She exits.

Elizabeth   Emma sat silently for a long while. But a few
minutes were sufficient for making her acquainted with her

own heart. A mind like hers, once opening to suspicion, made rapid progress.

Jane Why was it so much worse that Harriet should be in love with Mr Knightley, than with Frank Churchill?

Elizabeth Why was the evil so dreadfully increased by Harriet's having some hope of a return?

Sarah It darted through her, with the speed of an arrow, that Mr Knightley must marry no one but herself!

Jane Mr Knightley and Harriet Smith! It was a union to distance every wonder of the kind.

Elizabeth Such an elevation on her side!

Jane Such a debasement on his!

Sarah Oh, had she never brought Harriet forward! Had she left her where she ought, and where he had told her she ought! Had she not prevented her marrying the unexceptionable young man who would have made her happy and respectable in the line of life to which she ought to belong – all would have been safe! None of this dreadful sequel would have been.

Enter **Mr Knightley**.

Mr Knightley How do you do, Emma?

Emma How do you do? How are all the John Knightleys?

Mr Knightley All quite well.

Emma You have been with them for over a week?

Mr Knightley Yes. I returned this morning.

Emma You have some news to hear, now you are come back, that will rather surprise you.

Mr Knightley Have I? Of what nature?

Emma Of the best nature in the world – a wedding.

Mr Knightley If you mean Miss Fairfax and Mr Churchill, I have heard that already.

Emma How is it possible? (*A thought.*) Did you . . . call in at Mrs Goddard's?

Mr Knightley Mrs Goddard's? No, I had a few lines on parish business from Mr Weston and he gave me a brief account of what had happened.

Emma You probably have been less surprised than any of us, for you have had your suspicions. I have not forgotten that you once tried to give me a caution . . . I wish I had attended to it . . . but . . . (*She sighs.*) I seem to have been doomed to blindness.

Mr Knightley Time, my dearest Emma, will heal the wound. Your own excellent sense – your exertions for your father's sake – I know you will not allow yourself . . . Abominable scoundrel! He will soon be gone, however. They will soon be in Yorkshire.

Emma You are very kind, but you are mistaken. I am not in want of compassion. My blindness to what was going on, led me to act in a way that I must always be ashamed of, but I have no other reason to regret that I was not in the secret earlier.

Mr Knightley Emma, are you indeed – No, no, I understand you. Forgive me. He is no object of regret, indeed, and it will not be very long, I hope, before that becomes the acknowledgement of more than your reason.

Emma Mr Knightley, I really cannot let you continue in your error. I have never been at all attached to Mr Frank Churchill. I was tempted by his attentions, and allowed myself to appear pleased . . . He has imposed on me, but he has not injured me. That is the honest truth.

Mr Knightley He is a most fortunate man. Everything turns out for his good. He meets with a young woman at a watering place, gains her affections, cannot even weary her by negligent treatment. His aunt is in the way. His aunt dies. He has used everybody ill. And they are all delighted to forgive him. He is a fortunate man indeed!

Emma You speak as if you envied him.

Mr Knightley And I do envy him, Emma. In one respect he is the object of my envy.

Emma *looks away*.

Mr Knightley You will not ask me what is the point of envy. You are determined, I see, to have no curiosity. You are wise – but I cannot be wise. Emma, I must tell what you will not ask, though I may wish it unsaid the next moment.

Emma Oh, then don't speak it, don't speak it! Take a little time, consider, do not commit yourself.

Mr Knightley (*reluctantly*) Thank you.

Silence.

Emma (*taking pity on him*) Perhaps I stopped you ungraciously, Mr Knightley. If you have any wish to speak to me as a friend . . . if you wish to ask my opinion of any thing that you may have in contemplation . . . of a certain person . . . as a friend, indeed, you may command me.

Mr Knightley As a friend! Emma, that I fear is a word . . . No, I have no wish – stay, yes, why should I hesitate? I have gone too far already for concealment. Emma, I accept your offer – extraordinary as it may seem, I accept it, and refer myself to you as a friend. (*Pause.*) Tell me then, have I no chance of ever succeeding?

She turns, astounded, to him. He takes her hand.

My dearest Emma, for dearest you will always be, whatever the event of this hour's conversation, my dearest, most beloved Emma – tell me at once. Say 'No' if it is to be said.

She cannot speak.

I cannot make speeches, Emma. If I loved you less, I might be able to talk about it more. But you know what I am. You hear nothing but truth from me. I have blamed you, and lectured you, and you have borne it as no other woman in England would have borne it. God knows, I have been a very indifferent lover. But you understand me. Yes, you see, you understand my feelings – and will return them if you can. At present, I ask only to hear, once to hear your voice.

She turns to him.

Elizabeth What did she say? Just what she ought, of course. A lady always does. She said enough to show there need not be despair, and to invite him to say more himself.

Sarah However, she would have been too happy but for (*Sigh.*) poor Harriet. In time, of course, Mr Knightley would be forgotten or supplanted; but this could not be expected to happen early. Mr Knightley, always so kind, so feeling, so truly considerate for everybody, would never deserve to be less worshipped than now; and it was really too much to hope even of Harriet, that she could be in love with more than three men in one year.

Mr Knightley I have something to tell you, Emma; some news.

Emma Good or bad?

Mr Knightley I do not know which it ought to be called.

Emma Oh, good, I am sure. I see it in your countenance. You are trying not to smile.

Mr Knightley I am afraid, my dear Emma, that you will not smile when you hear it.

Emma Indeed! But why so? I can hardly imagine that anything which pleases or amuses you, should not please and amuse me too.

Mr Knightley Harriet Smith marries Robert Martin! (*She opens her mouth in amazement.*) You like it, my Emma, as little as I feared. I wish our opinions were the same.

Emma You mistake me, you quite mistake me. It is not that such a circumstance would now make me unhappy, but that I cannot believe it. How has it been possible?

Mr Knightley It is a very simple story. I arranged for Harriet to spend a few days in London with John and Isabella. Robert Martin went to town on business three days ago, and I got him to take charge of some papers which I was wanting to send to John. My brother asked him to dine with them that night . . . and the next. You know your friend best, but I should say she was a good-tempered, soft-hearted girl, not likely to be very, very determined against any young man who told her he loved her.

Emma   I am not sure that I know anyone best any more, but I do most sincerely wish them happy.

Mr Knightley   You are materially changed since we talked on this subject before.

Emma   I hope so – for at that time I was a fool.

Piano to the end.

Robert   Before the end of September, Emma attended Harriet to church and saw her hand bestowed on Robert Martin with so complete a satisfaction, as no remembrances, even connected with Mr Elton as he stood before them, could impair.

Jane   Jane Fairfax and Frank Churchill were married in November, attended, proudly and contentedly, by Mr and Mrs Weston, the Campbells . . . and the Dixons.

William   And Mr Elton was called on, in the intermediate month, to join the hands of Mr Knightley and Miss Woodhouse.

Elizabeth   The wedding was very much like other weddings, where the parties have no taste for finery or parade.

Jane   And Mrs Elton, from the particulars detailed by her husband, thought it all extremely shabby, and very inferior to her own. 'Very little white satin, very few lace veils; a most pitiful business!'

Robert   But in spite of these 'deficiencies',

Sarah   the wishes,

Robert   the hopes,

Sarah   the confidence,

Robert   the predictions

Sarah   of the small band of true friends who witnessed the ceremony,

Robert   were fully answered

Sarah *and* **Robert**   in the perfect happiness of the union.

Finis.

Michael Fry was born in London and studied at
Brimingham and London Universities. He has worked as a
director at the Young Vic, Lyric Hammersmith,
Nottingham Playhouse, Liverpool Everyman, Cambridge
Theatre Company, Southampton Nuffield, Chester
Gateway, Hawk's Well (Sligo), Edison Theatre (St Louis),
Bran Castle (Bucharest), Welsh National Opera and
Glyndebourne. He was Artistic Director of Floorboards
Theatre Productions from 1984 to 1988 and of Great Eastern
Stage, Lincoln, from 1988 to 1992. His adaptation of *Tess of
the d'Urbervilles* has been widely performed in England and
America, most recently at the Royal Exchange, Manchester.
Other work includes: adaptations of *Emma* and *The Great
Gatsby*; translations of Maeterlinck's *The Blue Bird*, Becque's
La Parisienne and Molière's *Les Fourberies de Scapin*; opera
libretti for *Les Parents Terribles*, *War and Peace* and *Dinner* (a
fragment). Since 1992, he has worked primarily in America,
as Professor of Acting at Webster University, St Louis;
Professor of Directing at Washington University and
Visiting Artist in Chicago, Minneapolis and New York. He is
currently working on a full-length study of adaptation,
Playing the Novel.

The Life and Times of
Fanny Hill

adapted from John Cleland
by April De Angelis

The Life and Times of Fanny Hill was first performed by Red Shift Theatre Company. It opened at the Gulbenkian Studio Theatre, Newcastle upon Tyne, on 11 March 1991 prior to a national tour and a run at the Battersea Arts Centre, London. The cast was as follows:

Fanny Hill	Laura Cox
Swallow	Maria Gough
Dingle	Mark Heal
Spark	Mark Jenkinson
Louisa	Jane Nash
Cellist	Helen Wickens

Directed by Jonathan Holloway
Designed by Charlotte Humpston

Part One

A mist.

Lights up on a still, posed figure, a man dressed circa eighteenth century. When lights are fully up he comes to life.

Voltaire   What a wonderful morning.
Absolutely wonderful. Très magnifique.
A morning when you wake up and think 'why, life is wonderful, after all!'
You think of things like trees and the wind and your heart leaps
And as you shave you wonder if this is the dawn of a whole new age . . .
My name is Voltaire.
I am on holiday.
I can tell you I am having a lovely holiday.
I love England.
I love it to death.
But France I hate.
France I spit on.
France is enough to drive a man to live abroad!

Here you are so modern, so successful.
You have liberty and plumbing.
What has France got?
Lots of people who know what time the king gets up
What time he has a piss
Powders his wig and so on.
Here, you have killed your king
Whoop!
And off came his head
And that is not such a bad thing.
Fuck his wig, eh?

The world may laugh at you and say
Pah, the English, so ugly and they do not wash.
But that is because you are so busy doing lots of trade.

Then your nation gets richer and you get freer
And so you are more free to get rich etc.

Yes, in England you have cast out darkness and superstition
and let the light of reason flood in.

Breakfast now. I'm hungry.
I tell you. I've seen the future and it works.
England.

Fanny Hill *has been lurking, dishevelled, in the background.*

Fanny   Over here, Monsieur!
Have you an itch that needs a scratch?

Voltaire   Mon dieu!

He crosses himself. Exits.

Fanny   French git!
I got nits off a Frenchie.
Nits are French, did you know that?

She begins to move, slowly, painfully.

It was cold last night.
Cold is bad for business.
Blokes don't like to tarry.
Frightened the frost will nobble their vitals.
No such luck.
Frost is after bigger catch.
Frost doesn't want a few sweaty fleshy inches
Frost wants everything.
Hands, feet, legs, bum.
Frost is after the whole of Fanny.
Wants to fuck me over once and for all.

(*Shouts to frost.*) You're not having me!
Not the price you're asking!

Fanny's fallen on hard times. Hard times.
Corners aren't as dark as they used to be
And customers are fussy.
What I say is, you don't need teeth to give good suck!
I wish it was always dark.
Black like inside a hat.

Then I'd do business.
Then I'd have a carriage and a parrot.
I haven't eaten for three days.
I could be dead on Sunday!
Bugger!

A man enters.

Hark! A spark!
Maybe my luck has changed.
I'll keep to the shadows.
God bless him, he approaches.
(*In a sweet voice.*) Morning, sir.
Have you a moment?
I need a hand for I am all unlaced.

Spark   I have reason to believe that you are the infamous Fanny Hill. Whore of this parish.

Fanny (*aside*)   Lord, a constable!
(*To him.*) Me, sir! No, sir!

Spark   My informants are reliable . . .

Fanny   There has been some abhorrent mix-up, officer, I may be out and about, sir, in these icy and sordid environs but I have a legitimate 'scuse. I am a widow of holy and reticent parts and as such I venture forth after morning prayers to walk my beloved pups. My husband, God rest him, bred assorted canines.

Spark   Where are these pups?

Fanny   Please, sir, it is a tragedy. As we veered into the vicinity of Hardudder St., hearing a loud 'pop', I know not of what genesis, my two pups took fright and in their quivering distress, bit through their silken reigns and legged it.

Spark   Legged it?

Fanny   Fled off – alas, such sweet and innocent doggies. The world may never see their like again. Turpin and Fudge I called 'em. One for it was black and fast, the other 'cos it was brown and slow.

Spark *pulls out a knife.*

Spark   See this?

Fanny   A knife, sir.

Spark   It likes old flesh.

Fanny   I've never so much as taken a boot to my doggies.

He pushes it closer to her.

Help!

Spark   Enough of your filthy conundrums.
You are Fanny Hill. That tart on the turn.

Fanny   I am, sir, but less of your turn.

Spark   A word.

Fanny   Spit it out.

Spark   I have something about my person that will be of particular interest to you.

Fanny   I doubt it.

Spark   Pardon.

Fanny   A sneeze. Pray continue.

Spark   Notifications of debts. Gambling.

Fanny   I abhor it. A woman that gambles is an iniquitous sight before man or God.

Spark   They've your signature.

Fanny   Since we've that proved give 'em here.

Spark   They're mine.

Fanny   Yours?

Spark   Purchased for a piddling sum. Their rightful owner having long given up hope of just recompense.

Fanny   Miserable turd.

Spark   Now you owe me.

Fanny   I understand.
My, we have come a long way round.
Well, what fleshly peculiarity are you after?

Which tickling trick that long and arduous service to my
noble profession has endowed me?

Pause.

What do you want? Jam, thongs or catskins?

Spark   Back off, strumpet.
I'm talking business.
I have a proposition.
Scientific.

Fanny   Go on.

Spark   A whore sells herself to one man at one time.
What if she could sell herself to fifty?

Fanny   She'd never get up again.

Spark   One hundred. Simultaneous.

Fanny   Impossible!

Spark   A thousand.

Fanny   Execrable!

Spark   Ten thousand!

Fanny   I must stop my ears to such numerous and
exhausting talk.

Spark   There is a way.

Pause.

I want you to write a book.
The story of your horrid career.
Thus servicing the multitude in one singular act.

Fanny   How disgusting! A book.

Spark   Ten per cent on sales and we'll forget the debts.

Fanny   Never. Books aren't meant for that sort of thing.
They're meant for educative purposes, holy instructions and
genteel pastimes.

Spark   Fifteen per cent.

Fanny   Done.

Spark   No double-crossing. Or I'll deliver the debts to the magistrate and you to Newgate. There's always room for one more trollop.

Fanny   I'll start work immediately.

Spark   Remember. No prating tales of hardship and denials. Think of the customer.

Fanny   I always do.

Spark   I'll be back.

Fanny   You're too kind.

Spark *flicks a coin onto the ground.*

Spark   An advance.

He leaves. She watches him go.

Fanny   May your balls shrivel up and your cock drop off.

She picks up the coin and holds it up.

Money!

This is as if she has uttered a magic word. A group of three women gather round her as if entranced by the coin. They freeze.

Fanny *breaks from the group. Comes forward. Speaks to the audience.*

Fanny   I have a confession.
My horrid career.
It has been horrid I'm sure of that.
But when I turn round fast to catch at it all I see is a blur of bedpans, or a bloke buttoning up.
You see my past has seeped out the crack between the days.
Temporary, I'm sure.
It will be back but not in time, I fear.
Not much of a one for remembrances, me.
Been kept busy.
And what's a past 'cept rotten dragging longings and memories of bad paths badly trod.
What good's that do a girl?
There is others though, who shall help me.
If my past is missing I shall ask them to find one for me.
That way a story shall be told come what may.

And I will write my book.
And get a percentage, after.

She rejoins her pose with the group.
Lights up on **Louisa** *and her.*

Louisa!

She tosses her a bottle.

I been looking for you.

Louisa *swigs at the bottle.*

Fanny   Louisa?
How's tricks?

Louisa   All right.

Fanny   I've heard they've been better.

Louisa   No.

Takes another swig.

Fanny   It's hard.

Pause.

It's hard.

Louisa   What?

Fanny   When you get a reputation.

Louisa   Reputation?

Fanny   Unjust.

Louisa   Reputation?

Fanny   People will talk.

Louisa   I'm fine.

Fanny   Spread things.

Louisa   Fine.

Pause.

Fanny   You worked in the theatre once.

Louisa   On the wigs. Combing 'em. Used to find all sorts.

Fanny   But you understand the medium.

Louisa   Beetles. Mice even.

Fanny   The art form.

Louisa   I left. The pay was crap.

Fanny   I want your help.

Louisa   Help?

Fanny   I want you to be me. Young and ravishably innocent as I was. Then you'll do things and I'll write 'em down.

Louisa   I dunno.

Fanny   People talk talk talk. Louisa.
Things get round fast.
Makes it hard, keeping body and soul together.

Louisa   I want a sovereign.

Fanny   You'll have one. We've got funding. Business sponsorship.

Louisa *takes a swig.*

Louisa   I don't do nothing without my friend.

She beckons **Swallow** *forward.*

Fanny   What's her name?

Louisa   Dunno.

Fanny   You could be mixing with all sorts.

Swallow   Swallow.

Fanny   What?

Swallow   My name.

Louisa   She's new.

Swallow   Like the bird.

Louisa   I met her on the streets.

Swallow   I can read.

Louisa   She's got class.

Swallow There is a garden in her face,
Where roses and white lilies blow;
A heavenly paradise is that place,
Wherein all pleasant fruits do flow.

Louisa That's poetry.

Fanny But no advantage.
She gets a shilling.

Louisa What do I do then?

Fanny Imagine.

Louisa What?

Fanny It's London. One fine morning.

Cellist Excuse me . . .

Fanny At the coach station . . .

Cellist I'm ever so sorry to . . .

Fanny You're a young girl, scarce fifteen, newly arrived to
the great metropolis.

Cellist *plays a note on her cello to interrupt.*

Cellist I can play a wide variety of . . .

Fanny Sit over there.

Cellist Oh. Thank you. Um. I was wondering . . .

Fanny Sixpence.

Cellist Oh.

*She seats herself with her cello. From now on she plays to accompany
moments, scenes.*

Louisa I feel stupid.

Fanny Close your eyes. Take a deep breath.

Louisa *does so. So does* **Swallow**.

Fanny You're all alone. Penniless.
An innocent and friendless orphan new to London.
What will happen?
Imagine.

Pause.

Well?

Louisa   I'll get screwed.

Fanny   That is a trifle bald, Louisa.

Louisa   It's the truth.

Fanny   But it lacks narrative.
The reader, as we all do, requires a little fondling before
being brought to the point.

Louisa   Oh.

Swallow *comes forward. She has her eyes closed.*

Swallow   Coming to the city is like I'm a flower picked and
thrown into the street.

She opens her eyes.

I think I have a feeling for it. Book writing. I've seen a book,
you see. Touched it.

She closes her eyes again.

A flower or a fish that is flopped onto stone as is gasping.

Fanny   Sweet bud, that is full of promise.

Swallow   Or . . .

Fanny   But quite enough to be going on with.

Louisa   How can it be like a flopping fish?

Fanny *holds* **Swallow**'*s face in her hands. Looks at it.*

Fanny   There's a resemblance. You shall be the young
Fanny.

Louisa   What about me?

Fanny   You can fill in.

Louisa   Fill in?

Cellist   A small role well played often gathers more
acclaim than the star part from a discerning and sympathetic
audience.

Louisa   Piss off.

Cellist   I just thought . . .

Fanny (*to* **Swallow**)   Shall we begin, dear heart?

Swallow *prepares herself.* **Louisa** *watches antagonistically.*
Swallow *looks about her, lost. Appears to be waiting. Sighs.*

Swallow   Left thus alone, in the heart of the throbbing
cosmopolis, absolutely destitute and friendless I began to feel
most bitterly the severity of my helpless strange
circumstances and burst into a flood of tears.

Fanny   Wonderful.

Swallow   Thank you.

Fanny   I will now enter the scene myself. Excuse me.

Fanny *goes to find a piece of costume in order to play the madam.*
Perhaps she always finds pieces from about her person?

Swallow   Listening. That's how I got my education.
I worked for this bloke. He was a poet.
He had this sore on his leg.
It dripped on the floor where he sat.
I had to clean it up.
Sit under his table and clean it up.
I used my hanky.
I used to hear him muttering, reading.
That's how I learnt things.
Wiping and listening.
Listening and wiping.
My hanky turned yellow.

Fanny (*calls*)   Ready?

She enters.

Sweetheart. Do you want a place?

Swallow   Yes please.

Fanny   What luck. I have come to this coach station in
search of a servant.
And since I cannot bear to think of such an artless,
inexperienced country maid wandering the streets of such a

very vile wicked place as London you must come with me. I
believe you might do, with a little instruction on my part.

Swallow   I will not hesitate to accept this offer of shelter
especially from so grave and matron-like a lady.

Fanny   Charming. This way.

They walk in a circle. **Fanny** *leads.* **Swallow** *follows.*

Swallow   My name is Fanny.

Fanny   Indeed!
I've not taken you for the common type of servant, Fanny.
Not for scrubbing.
But, if you are a good girl, to be my companion.
I'll be twenty mothers to you.

Swallow   Twenty!

Fanny   And you shall lie with a young gentlewoman, my
cousin.

Swallow   Thank you!
(*To audience.*) I was by the greatest good luck fallen into the
hands of the kindest mistress, not to say friend, the varsal
world could afford. I shall enter her doors with most
complete confidence and exultation.

Fanny *stops.*

Fanny   My abode.
(*Calls out.*) Phoebe! Phoebe!

A pause. She smiles ingratiatingly at **Swallow**. *Then looks pointedly
at* **Louisa**.

Phoebe!

Louisa (*ungraciously*)   I'm coming! I'm coming!

She enters the scene as Phoebe. She takes her time.

Oh sweet mistress, it's you.
How glad I am that you have returned. Such a good sweet
mistress.

Fanny   Well, I'm for bed. I'm dog-tired.
And I bet you are too, Phoebe.

Louisa   Shagged.

Fanny   This is the young gentlewoman I told you of,
Fanny. She will show you the way and be vastly good to you,
I'm sure.
Good night.

Fanny *retires to scribble.*

Swallow   Good night . . .

Louisa *walks over to the bed.* **Louisa** *has begun to take off some
clothes.*

Swallow   So. This is where we are to sleep.
It's a bit early. Not yet lunch time.

Pause. **Swallow** *begins to take off some clothes.*

Louisa   Don't hang about.

Swallow   I have heard how several maids out of the
country have made themselves forever by preserving their
virtue and this so winning their masters that they married
'em and kept them coaches and they lived vastly grand and
happy and some of them came to be duchesses.

I don't know how I will sleep.

Swallow *follows* **Louisa** *to bed.*

Swallow   Good night, Phoebe.

Louisa   Good night, Fanny.

As they get into bed **Louisa** *gives* **Swallow** *a kiss on the lips.*

Swallow (*aside*)   This was new. This was odd.

Louisa *kisses her again.*

Swallow   But not so bad.
Perhaps it is the London way to do things.
A way to show pure kindness.
I am such an unpractised simpleton perfectly new to life that
such things are unknown to me.
Still, I will not be behind hand but return the embrace with
all the fervour that innocence knows.

Swallow *kisses* **Louisa** *back.*

A pause. **Swallow** *calls over to* **Fanny**.

Swallow   Miss Fanny, what shall I do now?

Fanny   Use your imagination and if you can't do that, think of your shilling.

They find a series of positions to illustrate this next speech. The positions change at intervals.

Swallow   Encouraged by this her hands became extremely free and wandered over my whole body with touches, squeezes, pressures, that rather warmed and surprised me with their novelty than shocked or alarmed me.
Every part of me was open and exposed to the licentious courses of her hands which like a fire ran over my whole body And thawed all coldness as they went.
Not content with the outer posts she now attempts the main spot, that sweet seat of exquisite sensation which till that instance had been quite innocent.
I should have jumped out of bed and cried 'help' against such odd assaults but her lascivious touches had lighted up a new fire, a strange pleasure that wantoned through all my veins, I was confused, transported, out of myself . . .

A man enters.

Dingle   Hello.

Everything stops. They all look at the man.

Pause.

What are you doing?

Louisa   We're writing a book.

Dingle   Oh.

Fanny   Any objections, sir, or may we continue unmolested with our literary activities?

Dingle   Don't mind me.
If I may make so bold I would like to introduce myself.
My name is Dingle.

Fanny   Fanny Hill. You're standing in our best bedroom so to speak, Mr Dingle.

He jumps aside.

Dingle   I do beg your pardon.

Louisa   I seen him before. Hanging about like an old tooth.

Dingle   A man must take the air, miss.

Fanny   We digress. Let us put Dingle in parenthesis and continue.

Dingle   Please. Don't do that. I wish to remain, Miss Fanny. May I?

Louisa   What for?

Pause.

Dingle   I would dearly love to learn the art of quill-driving.

Fanny   That can be arranged.

Dingle   I'm indebted.

Fanny   Precisely. Ten shillings.

Dingle   Ten shillings!

Fanny   It's an educational experience.

Dingle   I am temporarily at a low ebb, so to speak.

Fanny   How much?

Dingle   Tuppence and a piece of cork though that is slightly chewed.

Fanny   Here.

She holds out her hand. He gives it to her.

You're on the slate.

Dingle   I have seen better days. I used to own half a ship.

Louisa   In a bottle.

Dingle   A regular sea-going vessel, Miss.

Fanny   Returning to our incarnations of pleasure . . . young Fanny having had the first sparks of delight tossed onto her kindling is now rigged out to be a proper lady.

Swallow *spins round.*

Swallow   A Brussels lace cap.

Fanny   Braided shoes.

Louisa   Silk stockings.

Cellist   A white lute-string flowered with silver.

Dingle   'Tis a giddy age.

Swallow *stops.* **Fanny** *arranges her more revealingly. They look as if into a mirror. The others hold still.*

Fanny   I was tall and barely turned fifteen.
My shape owed nothing to stays.
My hair was a glossy auburn flowing down my back in natural buckles and not a little setting off the whiteness of a smooth skin.
My eyes were as black as can be imagined
And my bosom finely raised, though one might discern rather the promise than the actuality of the firm round breasts that would soon make good.
This is, I own, strong self-praise, but should I not show gratitude to nature?
Why suppress, through affectation of modesty, the mention of such valuable gifts?
Plus, a reader likes things fleshed out.

The others reanimate.

I'm sure you're keen to assist us, Dingle.

Dingle   If it is an honest book, Miss Fanny.

Fanny   Sir, 'tis the stark naked truth.

She holds out her hand. He accepts. They all get into position. A tableaux for the next scene, a bit like a photo. **Fanny** *stands back to check everyone, then rearranges* **Dingle** *into something of a grotesque figure. They hold the pose.* **Fanny** *breaks it.*

Fanny, sweetness?

Swallow   Yes, Mother Brown?

Fanny   You look plums in sugar today.
Allow me to introduce you to my esteemed coz. Mr Crofts.

She indicates **Dingle**. *He bows his head.*

A very fine gentleman.
Isn't that right, Phoebe?

Louisa   Yeah. Very fine.

Fanny   Not above sixty and with his own chariot.
More, he is violently smitten with you at first sight.

Dingle *stares at* **Swallow**. *A pause.*

Fanny   Now Phoebe and I must leave on pressing business.
Farewell.

They start to leave.

Swallow   Wait!
He is looking at me goats and monkeys.

Fanny   As I said. Important business.

Swallow   He is staring at my bosom.

Fanny   Sir, be very tender of the sweet child.
Phoebe!

They exit. **Dingle** *stares at* **Swallow**. *She is uncomfortable.*

Swallow   Alone!
I stole corner glances at him, then looked away in pure
horror and afright, which he attributed to nothing more than
maiden modesty.

Dingle *gives a grotesque smile.*

Dingle   Come over here, poppet.

Swallow   No. You are a liquorish old goat.

Dingle *laughs.*

Swallow   Imagine a short ugly man who looks . . . dead.
And has great goggly eyes as if he were being strangled.
Fangs.
Breath like a lavvy.

And when he smiled it was horrible if not downright dangerous to a woman with child.

Dingle *breaks out of character*.

Dingle   You can't put that in!

Swallow   He lavished great sums on such wretches as could pretend to love his person whilst to those who had not the art to dissemble he behaved brutally.

Dingle   It's slander!

Swallow   He thought he was born to please women, though he could best please them by his extinction.

Dingle   Scurrilous libel!

Fanny   Advance, Dingle!

Dingle, *back in character, moves towards* **Swallow**. *She attempts to avoid him.* **Dingle** *stumbles after. He may grab hold of her but does not have an easy time of it.*

Fanny *writes*.

Swallow   The monster squats by me, flings his arms about my neck, draws me forcibly towards him and obliges me to receive his pestilential kisses. He tears off my handkerchief and pushes me to the settee. I feel his hand on my naked thighs which are crossed and which he endeavours to unlock. Oh, then! aroused out of my passive endurance I sprung from him with an activity he was not prepared for, flung myself at his feet and begged him not to hurt me.

Dingle   Hurt you, my dear?

Swallow   Says he.

Dingle   Has not the old lady told you that I love you and shall do handsomely by you?

Swallow   Do not hurt me, Mr Crofts.

Dingle   Hurt you?

Swallow   I shall love you dearly . . . if you go away!

Dingle   Saucebox!

Swallow I am talking to the wind.

Dingle Hurt you?

Swallow The disorder of my dress proves fresh incentive. Snorting and foaming . . .

He snorts and foams.

Together With lust and rage . . .

Swallow He seizes me and tosses my petticoats over my head.

She gives a cry. Struggles.

I struggled with indignation! I died with terror!

Dingle I am unbuttoned!

Dingle *goes to close in with a final lunge.* **Swallow** *rolls over/moves. He misses. He collapses with a cry of dismay.*

A silence.

Swallow *sits up.*

Swallow He had it seems, brought on, by his eagerness and struggle, the ultimate period of his hot fit of lust, which his power was too short-lived to carry him through the full execution of.

Pause.

He came too soon.

Dingle Strumpet.

Swallow It's all over my petticoat.

Dingle Country modesty! I know what's second-hand goods. You've left your maidenhead with some village hobnail and come to dispose of your skim-milk in town!

Fanny Louisa, fetch Mr Dingle some refreshment. He's put in a good morning's performance.

Louisa *gets a gin bottle. Swigs it herself.*

Swallow My petticoat . . .

Fanny It'll dry out.

Swallow *sits dabbing her petticoat.*

Fanny (*to* **Cellist**)   A little mood music, I think.
In order to succour my scribbling.

Cellist *complies.*

Fanny   Funny. I keep 'xpecting some sound, some sight;
the toss of a petticoat or a groan perhaps, to jog my memory.
To slip me my past.
But no.
Still, early days.

Cellist   Early days.

Fanny *writes.*

Dingle   Miss . . . Louisa?

Louisa   What?

Dingle   That was the name of my ship.

Louisa   What?

Dingle   Louisa.

Pause.

A good ship. She sailed remarkably fast.
You could send her to sea at easy expense.
First I only had one sixteenth of her.
Then I saved and saved till I had a whole half.
A whole half.
Don't take me wrong, Miss Louisa.
There was a woman on the front of my ship.
She was made of wood. She had two big blue eyes.
Mind you, she only had a top half. No legs.
Her mouth was red.
She looked like you.

Louisa   She was made of wood?

Dingle   Oak.

Louisa   Even her tits?

Dingle   I never looked.

Louisa   They must have been.

Dingle   I never looked.

Louisa   She would've got cold. All them waves, splashing her. She must have thought of you, all snug and tucked up at night. And her. Freezing.

Dingle   She wasn't alive.

Louisa   Not like me.

Dingle   No.

Louisa   No. She was hard, whereas me, I'm soft. Wood tits aren't as good as the real thing.

Dingle   Miss Louisa!

She laughs.

Swallow (*to* **Fanny**)   One day he found me.
The bloke I worked for.
Touching his book.
He was a gentleman though.
He didn't scold me.
He read me a poem.
There cherries grow which none may buy
Till 'Cherry-ripe' themselves do cry.

Fanny   Enchanting. I can see you've a flare.

Swallow   A flare?

Fanny   For books.

Swallow   I have?

Fanny   I'd say.

Swallow   Is Mr Crofts coming back?

Fanny   No, dear heart. He has been incarcerated for illegal contraband practices.

Swallow   Oh, good.

Fanny   Ever onwards, else our readers will be salivating themselves for chapter two: 'The Mysteries of Venus'.

An Intro on the cello.

Louisa (*sings*)   There is a thing long and stiff
And at the end there is a cliff
Soft moisture from it doth grow
And makes fair ladies pleasant grow.

Swallow   What is it?

Louisa   A pen.

Swallow   You've got a nice voice, Louisa.

Fanny   It is twelve noon. The shutters are down. The house
is quiet. Young Fanny and Phoebe happen to be in Mother
Brown's closet, resting on the settle bed, when they hear a
rustling in the bed chamber.

She makes sounds of rustling.

Swallow   What's that?

Louisa   It is a rustling in the bed chamber.

Fanny *draws a curtain round the bed. Lights focus on this.* **Louisa**
and **Swallow** *go one either side of the curtain.*

Louisa *and* **Swallow**   We instantly crept softly and posted
ourselves so that, seeing everything minutely, we could not
be seen.

Swallow   By then my native purity had been corrupted by
all the frolic, thoughtless gaiety and dirty talk of the house.

They draw the curtain back or it is drawn back.

Louisa *and* **Swallow**   Then who should we see but the
venerable mother abbess herself handed in by a tall, brawny,
young horse grenadier, moulded in the Hercules style.

We see **Fanny** *with* **Spark** *disguised as a horse grenadier. He should
be partly masked so as not to become a 'real' character. They pose.*

Louisa *and* **Swallow**   Oh, how still and hush did we keep
our stand . . .

*The pose breaks. A purse is exchanged. They go straight to work. A
dumbshow is enacted. Music accompanies this.*

But madam was so taken up with her present great concern
that she had no attention left over to care for anything else.

Louisa   They got straight down to essentials.

Swallow   He laid her down pretty briskly –

Louisa   And canted up her petticoats.

Swallow   Her face blushed –

Louisa   With brandy.

Swallow   But soon I stared with all my eyes at a thing that entirely engrossed them . . .

Louisa   Her sturdy stallion had now unbuttoned and produced . . .

Swallow   And produced . . . his willy.

Fanny *interrupts.*

Fanny   And produced that wonderful machine, that treasure.

Louisa   That object.

Fanny   That sweet cause of my complaint.

Louisa   That piece of furniture.

Fanny   That flesh brush, capital part and beloved guest.

Louisa   That conduit pipe.

Fanny   That engine of love assaults.

Louisa   Bit of gristle.

Fanny   That maypole, pleasure wedge, love truncheon, plenipotentiary instrument and is someone taking notes?

Dingle *hurries to do so.*

Dingle   Sorry.

Dumbshow continues.

Louisa   He mounts.

Swallow   And is engulfed.

Louisa   The bed shook.

Swallow   The curtains rattled.

Pause.

Will he not give her a mortal wound?

Louisa   True, there are a great diversity of sizes in those parts owing to nature, childbearing and frequent overstretching by unmerciful machines but believe me we would take a great deal of killing.
He thrusts.

Swallow   She heaves.

Louisa   At first gentle and regular . . .

Swallow   But presently the transport began to be too violent to observe any order or measure . . .

Fanny *and the grenadier follow cue.*

Louisa   Faster.

Swallow   And faster.

Louisa   More furious.

Swallow   And furious.

Louisa   She spurs him on.

Swallow   Till he can hardly keep his saddle.

Louisa   Oh no! I can't bear it! She cries.

Swallow   I am going to die!

Louisa   She throws her arms about wildly.

Swallow   Gives a deep sob.

Louisa   And dies in an agony of bliss.

They let the curtain drop.

Louisa *and* **Swallow**   We were thrilled to the soul and our emotions had grown so violent that they almost intercepted our respiration.

They breathe out heavily.

Swallow   Such a sight had given the dying blow to my native innocence.

She approaches **Louisa**.

Now I am all stirred up and aglow with stimulating fires.

As she goes to embrace **Louisa**, **Fanny** *steps between them, through the curtain and separates them.*

Fanny But young Fanny was pining for more solid food and would not be put off much longer with this foolery of woman to woman.

Swallow Oh.

Louisa Please yourself.

Fanny It's not what gentlemen read books for.
I thought you had a feeling for books.

Swallow I do.

Fanny I might have mistook you.

Swallow No.

Fanny We're writing for a market.

Dingle Herrings.

Fanny How's that, Mr Dingle?

Dingle It's no good shipping herrings to the Spanish, Miss Fanny. They have an aversion.

Fanny Quite so. Shall we tilt our prow at the ensuing scenario?
I have made notes.

She reads. **Swallow** *sits centre stage.*

Adieu all fears of what man could do to me!
I would have pulled the first of that sex that presented himself off the streets and offered him my bauble. I wanted no more of Phoebe. Everything there so flat, so hollow . . .
I'd only obliged before out of fear of displeasing her . . . but now, for my part, I was filled with ardent desires for the main dish, the essential specific!

Swallow Ardent desires for the essential specific . . .

Fanny Exactly!

Swallow *looks about her. Fetches a pillow or a bundle of some sort. The space clears. She is left alone.* **Fanny** *is looking on. Lights focus on* **Swallow**. *She looks at the pillow.*

Swallow   An eye.
Two eyes.
Eyelashes.
Red lips like a bee has stung them.
Curly hair.
All disordered.
Heavens what a sight!
A boy.
A young gentleman.
He is fast asleep in Mother Brown's chair.
Left there by his thoughtless companions who got him drunk, dumped him and went off for a screw.
Trembling, I took one of his hands in mine and woke him as gentle as possible.
What time is it, he asks?
Six o'clock, I replied.
His eyes had fires in them.
I could not help it but I touched his cheek.
He kissed me.
It was the first kiss I had ever relished from a man in all my life.

Pause.

Love.

Pause.

He said he was so struck with me that he asked if he could keep me.
Rash, sudden and dangerous as this offer might be from a perfect stranger, a giddy boy, the prodigious love I was struck with for him put a charm in his voice there was no resisting!
Yes, I said, yes!
Then we escaped from Mother Brown's bawdy house and went to a pub and drank hot chocolate.

Pause.

Love.

Pause.

His name was . . . Charles.

Fanny Charles?

Swallow Yes.

Fanny Who the hell's Charles?

They all gather round. **Swallow** *stays sitting in the middle of them, looking up.*

Swallow A gentleman.

Fanny Gentleman?

Swallow I'm in love.

Fanny Oh yes?

Swallow Yes. I've escaped with him.

Fanny And then what?

Swallow Nothing. We are very happy.

Fanny And that's it?

Swallow That's it.

Fanny 'I was very happy and that's it.'
I can't write that.

Swallow We are happy.

Fanny You can't end a book on chapter three.
Too thin. It wouldn't sell.
He'll have to go.

Swallow No.

Fanny Yes.

Swallow No.

Dingle Perhaps he could be struck on the head by a blunt object whilst strolling on the dock side. He would then fall into the waters and drown without ever regaining consciousness.

Swallow No.

Louisa He could choke on a crust.

Swallow No.

Cellist   Or be gored by a stray bullock.

Swallow   He was to come back. I'm having his baby.

Pause.

Fanny   How did that happen?

Swallow   What?

Fanny   That.

Swallow   We loved each other.

Fanny   How?

Swallow   You know.

Fanny   Did it hurt?

Swallow   No.

Fanny   Not even the first time?
That's funny. It usually hurts the first time.
Don't it, Louisa?

Louisa   I've had worse.

Swallow   A little. Perhaps it hurt a little.

Louisa   Best to stuff your petticoat in your mouth and bite
down hard.

Cellist   Or recite a little rhyme.

Fanny   It hurts but they do it. They go ahead and do it.
Don't they, Mr Dingle?

Dingle   That is God's will, Miss Fanny.

Fanny   It would be.

Swallow   Charles was very kind.

Fanny   Oh, I can see it all.
Come, come, my dear, says he.
Let me show you a room with a fine prospect over some
gardens . . .

Swallow   There was a view . . .

Fanny   But we know what prospects he had in mind.

Swallow   I was dying with soft fears and wishes . . .

Fanny   He starts the main attack . . .

Swallow   I told him my flower was yet uncropped.

Fanny   He snorts in disbelief!

Swallow   The truth is powerful!

Fanny   He shoves it in.

Swallow   I tell him I cannot bear it.

Fanny   So he gives it a grease . . .

Swallow   He kisses my falling tears.

Fanny   And carries on. He lets himself be borne headlong away by the overmettle of that member exerting itself in native rage. He breaks in, carrying all before him and with one violent merciless lunge sends his pole imbrued and reeking with virgin gore right up the very hilt of you. Charming.

Swallow   But Charles employed such warmth to soothe, caress and comfort me in my complainings, even bringing me a cordial, that presently I drowned all sense of pain in the pleasure of seeing him, of thinking I belonged to him, he who was the absolute dispenser of my happiness, my fate.

Fanny   I bet he wanted to try again in five minutes.

Louisa   I lost mine off of a young gentleman of the cleaver.

Cellist   I beg your pardon?

Louisa   A butcher.

Fanny *indicates that she is about to start work again. The others leave centre stage.*

Fanny   Well, now, young Fanny. I am your present landlady. Mrs Jones. I'm come to give you some news. Charles will not be back for roughly four years.

Swallow   No!

Fanny   A jealous relative has had him bundled aboard a ship headed for the south seas. Tragic. I doubt you will ever set eyes on him again. Those voyages can be highly perilous and the native women most flirtatious.

Fanny *tosses the pillow aside.* **Louisa** *sits on it.*

Louisa   Oh, Charles!

Swallow   What about the baby?

Fanny   You lose it.

Swallow *gives a small cry.*

Swallow   No . . .

She sinks to the floor.

Fanny   Art requires sacrifice.
You may call me hard-hearted but I merely place myself
upon the altar of literature.
An encumbered heroine is a sentimental liability, especially
in a book of this *œuvre*.

She turns to **Swallow**.

Look!
Your health is returning to you even as I speak. You are
welcome to stay in these lodgings as long as you please,
Miss Fanny, but you owe me twenty-three pounds and
seventeen and six pence and I would not like to see you rot in
Newgate.

Swallow   Newgate?

Fanny   Hush. Can you sit up?

Swallow   I think so.

Fanny   Here. Eat this.

She hands her a chicken leg.

Swallow   I'm not hungry.

Fanny   Nonesense. When you've got down half a partridge
and four glasses of wine you'll feel much better.

Swallow   I've a melancholy.

Fanny   Sorrows pass.
Besides. I have a gentleman to visit you.
Mr H as he wishes to be known.

He has a large diamond ring and has heard of your misfortunes and is willing to serve you.

Swallow   I don't want to see anybody.

Fanny   This is no time for personal preferences.
Make your market while you may.
I'll send him up.
Try to look a little cheerful.

Dingle *is ushered in*.

Dingle   Good afternoon.
I have heard of your terrible misfortune and have come to visit you.
Where shall I put my clothes?

Swallow *bursts into tears*.

Dingle   Please. Please do not distress yourself.
You have had a cruel plunge for one of your youth and beauty.
Have you got any hangers?

He begins to take off his clothes.

Swallow   I am lifeless.

Dingle   You'll feel differently in a day or two.

Swallow   I do not care what becomes of my wretched body.

Dingle   You say that now . . .

Swallow   I don't care if I die.

Dingle   Violent passions seldom last.

He gets into bed with **Swallow**.

Swallow   Maybe I am dead.

Dingle   And those of women the least of any.

Swallow   A dead cold corpse . . .

Dingle   Please, Miss Fanny!

Swallow   Soon I will begin to stink and fall apart!

Dingle   Do you want your ten shillings or not?

A pause.

They begin a dumbshow of intercourse.

Fanny   My! How the animal spirits do rush mechanically
to their parts!

Swallow (*whispers*)   Drink to me only with thine eyes,
And I will pledge with mine;
Or leave a kiss but in the cup
And I'll not look for wine.

By now the whole scene has faded.

Cellist   There are not, on earth at least, eternal griefs.
Some are, if not at an end, at least suspended.

She gives a flourish on her cello.

Activity. **Swallow** *jumps up.* **Fanny** *hands* **Swallow** *a loop on a
stick (a peep-hole prop).*

Swallow   I am now some seven months with Mr H.
And am kept in comfort and style.
One day I return from visiting . . .

She mimes returning.

And finding the street door open . . .

She mimes finding the door open.

I enter without knocking.

She enters.

Fancying I heard my maid's voice, I stole softly to the door
which afforded a very commanding peep-hole.

She lifts up the hand held peep-hole. As she does so **Dingle** *and*
Louisa *take up their positions.*

And there I see Mr H pulling and hauling at this coarse
country strammel.

The tableau comes to life.

Louisa   Pray, sir, don't, sir. Let me alone. I am not for your
turn. Sure, you cannot demean yourself with such a poor

body as I? Lord, sir, my mistress may come home, I must not indeed. I will cry out. I will cry out.

Pause.

I think it will be easier if I sit on the table.

She sits on the 'table', pulls him towards her and makes very short work of him. She pushes him away, takes some money from his pocket . . .

Supper at seven then . . . sir.

She curtsies. Swaggers off. He attempts to recompose himself. Staggers off.

Swallow   This was provocation!
Only revenge could restore me to perfect composure.

She tosses aside the peep-hole.

Mr H had taken into his service a fortnight before a very handsome young lad. Scarce turned nineteen, fresh as a rose and as pretty a piece of women's meat as you were likely to see.

Louisa *appears on cue. Dressed as a boy.*

Swallow   His chief employ was to carry letters and bring messages between his master and me.

Louisa   Morning.

Swallow   Hitherto I had only taken notice of the comeliness of the youth, but now I began to look on this stripling as a delicious instrument of my resigned retaliation.

Louisa   Here's your letter.

Louisa *holds out a letter.*

Swallow   I could not help observing that this lad eyed me in a bashful, confused way. My figure it seems had struck him.

She takes the letter provocatively, screws it into a ball and throws it some distance.

I have dropped it.

Louisa   You have dropped it.

Louisa *picks it up and attempts to smooth it out. She awkwardly
hands it back.* **Swallow** *does not take it.*

Swallow   Boy, have you a mistress?

Louisa *shakes her head, no.*

Swallow   Is she prettier than me?

Louisa *shakes her head, no.*

Swallow   Has she got smaller feet?

A pause.

Come here.

A pause.

Are you afraid of a lady?

She takes **Louisa***'s hand and places it on her breast.*
A pause. They go to kiss and at that moment **Fanny** *tosses something
into the scene that rattles on the floor and breaks the moment. It is a sock
stuffed so as to make a mock penis.*

Louisa   What's that?

Fanny   What's it look like?
It's a representation, Louisa.
You've seen plenty of these before.

Louisa   Not like that I haven't.

Fanny   It's the sceptre-member. Now get on with it.

Louisa *puts in on the floor in front of them both.*

Louisa   I stole my hand upon his thighs . . .

Swallow   Down one of which I could feel a stiff, hard body.

Louisa   The essential object of enjoyment.

Swallow   Curious then and eager to unfold so alarming a
mystery, I played with his buttons.

Louisa   Which were bursting ripe with the active force
within.

Swallow *and* **Louisa**   When lo! His waistband and foreflap
flew open at a touch . . .

Louisa *picks it up and holds it up.*

Louisa   And out it started!

Swallow   And I saw with wonder and surprise a maypole of so excessive a standard that had the proportions been observed it might have belonged to a young giant.

Louisa *holds up the sock again.*

Louisa   It was fucking enormous.

Swallow   And set off by a sprout of black curling hair at the root. Through which the fair skin showed as in a fine evening the clear light shows through the distant branch work of trees o'er topping the summit of a hill.

Louisa   He had nice pubes.

She tosses the sock to **Swallow**, *who catches it.*

So I offered him a full view of mine. Plus the whole region of delight and the luxurious landscape round it. All the secrets of that dark and delicious deep. I made myself as open as possible.

Swallow   Oh, how it did batter and bore against me!

She beats it against anything to hand.

Stiffly, in random pushes, now above, now below its point.

Dingle   Careful!

Swallow *keeps hitting.*

Swallow   Battering and boring.

Dingle   Miss Fanny, I protest!

Swallow   Boring and battering.

Fanny *calls from offside.*

Fanny   Till burning with impatience I guided him gently in for his first lesson of pleasure.

Swallow *stops.*

Louisa   A favourable motion from me . . .

Fanny   Met a timely thrust of his and so he gained lodgement.

Swallow   He pursued his point by violent and most painful piercing thrusts. Get out! I cried.

Fanny   Not meaning a word of it. And so he kept his post.

Louisa   All his looks and motions acknowledged excess of pleasure which I began to share for I felt him in my very vitals.

Swallow   I was quite sick/

Fanny   With delight.

Louisa   Our pleasure increased deliciously. At the height of fury I twisted my legs around his and drew him home and kept him fast as if I sought to unite our two bodies.

Swallow   Then we stopped.

Fanny   A pleasure stop.

Louisa   As delicious perhaps as the crowning act of enjoyment itself. Kissing, toying, clipping, whilst that delicate glutton, my nethermouth, as full as it could hold, kept palpitating with exquisite relish the morsel it so deliciously engorged.

Fanny   Nature could not long endure a pleasure that highly provoked without satisfying it.

Louisa   So we pursued it to its darling end. Nor lay I inactive on my side but encountered him with all the impetuosity of motion I was mistress of.

Swallow   And soon.

Louisa   The sweet urgency of action raised the titilation in me to its height and loath to leave behind the partner of my tender joys I employed all the forwarding arts I knew to promote his keeping my company to the journey's end.

Swallow   What did you do?

Louisa   I squeezed his globular appendages.

Swallow   Oh.

Louisa   And then the symptoms of sweet agony!

Louisa, Swallow, Fanny   The melting moment of dissolution when pleasure dies by pleasure and flings us into an ecstasy breathless fainting lost entranced . . .
Then the hot warm floods and liquid streams
And after, voluptuous, fast locked in arms langour.

Pause.

Louisa   Soon we were ready to try again.

Dingle   No! Louisa!
This is too much.
This book, Miss Fanny!

Fanny   Is coming on apace, Mr Dingle.

Dingle   But who will read it?

Fanny   Those that can pay good money for it.

Louisa   Once again I advance . . .

Swallow *mimics* **Louisa***'s movements.*

Dingle   Louisa! I hear Mr H returning!

Swallow   I reached out . . .

Dingle   His foot is on the stair . . .

Louisa   We embraced!

Both **Swallow** *and* **Louisa** *are miming an embrace.*

Dingle   He is returned! He is returned!

Dingle *assumes Mr H's character.*

Oh, horror! Horror!

Swallow   I screamed.

She screams.

And dropped my petticoat.

Louisa   The thunderstruck lad stood trembling and pale.

Swallow   We stood before him like criminals.

Dingle   What have you to say for yourself?
To abuse me in such an unworthy manner and with my own
servant. How have I deserved this?

Swallow   I have only done what you have done.
I had not a single thought in wronging you till I saw you
taking liberties with my own serving wench last Tuesday.
That has driven me to this course which I do not pretend to
justify.
This young man is faultless.
I seduced him to make him the instrument of my revenge.
He is innocent and I am guilty and entirely at your mercy.

Dingle   Madam, I take shame to myself and confess that
you have fairly turned the tables on me. I own too that your
clearing of this rascal here is just and honest in you.
However, there can be no comparison between my
provocation and yours, for I am a gentleman and you are a
tart.
And so, renew with you, madam, I cannot!

Swallow   But . . .

Dingle   The affront is too gross.
You've got a day to get out.

Swallow   Very well.

Dingle   And give me that.

He takes the stuffed sock.

This is my sock and it has been most vilely ill-used. Goodbye.

He exits. **Louisa** *follows him.*

Swallow   I am once more adrift.
Cast out into a world cold, hard and bargaining.
What will become of me?
Alas, I have nothing . . . but fifty silver guineas.
And any woman of pleasure knows how little long that may
last her . . .

Swallow *wanders to the sidelines.*
Fanny *is scribbling.*

Cellist   I had a thought.

Fanny *continues to write.*

Cellist   If I need to remember things I usually tie a knot in something.

She indicates her skirt which has a knot in it.

A knot. To remind me.
To help me remember.
I tie a knot in something.

A pause.
Cellist *coughs. She exits.*
Fanny *is scribbling.*

Louisa   I need my money.
I need it now. Today.
My sovereign.
You promised.

Pause.

I need it later then.
Later.
But I need it.

She begins to exit.
Dingle *catches up with her.*

Dingle   Miss Louisa!

A pause.

There was a wild night once.
Wind and a storm.
A heavy sea.
My ship.
So much water in the sea.
Soon she became waterlogged.
So light but she became waterlogged.
All hands on ship! someone shouted.
But still she sank like a weight.
That was a dark night.

Louisa   You wanted comforting.

Dingle   I did need comfort.

Louisa   Still, I expect you couldn't afford it then, eh?

She leaves. He follows.

Swallow   I sat under the table, wiping.
I used to like listening.
Poetry. Beautiful. Nice.
The shepherd swains shall dance and sing
For thy delight each May morning;
If these delights thy mind may move,
Then live with me and be my love.

Spark *comes on. Watches her.* **Swallow** *regards him with alarm.*
She runs off.
Fanny *scribbles.* **Spark** *taps his cane on her table.*

Fanny   It's you. What an unlooked for pleasure.

Spark   I was just passing.

Fanny   We're half way.

Spark   Speedy work.

Fanny   I've learnt never to entertain time-wasting
unnecessaries, like excess biographical material or knickers.

Spark   Most commendable. When can I have my book?

Fanny   You can't hurry art.

Spark   Oh, I'm not so sure.
Art, like everything, must have one eye cocked on the
market. And if the market looks your way, it's a chaste soul
that can refuse its goodly embrace.
Indeed t'would be unnatural!
For an appetite is a healthy thing.
And appetites must be fed.

Fanny   I griddle as fast as I can.
Soon I will be out of paper!

Spark   Write smaller.
I will return.

Fanny   I await you in breathless expectation.

He exits.

His book. His book.
It's my book. Mine.
Oh, I can see myself opulent.
Money. No more ice nights.
No more vomit stinking gobs and poxy pricks.
No.
He may be a driblet of dung but his idea's priceless.
Priceless and I'm having it.
My book. Mine. Mine.

Pause.

So far six fucks.
That's more than most of you get in an evening.

She puts down her pen.
Lights down.

Part Two

The cello plays. The whole cast are in a tableau of copulating, bizarre.
It moves as one thing, like a machine. It gets frenetic and then dies.
Everyone 'dies' together. The machine collapses, sags. **Fanny** *speaks.*

Fanny Dear reader,
I imagined you would have been a trifle tired, nay, cloyed,
with the uniformity of adventures and expressions
inseparable from a subject of this sort, which, after all, has at
bottom a thing eternally one and the same.

But no.
Here you are returned for book two.
You may well be duller than I thought
And unable to concoct better for yourselves.
Poor lambs.

Still, you will appreciate my problem.
A certain repetition is inevitable.
And let's face it those awful words,
Joys, ardours, ecstasies, et cetera employed so regular in the
practice of pleasure tend, like an old mattress to flatten with
frequency and lose all bounce.

My advice on such matters is this:
Use your imagination.
That will give life to colours worn dull by frequent handling.

As for the mincing metaphors and affected circumlocutions I
employ to describe that old last act, don't blame me.
I am merely avoiding the whip of the censor which you, the
darling public, have erected for your own moral protection.

Look at me now, speechifying.
I must obey my own rules
And immediately grab hold of the main parts of my story.

She reaches over and grabs **Dingle** *by the crotch. He responds with an*
expression half pain/half pleasure. Simultaneously we hear a long note
from the cello.

Tempus fugit, Mr Dingle.
Are you with us?

Dingle   I think I may stay, Miss Fanny.
A voyage once embarked upon should not be lightly
abandoned.

Louisa *turns round. We see that she is heavily pregnant.*

Swallow   Louisa!

Cellist   Louisa!

Dingle   Louisa!

Fanny   What fast work.

Dingle   Who's is it?

Louisa   Yours.

Dingle   Mine!

Louisa   Wretch! Pisspot! Rascal!

Dingle   There's been some mistake.

Louisa   Treat a poor girl so!

Dingle   Upon my life, Miss Fanny . . .

Louisa   I am undone!

Dingle   I swear.

Louisa   Dog-breath. Will you not even pay for the upkeep?

She holds out her hand.

Dingle   Pay?

Louisa   Shag-bag. Villain. Pimp. I will call a constable.

Dingle   I beg you . . .

Louisa *laughs. She pulls a pillow out from under her skirt.*

Louisa   An easy birth.

Swallow   Louisa . . .

Louisa   I've been earning a few dirty and dishonest pence
down Sadler's Wells. Gulling a few culls.

Dingle   A swindling trade.

Louisa   Yeah.

Fanny   Come come. Enough chattering.
I hear the muse calling.

Louisa   When am I going to get bleedin' paid?
I need it, soon, my sovereign.

Fanny   In good time. In good time.
(*To* **Swallow**.) Are you ready my sweetling?

A cello note.

Swallow   I am all alone in the world.
The streets smell of piss.
There's a frost and someone is huddled on the ground dead
or begging.
I'm lost.
The night is dark.

Fanny   Good evening.
May I introduce myself? I am Mother Clap.
A middle-aged, discreet sort of woman.
May I offer you my cordial advice?
There is no one more acquainted with the wicked part of
town than I.
So who is fitter to guard and advise you than I?

Swallow   Well . . .

Fanny   No one.
I keep a house of conveniency.
Promoting schemes of pleasure and unbounded debauchery.
However, I content myself with a moderate profit.
I am a gentlewoman born and bred, reduced to this course
through dire necessity
And the delight in encouraging a brisk circulation in the
trade.
Here is my card.
We've a Covent Garden address you'll see, and only serve
customers of distinction,
No turds.
Au revoir.

Swallow *accepts the card. Looks at it then at the audience.*

Swallow   Thus I passed from a private devotee of pleasure to a public one. Thereafter being able to dispose of myself for the general good of all.

Fanny (*aside*)   A natural market expansion.
(*To* **Swallow**.) Welcome.
We sit in the window here, see.

Cellist, Fanny, Louisa, *all sit in a row as if facing a window. They are all sewing a large sheet.* **Dingle** *does the scripting in this scene.*

Fanny   Demurely employed on milinary work.
A cover for traffic in more precious commodities.

Swallow *takes her place amongst them.* **Louisa** *whistles.*

Louisa   Here's a spark!

They all pose and smile. They watch him pass by in unison. Then the pose immediately drops indicating that he has passed by.

(*Calling after him.*) Mulc's dropping!

Cellist   Sometimes we have a great deal of time on our hands.

Swallow   Oh.

Fanny   Which we employ by entertaining each other with stories of critical periods in our personal history.

Louisa   I had a fucking weirdo once.

Fanny   Louisa!

Louisa   He could only come if he watched me naked strangling a pigeon.

Cellist   Goodness.

Fanny   That is hardly the stuff of literature.

Louisa   I told him, I hope you've brought your own pigeon.

Fanny   We usually select a topic. Don't we, girls?

Louisa Yeah. 'Love, laughter and the joys of a goat's gut condom', or how I avoided getting up the duff.

Cellist Perhaps we could discourse upon safety matters? How to prevent the admittance of blunt and dangerous implements into the boudoir.

Louisa What? Please enter but leave your dick on the doormat?

Cellist Hammers, I meant, or knives . . .

Fanny Please. These are unsavoury practicalities and likely to snag at a smooth read. I suggest 'when first we changed the maiden state for womanhood'. Louisa. May we have your story, dearest?

There is a silence. **Louisa** *does not comply.* **Fanny** *prompts her.*

You came from a farming family, remember?

Louisa Oh yeah.

Pause. **Fanny** *continues to prompt.*

Fanny But your mother and father didn't like you a bit. So they chucked you out.

Louisa Oh yeah.

Fanny You took the road to London.
After twelve miles you stopped in weariness and bawled your eyes out.
Just then a sturdy country lad approaches with his travelling equipage.

Louisa His what?

Cellist It's a euphemism.

Fanny It's a suitcase.
Anyway. You and he travel on together.
He says you both should pass for man and wife.
You agree, never dreaming of the consequences.

Louisa Oh no.

Fanny So you get to an inn, say you're married and they go and put you in the same bed.

She uses the thing they are sewing as a bed sheet.

Being so incredibly innocent you thought nothing more of going to bed with a young man as with a dairy wench.

Louisa   That's me all over.

Fanny   It was a bitter night. Brrrr.

She shakes the sheet as if shivering.

And so the two of you nestled close for warmth. Oh! how powerful is nature and how little is wanting to set it into action.

She pulls the sheet over them.

The strange tickling heat.
His thigh between yours.
Your mouth full of tongue.
The king member alert.
The piercing pain that makes you cry out.

Louisa   Bollocks.

Dingle   Shall I note that, Miss Fanny?

Fanny   Excise it, Dingle.

Louisa   Her needle.

Cellist   Sorry.

Louisa   Stuck it in me.

Cellist   I became deranged in the flurry.

Louisa   It hurt.

Fanny   Suck it, my precious, and then continue.

A pause.

Louisa?

Louisa   I came from a village.
But I weren't innocent,
I'd done it loads of times.
Especially at harvests.
Men and women.

Fanny   The story.

Pause.

Louisa   Then this thing happened.
The whole village had to go.
Flat.

Fanny (*impatient*)   Yes, yes.

Louisa   The whole land was becoming one big farm
For miles and miles and it was an act of parliament.
And the village went quiet and rotted
And the people went quiet and faded
And I drank and fucked
And then I couldn't get work.
Not enough.
Work got thin
Like a bad crop.
I got hungry
Day after day after day after day
Like a knife
In the guts.
So then I got on the London road
But I never met a lad
I met a girl
She had arms like twigs
And she never asked me nothing
But if I had some bread or a potato
And then she took me where she lived, dead place,
And I went in through the door
Which was low
And the place stank
And there were three dead people
All curled upon the floor
And two of them were children
And one was the mother
And they had straw in their mouths
Which they'd been eating.
And I left.
When I got to London I drunk and fucked some more

Only I got paid for it.
They took the land but they left the bodies.

Pause.

Fanny   My readers do not want the sordid stink of
suffering, they want a hard-on.
Still, salvation is at hand.
Look. Here is a customer.

She pulls back the sheet. They are lewdly exposed. **Dingle** *scurries to
serve in the scene.*

It is Mr Norbert.
Originally a gentleman of great fortune and constitution,
both now sadly impaired by his over violent pursuit of the
vices of the town.
Having staled all the more common modes of debauchery he
has fallen into a taste for virgins in which chase he has ruined
many of that number sparing no expense to further his end.
Afternoon.

Dingle   Afternoon.

Fanny   Trade is very good at the moment, very good.
The wind has blown something my way, Mr Norbert.
Blown all the way from Preston.
That I believe is where she comes from,
Intact.
(*Aside.*) He's like a dog drawn to a bitch.
Her name is Fanny.

The others move aside from the scene. **Fanny** *hovers.*

Dingle   How d'you do?

Swallow   Well, thank you, Mr Norbert.

Dingle   How old are you?

Fanny   She's sixteen.

Dingle   And new to town?

Fanny   Pristine.

Swallow   I am learning to make hats and live with this kindly milliner.
Hats are fascinating and come in different sizes.

Dingle   Gosh.

Fanny (*aside*)   He will pay a dazzling sum.

The others begin to prepare the next scene. Bringing a candle and a jar with a blood-soaked sponge in it.

There is in men, once they are caught by the eye, a fund of cullibility that their lordly wisdom little dreams of. It would be a sin not to make market of such fellows. They make good dupes. We make a good fifty quid.
The night is fixed!

The candles are lit.

Dingle *and* **Swallow** *are alone. He approaches.*

Swallow   No.

Dingle   Yes.

Swallow   No.

Dingle   Yes.

Swallow   No.

She gives him a push. He overbalances.

Dingle   My dear.

Swallow   Go away.

Dingle   Don't be afraid.
Come to me, my sweet, untouched goods!

He gets close to her. Begins to unbutton.

Swallow   I shall be ruined, I shall.
Lord, what are you about?
This is bitter usage!
Help! Help!

Dingle   Innocent, innocent.

Swallow   What is that?

Dingle   What?

Swallow   That.

She points to his crotch.

Do not bring it near me, for I do not like the look of it.

He laughs. Climbs on top of her.

I am afraid it will kill me!
(*Aside.*) His machine is of one of those sizes that slips in and out without being much minded.
Lord! I was never so used in all my born days!

Dingle   Just a little wider.

Swallow (*aside*)   I suffered him to lay my thighs aside but watched the direction and management of his point so well that no sooner than his instrument's tip touched my cloven inlet, as he fatigued and toiled to get it in, I gave a timely jerk and cried 'Oh, I shall die', 'You have killed me' et cetera, all accompanied by the proper gestures and followed by a scream as if he had pierced me to the heart.

She gives a piercing scream.

I then shook him off with some violence.
I'm sure he held me the dearer for it.

Dingle   Oh, rapture! Oh, my little unimpaired cargo.

He climbs back on top of her.

Come, come. The worst is certainly past. With a little courage and consistency I shall get it over once and for all. And ever after you shall experience nothing but pleasure.

Swallow (*aside*)   Surely not of his making!
Little by little I suffered myself to be prevailed upon, spreading my thighs insensibly and yielding him liberty of access so that he got a little within me.

Dingle   Ah!

Swallow   But I worked the female screw so nicely (*She twists.*) that I kept him from the easy mid-channel direction and by dextrous wreathings and contortions (*She wreaths and contorts.*) created an artificial difficulty of entrance which made him win me inch by inch with the most laborious of struggles.

Dingle (*struggling*)   Inch by inch.

Swallow   At length, with might and main, he winds his way completely home and gives my virginity, as he thought it, the final *coup de grâce*.

Dingle *makes appropriate grunting noises*.

Swallow   He was like a cock clapping its wings over his downtrod mistress.

Dingle *makes a triumphant sound something like a cock crowing*.

Swallow   Whilst I lay acting the deep wounded, undone and no longer maid.
(*To him*.) Alas! I am ruined!

Dingle   There, there. Do not cry.
I must get a little sleep.

He falls asleep.

Swallow   You will ask whether all this time I enjoyed any perception of pleasure? I assure you, little or none, except perhaps towards the latter end when a faintish sense of it came on mechanically from so long a struggle.

She gets up quietly and fetches the jar with the sponge.

A tumbler full of blood.
A sponge that requires no more than gently reaching the hand to it and when it is taken out and squeezed between the thighs, it yields plenty enough to save a girl's honour.

She squeezes the blood over her thighs, her shift, she rubs it in a bit.

And I will make thee bed of roses
And a thousand fragrant posies.

Mr Norbert. Mr Norbert.
Blood.

Dingle   My jewel.

Swallow   Blood. Blood.

Fanny   One blood is quite enough.

She continues writing.

Louisa (*to* **Swallow**)   You're getting it everywhere.

Swallow *continues to dab herself.*

Dingle   She is merely working with industry, Miss Louisa.

Louisa   Industry?

Dingle   Hard work. Honest hard work.
There are laws.
Whatsoever thou sowest.
I worked hard.
First I owned one sixteenth . . .

They speak the next two lines simultaneously.

Louisa   . . . of a ship and then I owned half.

Dingle   . . . of a ship and then I owned half.

Pause.

And then it sunk.
But, you see, I'd been caught in a net,
Tangled in it.

Fanny   How does one spell 'bifurcate'?

Dingle   Adrift on a sea of intemperateness.
Tempted.
Then those same pure laws
That elevate man to his highest condition
They cast me down.
A storm of retribution.
You see my point.

Louisa   I got headache.

Fanny   'Globule'?

Dingle   Things eating away at my pure condition,
crumbling soft timber, like a pox.

Fanny   'Hirsutc'? Or shall I put plain old 'hairy'?

Louisa   Headache. (*To* **Dingle**.) That's you.

Dingle   Crumbling, Miss Louisa.

Louisa   Lice-shag!

He moves away.

Swallow   Have we finished?

Fanny   I've not yet reached my optimum target of encounters.

Swallow   What do I do now?

Fanny   You stay with Mr Norbert and become his mistress.

Swallow   And we will sit upon the rocks
And see the shepherds feed their flocks.

Cellist   Did you ever know a Mr Norbert?

Fanny   Who?

Cellist   A Mr Norbert?

Fanny   I did it in the dark a lot. It's hard remembering things in the dark. The Norberts from the Dashwoods from the Drybutters.

Cellist   Oh.

Swallow   I stayed with Mr Norbert.
Sometimes he would sit me stark naked on a carpet by a good fire and contemplate me for an hour, kissing me in every part, the secret, critical one – far from being exempted – receiving the most homage. His touches were exquisitely wanton and luxuriously diffused as if by his invention he meant to make up for his capital deficiency. For after he had gained an erection it would melt away in a washy sweat that provokingly mocked my eager desires.

Cellist   I think I would like a man with a capital deficiency.

Fanny   Who asked you?

Cellist   Luxuriously diffused sounds rather nice. That's all. Better than all the puffing and blowing.

Fanny   Puffing and blowing?

Cellist   Yes.

She demonstrates.

Like that.

Fanny   Arch Jade! The demise of such practices leads to all sorts of unmentionables which I will not hesitate to immortalise in print.

She takes centre stage. Joining in.

(*Sings.*) One day when Norbert's wand was too weak
I was approached as I walked in the street
By a young sailor, who kissed me sweet.

Louisa   At first I said 'Sir'!
Who do you think you are

Fanny   But then I went with him to a local bar,
Not far.

He fell directly on board me
And without more ado
He pulls out his splitter

Louisa   And I said ooh

He'd been at sea a terrible while
The longer the better
I replied with a smile.

Fanny   Sir, I said, watch it, you're at the wrong door.
Any port in a storm dear, he jested, cocksure.
Still, he altered his course and came in the right door.

Oh we made waves and we splashed and we foamed
I had a good swim
And then I came home.

Louisa   Where have you been, says Mother Clap
And when I tells her she gives me a slap.

Together   It's a risk to your health to be free with your flesh,
So opened legged, so salacious

Louisa   So I promised never more a venture so rash

Fanny   'Specially for no remunerative cash.

Cellist   I think I would still prefer one of Mr Norbert's propensities.

Fanny   A fondler.

Cellist   Yes.

Fanny   Well, hard luck, 'cos he dies.

Cellist   Poor Mr Norbert. I wish I'd never said anything.

Fanny   He departs due to a debauch of drinking.

Dingle   Amen.

Fanny   Flinging young Fanny here back onto the open market.

Swallow   No condition of life is more subject to revolutions than that of a woman of pleasure.

Music. Stage clears as **Spark** *enters.*

Spark   Revolution?

Fanny   Kind benefactor.

Spark   Can the winds of change have blown as far as this foul corner?

Fanny   Happily, no. That sort of thing is best left to abroad.

Spark   I am of a revolutionary outlook.
I've read Rousseau.
It is my belief that things are only good or bad in reference to pleasure or pain. That we call good is apt to increase pleasure in us. Ergo, to fuck is good.

Fanny   How nicely put.

Spark   I have cast off the abrasive shackles of conformity.

Fanny   Talking of abrasive shackles . . .

Spark   And live a libertine's life.

Fanny   I need a little help.
A few moments of your time. We were just about to evoke the scenario of the rod.

Spark   Indeed.

Fanny   There are some poor few under the tyranny of this cruel taste.

Spark   Perverts.

Fanny   Some require it to quicken those flagging, shrivelly parts that rise to life only by virtue of a sharp thwack and others just fancy it. Dreadful.

Spark   What does it entail?

Fanny   A rod.

Someone throws her a rod.

And some rope.

And some rope.

I keep the rod.
The recipient of the lash has their hands tied.

She signals. Someone comes and ties his hands.

And that is how the whole beastly and offensive business begins.

Spark   I see.
It cannot be enjoyed.

Fanny   Some miserable wretches achieve a vestige of titillation, yes.

Spark   Impossible.

Fanny   You are a man of the new age.

Spark   I am.

Fanny   Then allow me. An experiment. Scientific.

She gives him a slight tap.

Anything?

Spark   Nothing.

She hits him again.

Fanny   That did not hurt?

Spark   No.

Fanny   Or that?

Spark   Nor gave me any pleasure whatsoever.

Fanny   Tut tut.
As little bothered as a lobster by a flea bite.
I'll try a little harder.

She hits him.

Spark   A little discomfort but I assure you not the slightest arousal.

Fanny   Fancy that.

Hits him hard.

Spark   Ow!

Fanny   A result!

Spark   But no gratification.

Fanny   P'raps due to a wilful disposition?

Spark   The experiment is clearly defunct. Untie me.

Fanny   So soon? I 'xpect you was a handful at school.

Spark   Untie me. Bulk-mongerer.

Fanny   Don't turn nasty. This is science, remember.

She hits him again.

Spark   Ow!

She pokes him with the rod. Knocks him to the floor. Climbs over him.

Fanny   I smelt desire. I'm sure I did.
Procured at the hands of pain.

Spark   Liar.

Fanny   I saw it I did.
A stirring.
Your little wren peeping its head out of the grass and shuddering into life as each lash skimmed the surface of your cliffs so chubby and white cheeked.
Ergo, what a turn-up.

She laughs.

Spark   I'm giving you one more chance. These ropes.
Loosen them.

Fanny   There is talk of revolution.
Oh yes.
Right here.
This rod, for instance, is sharp.

Spark   Festering baggage.

Fanny   How foolish to misprize an armed woman and in
your position.
Now you will hear my business.
As you know I have been engaged in artistic endeavours
aimed at pleasuring a grateful readership.
My memoirs.
Well, my book is my book.
I have written it and I will put my name to it and take all the
profits and be excessive rich.
Oh, people will scrape low for me, very low.
I shall attend literary salons and chaff about being a tart and
I shall wear impertinent headgear and be constantly
accompanied by three singing birds and I will have diamond
heels and eat only the icing off of cakes and if I wake at night
a brawny chap shall sing to me and there will be a hundred
silver bells strung about my person and my cats shall be
scented and I shall swig grog and daily masturbate before a
thundering warm fire in my boudoir and you can piss off,
pimp.

Spark   I still have your debts.

Fanny   Trifling things soon dealt with.

Spark   Stinking whore.

Fanny   Arse breath.
Find someone else to pick out your splinters.
Untie his feet.

Someone does so.

Spark   This is not the end.

Fanny   Farewell. It's been a pleasure.

Spark   I'll see you in the stocks.

He goes.

Fanny   A triumph!
Life takes such strange turns.
I feel quite elevated.

Pause.

I almost remembered something then.
A good sign.

Cellist   How fortuitous.

Fanny   Exactly. I'd have two pasts then. A real one and
one to make money with.

She kisses her book. **Louisa** *gives a gasp.*

Louisa   Christ!

She doubles up.

Christ!

Fanny   What's the matter?

Louisa   I'm shaking. Look, shaking.

Fanny   We've got to get on.

Louisa *gives a short cry.*

Louisa   Can't stop.

Dingle   She's shaking.

Louisa   Cold and bloody shivering.

Dingle   And white.

Fanny   You took something.

Louisa   Powder. Tasted of metal.

Fanny   The cure'll probably finish for you.

Louisa   I paid for 'em.

Fanny   You was ripped off.

Louisa   I've got a pain.

Dingle   She's sick.

Louisa   Get lost.
(*Sings.*) So I promised never more a venture so rash . . .
Can't sing.

Pause.

I owe 'em my sovereign.

Fanny   Life is expensive.
Next is the story of Louisa and the good-natured idiot, Dick.

Louisa   I'm resting!

Fanny   He is a seller of nosegays.

She tosses **Dingle** *something he can use as a nosegay.*

He is strong as a horse though in somewhat ragged a plight
and smelly.

Louisa   I'm not doing it.

Fanny   A wayward fancy seizes Louisa.

Louisa   No, I said.

Fanny   She winks at him. Asks him upstairs.

Dingle   She has a strange longing to be satisfied.

Louisa   No!

Dingle   She encourages him with her eyes.

Fanny   He drops his baskets.

Fanny *repeats bits of* **Dingle***'s litany as she makes notes. She almost
overlaps with him.*

Dingle   Through his rags she discovers his thighs and then
the genuine sensitive plant . . .

Fanny   Sensitive plant . . .

Dingle   . . . which, instead of shrinking from her touch,
joys to meet it and swells and vegetates . . .

Fanny   Vegetates . . .

Dingle   . . . under it. The waistband unskewers to reveal
the whole of Dick's standard of distinction in full pride and
display and such a one . . .

Fanny   Such a one!

Dingle   It was positively of so . . . so tremendous a size it . . .

Fanny   So tremendous a size . . .

Dingle   It astonished and surpassed all expectation, its enormous head . . .

Fanny   Enormous head . . .

Dingle   Seemed not unlike a common sheep's heart.

Fanny   A common sheep's heart!

Dingle   You may even have trolled dice securely on the broad back of the body of it . . .

Fanny   And the length too was prodigious. Oh, Louisa's appetite was up.

Louisa   It weren't!

Dingle   The springs of his organ were wound to an extreme pitch.

Louisa   I'm going to puke.

Dingle   She took the fall she loved . . . onto the bed.
He faithfully directed his label of manhood, his battering point . . .
And his joys become furious . . .

Fanny   Furious . . .

Dingle   His eyes shoot fire. His teeth churning, his face glowing, his frame raging . . .

He has approached **Louisa** *and has grabbed her.*

Louisa   Let go!

Fanny   Raging . . .

Dingle   Ungovernable, butting, goring, wild, overdriven,

Fanny   Goring . . . and what?

Dingle   He ploughs up the tender furrow.

Louisa   Let go of me!

Fanny *whispers as many of these words as she can follow.*

Dingle   Nothing can stop, blind rage, piercing rending
tearing splitting . . .

Louisa *breaks free.*

Louisa   LET GO!

Dingle   Splitting . . .

Louisa   My turn.

Dingle (*quieter*)   Splitting . . .

Louisa   Now I shall tell you about mine.
My favourite bits.
My choice bits which give me hot nights.

Dingle *shies away.*

Louisa   My mouth, my small tongue ever ready,
My little woman in a boat.

He puts his hand on his crotch. **Louisa** *drives him back now.*

She won't bite,
but can be ravishingly touched by me or others.
Such exquisite vibrations, such shudderings.
Such delicious delirium and drenching pleasures, such
riotous times and sweet excesses.
All mine.
Mine mine mine.
Yes.
Oh yes!

Fanny   That is all very well, Louisa, but not for my book.
Gentlemen are more interested in their own bits.

Louisa *continues to attack* **Dingle**.

Louisa   Come on then. Come on.
Now.
Let's see your label of manhood now.
Let's see the lank and flapping thing!
Let's have more insupportable delight.

He backs away a bit; puts his hand on his crotch.

No?
Pity.
I want a drink!

She sits down heavily. She seems ill.

Dingle   Miss Louisa.

Pause.

Miss Louisa.

He approaches.

You're poxed.

Louisa   I want a drink.

Dingle   Poxed. Poxed a hundred times over.

Louisa   Come closer and I'll spew.

Dingle   I came here for you.

Louisa   What?

Dingle   For you. To rescue you.

Louisa   Me?

Dingle   From drowning. Sinking.
I have submitted myself to foul and licentious practices for
your sake, Miss Louisa, for your sake only.

Louisa   Nutter.

Dingle   I am your salvation.
Profane things are practised here in our very streets which
have made this city a second Sodom!

Louisa   Get away.

Dingle   You must renounce your way of life and come with
me.
Here is my card. I won't use force.
It's all voluntary.

He holds out a card. She does not take it.

I am in disguise.
I belong to an organisation.
We call ourselves 'night walkers'.

We walk out and about at night, saving souls.
That's when I spotted you.
We are out to end the horrid debauchery of the age.

Louisa   Fucking help.

Dingle   It starts with the harlot. That's you.
You tempt us. You turn us off course.
We neglect things. We lose money. Then we steal to pay for
your filthy services. This leads to quarrellings and fightings,
clamours of 'murder', breaking of windows and other
tumultuous riots, routs and uproars. Property is lost. The
state is enervated. The pox spreads to wives and families,
soldiers and sailors and they are effeminated. Sailors are
effeminated and ships sink. Ships sink. They sink. You sunk
my ship.

Louisa   I never bleedin' touched it.

Dingle   Ships are lost. Trade is lost. Colonies are lost. Wars
are lost. The whole country is lost. Lost.

Fanny   I fear you have a case of rumpled premises, Dingle.

Dingle   I will be heard, Miss Fanny. I will be. You must
think of your future life, Louisa.

Louisa   I want to get through this one.

Dingle   Repent.

Louisa   I'll eat now and pray later.

Dingle   Turn your back on evil.

Louisa   It's only sticking a penis up me and twiddling it
about a bit.

Dingle   Once a whore always a whore.

Louisa   You've dabbled. I've seen you. Round here.
Before. Maybe even done you.

Dingle   I paid. I paid. My Louisa sunk.

Louisa   Go home.

Pause.

Dingle   You're dying.

Pause.

Dying.

Louisa   No.

Dingle   Dying.

Louisa   What do you know?

Pause.

I'm fine.

Dingle   You're burning now.

Louisa   Fine.

Dingle   A death fever.

Louisa   No.

Dingle   A hell fever.

Louisa   No.

Dingle   Dying.

Pause.

I know a place. A hospital. A pure place.

Fanny   All this morbidity! And with our end in sight. I suggest you bugger off, Dingle, and leave us to our art.

Dingle   Death and damnation, Miss Louisa!

Pause.

I pity you.
I had hoped to save you but see I am too late.
Fanny Hill. I do not know strong enough terms with which to express my repugnance for your opus.
Goodbye.

Fanny   He has a certain dexterity of phrase, I'll give him that.

He begins to leave.

Louisa   Wait!

Pause.

Wait.

She gets up.

Fanny   Louisa?

Swallow   Louisa?

Louisa *looks at them and follows* **Dingle** *out.*

Fanny (*shouts*)   Louisa!

Cellist   They've gone.

Fanny (*calls after them*)   I'm not paying you!

Pause.

(*To* **Swallow**.) I still have you left, my little bird. You will
help me finish my story.

Cellist   She's got blood on her face.

Fanny   Spit on your hanky, rosebud, and wipe your face.

Cellist   It's on her dress too. Blood.

Swallow   A gown made of the finest wool
Which from our pretty lambs we pull.

Nothing happens. **Cellist** *offers* **Swallow** *her hanky.* **Swallow**
takes it. Begins to wipe her face.

Cellist (*to* **Fanny**)   Did you have a daughter, ever?

Fanny   I might have. I might not.

Cellist   I just wondered.

Swallow   Wipe, wipe, wipe.

Fanny   Let us have a lively tune.

Cellist *complies.*

Fanny   We've had a glut of pleasure already, but why stop
there?
We will resume our history.
It's time young Fanny met a rich old gentleman.

Swallow   Come live with me and be my love.

Fanny   A rational pleasurist. Much too wise to be ashamed
of the joys of humanity and with a fat bank balance.

Swallow   Wipe, wipe my face. It's all over my face.

Fanny   Come along. You've been such a good girl to Fanny thus far, it would be a shame to let her down at the very denouement. I shall give you a pretty setting. The park. Plenty of foliage plus ample opportunities for hasty concealment. What do you say?

Swallow   I lied about the wiping.

Fanny   Never mind that.

Swallow   It wasn't a sore but it ran down his leg.
Sometimes he stuck it in my mouth where I sat but I
wouldn't swallow, I spat it out later.
Sometimes he let me touch his books.
His room was warmer than the rest.
He always had a fire and a plate of apples.
I liked his voice when he read,
It tangled with the words,
Like bits of music.
I always wiped up after.
But then I got bigger and I couldn't wipe that up, no.

Fanny   You meet the old gentleman in the park.

Swallow   Then he told me to go.
He wouldn't look in my eyes.
No more words.
No more soft words.
No more shepherds.
I left.
I walked for four days.

Fanny   The old gentleman makes you sole executrix of his will in an indecent short time.

Swallow   I couldn't go home like it.
So I went to a new place.
I knocked on the door of the church-warden but he would not open it.
So I sat on his step.
In the morning they made me leave the parish because I had a belly on me and they did not want it born where they would

have to upkeep it.
They were poor and hardworking they said and I must go
elsewhere.
So I went in the fields.
In the snow.
Later there was blood in the snow and I moaned in it and
staggered a mad dance in it and the baby came.

Fanny   An indecent short time.

Swallow   I carried her all day and she was screaming.
Sometimes I sat in the snow.
I did not know what to do.
In my mind I called her Annie.
I did not know what to do.
So I tied her in my hanky and came to a river
Then I dropped her in the river and she did float a little and
sink fast.
She was light but she sank fast.

Fanny   A short time.

Swallow   That is murder.

Cellist   Murder . . .

Swallow   There are not nice words for it.
To kill a child, but I did not know how to keep her.

Fanny   What does the old gentleman ask of you?

Swallow   To bite the ends off his gloves.

Fanny   Lovely. You've got an imagination.

Swallow   There was a girl burnt at Iveschester.
She was strangled by having the stool taken from under her.
She killed her baby. It took them six weeks to find her.

Fanny   Silk or kid, the gloves?

Swallow   They always find you. Annie will float into a port
and they'll come and get me.

Fanny   Not yet.

Swallow   They they'll burn me.

Fanny   You've got too much imagination.

Swallow   I want to ask you. I've been thinking.
Put me in your book.

Fanny   So close. So close to the end.

Swallow   I did not know how to keep her, write that.

Fanny   We can finish before dark, if we hurry.

Swallow   People will hate me otherwise.
Shout at me when I'm burning.
They'll hate me for ever and they won't know.
Write me in your book so they won't hate me.
Don't write soft things. Write me.

Fanny   That's not how the world goes.

Swallow   How does it go?

Fanny   That sort of thing won't sell.
It would be like reading a report.

Swallow   They strangled her first so as to stop her talking
out. Saying things. True things.

Fanny   Who'd want to read a thing like that?

Swallow   They choke you off at the neck.
Put about me in your book.
It's not the dying.
Dying is quick, quite. It's the being hated.
Being hated goes on.
I might lie in a grave wanting to tell.
Twisting about.
Put me in your book, please.

Pause.

Just a page.

Pause.

Fanny   No.

Swallow   She cried so much I tore out some of my hair.
I left that in the snow too.
Goodbye.

Fanny Where are you going?

Swallow Which way?

Fanny No one will look for you here. Not today.

Swallow They found her in six weeks.

She goes.

Fanny (*calls*) You're better off here than anywhere else.

Cellist She's gone too . . .

Fanny She was better off here than anywhere else.

Pause.

Fuck!

Pause.

This book needs one last fuck.

Pause.

I'll have to do it alone.
That's life for you.

She prepares herself.

I intend this last fuck to be a very happy fuck. Proving that a whorish life is a rewarding life. And if the sober amongst us object I have this to say: A fart upon you.
Music please.
That last old rich gent inadvisedly runs to a window on an alarum of fire and stands there naked and exposed to the fatal impressions of the damp night air. Which prove fatal.

A funereal note.

I was then in the full bloom of my youth, and being his sole heiress and executrix, rolling in it.

A happy note.

But alas, how easily is the enjoyment of the greatest sweets in life poisoned by regret for an absent one who was horribly snatched from me and bundled aboard ship and who I had not now laid peepers on for two years.

A sadder note.

Anyway, one night I drove to this inn and I called to this coachman to fetch me down, he had on a great cape and a hat which flapped about his chops, and as he approached the thing flew off, owing to a freak gust, and there he stood. Everything went misty and I shot into his arms crying 'My life! My soul! My Charles!' And then I swooned away under the agitations of joy and surprise.
A crowd gathered.

Dingle and **Spark** *walk on still in shadow.*

Fanny   My dearest Fanny, says he, can it be you?
And then we snogged.
Unutterable delight! Sweet confusion!
We hired a private room immediately.

Spark *walks in.*

Spark   This is a love story.
Your customers won't want this slop, Fanny.
They want their appetites fed. They want meat.

Fanny   I'm getting to the meat. What's it to you, anyway?

Spark   Disinterested advice, that's all.

Fanny   I was soon laid in bed, and Charles, after a short, prelusive dalliance, lifted up my linen and his own and laid his bare chest next to my bosom, beating now with the tenderest alarms.

Dingle *comes in.*

Dingle   Filth! Pure and unadulterated.

Fanny   I loved Charles with all my heart.

Spark   They don't want romance, they want flesh.

Fanny   The powers of solid pleasure thickened upon me. I could not help feeling the stiff stake of my supremely beloved youth bearing hard and inflexible against my thigh.

Dingle   It's dirt.

Fanny   Charles, my love.

Spark   Where is the dirt?

Fanny   I was now in touch at once with the instrument of pleasure and the great seal of love, two mingling streams which poured an ocean of intoxicating bliss on such a weak vessel as me that I lay overwhelmed, absorbed, lost in an abyss of joy and dying of nothing but immoderate delight.

Cellist   Oh, well done, Miss Fanny!

Dingle   Vice!

Spark   Still a trifle fleshless.

Fanny   I feel the delicious velvet tip! Oh, my pen drops from me in ecstasy!

Cellist   Oh, my!

Fanny   Description deserts me!

Cellist   My, my!

Fanny   I had now taken in love's true arrow and soon began the driving tumult on his side and the responsive heaves on mine.

Cellist   Goodness!

Fanny   How can I do justice to that sweetest of sensations accompanied by the stiff insinuation all the way up?

Cellist   How?

Fanny   Sparks of love fire ran all over, blazing in every vein, every pore of me. Soon our joys grew too mighty for utterance! And oh!

Cellist   Oh!

Fanny   That touch! That voluptuous intermixing! How delicious! How poignantly luscious! Now!

Cellist   Now!

Fanny   I felt it to the heart of me, now!

Fanny *gives a final gasp*.

Dingle   Sex!

Spark   Romance!

Fanny   My book has mixed them both, sirs, into the greatest of joys!

Cellist   Bravo, Miss Fanny!

Fanny   Thank you.
Charles and Fanny are soon married and live happy and wealthy ever after.
Thus I have satisfied both the square and the scurrilous amongst you.
I shall be rich!

She kisses her book.

Cellist   I thought that last passage quite . . . diverting.

Fanny *kisses it again.*

Spark   Is that it? The book?

Fanny   It is. My sweet salvation.

Dingle   Diverting, she called it.

Fanny   Entertaining, enlightening, pleasuring.

Spark   I've come for it.

Fanny *laughs.*

Fanny   I told you. It's mine.

Dingle   Diverting.

Spark   The book.

Fanny   No.

Dingle (*indicating* **Cellist**)   If it should fall into the hands of the likes of her. An innocent wench. Where would it lead?

Cellist   Where?

Spark   I'm afraid you have little choice in the matter.

Fanny   Once a pimp, always a pimp.

Dingle   Reading has spread to all sorts. You can't see a woman but she has a newfangled novel tucked into her purse.

Spark   New laws.

Fanny   New laws?

Spark   The contagation of licentious publications are fatal to the unguarded minds of the youth of both sexes.

Dingle   Not to mention servants and women.

Spark   We're on state business.

Fanny   What business?

Dingle   There are worse fates than illiteracy!

Spark   This book is an insult upon religion and good manners.

Dingle   Nakedness and books are dangerous. I'm in this organisation. Here is my card.

Fanny   A gob on your card!

Spark   If you're going to show vice, it must disgust. Not please.

Fanny   A book can please as nature pleases!

Spark   While art must imitate nature it is necessary to distinguish those parts of nature which are proper for imitation.

Dingle   Your book is about nothing but copulation!

Fanny   Some books are about nothing but ships and there are no objections.

Dingle   This book is merely an account of the flesh trade.

Fanny   The whole world does a trade in that, Mr Dingle. Nothing's free or haven't you noticed?

Spark   This book is an inflammatory text and fit for the fire.

Fanny   The fire!

Spark   In the wrong hands it could be the beginning of a serious decline.

Dingle   Good novels are about decent married people raising a family!

Spark   So. Give it to me.

Fanny   No!

Dingle   The book is perilous!

Fanny   To a fool. But are fools worth the least attention?

Spark   Hand it over.

Fanny   No! I will not let you have it. Never! No!

Spark   Then I shall fetch a bishop.

Fanny   A bishop?

Spark   And a justice. The penalties are most severe.

Pause.

Fanny   I am ruined.

She still holds onto her book.

Dingle (*calls*)   Louisa!

Louisa *enters. She is dressed in grey, tight, constricting clothes, her hair is scraped back. She carries a large iron box and some keys. She does not look about her.*

Fanny   Louisa! It's me. Fanny.

Pause.

We cannot let them do this.

Louisa *unlocks the big iron box. She holds out her hand for the manuscript.*

Fanny   Louisa?

Dingle   The obscene knows no bounds. It flies into the remotest corners of the earth, penetrating into the obscurest habitations and corrupting the simplest hearts.

Louisa   There's nothing you can do.

She takes the manuscript from **Fanny** *and places it in the box.*

Dingle   This is our strong box. Treble-locked. I belong to this organisation. We have collected nearly one thousand lewd prints, four hundred and seventeen books, French and English, and well over sixteen hundred bawdy common songs.
It's a beginning.
Well, I've work to do. I cannot stay.

May you see the light, Miss Fanny.
Good day.

He exits.

Spark   Perhaps this has shown you your place in the world.

Fanny   Hypocritical ponce! My only satisfaction is in
knowing that your profit too is scuppered!

Spark   Oh no. No.

He laughs.

You labour under a misapprehension, Miss Fanny. I am
starting a whole shining new enterprise. Yes, books must be
spanking clean and free from the sordid infiltrations of desire
but there will still be a market for such carnalities.
And where there is a market there is a way.
And where there is a prohibition there is a profit.
And I intend to make it, under the counter so to speak.

Fanny   You could never write a book.

Spark   No. But then I won't need to. I'll be dealing in pure
sleaze, no storyline.
Times change and one must move with the times.
So, I'll say my goodbyes.
The pleasure's been all mine.

Fanny   May your globular appendages be ulcerated.

He salutes. Exits.

Louisa! Louisa! Don't let them do it!
Slip it back to me! On the quiet.

Louisa   I can't.

Fanny   Why?

Louisa   I'm a Magdalen girl now.

Fanny   Magdalen?

Louisa   Like a church. Like a hospital.
Up at five. Sweat out our badness in the laundrys.
There's loads of us. Then we've work to do.
I collect things. Songs.

Fanny   You weren't dying.

Louisa   Wasn't I?

Fanny   No.

Louisa   I would have done. Soon enough.

Fanny   Delicious delirium.

Louisa   We're forbidden to speak of the past.
We're in bed by nine. Lights out ten past.
Hands on top of the covers.

Fanny   Lord!

Louisa   Things are changing, Fanny. Stiff collar times are coming. We take baths in our petticoats.

Fanny   What for?

Louisa   I dunno. They chopped off the king's head in France. And the Queen's. There's blood on the streets. We don't want it happening over here.

Dingle (*calls from offstage*)   Louisa!

Louisa   I've got to go.

She starts to close the box, then remembers.

I nearly forgot. I've a song to put in the box.

She opens the box and sings into it.

(*Sings.*) My lady has a thing most rare
Round about it grows much hair
She takes delight with it in bed
And often strokes its hairy head.

Fanny   What is it?

Louisa   A lap dog.

They both laugh raucously.

Dingle (*calls*)   Louisa!

Louisa   I must go.

She shuts up the box. Composes herself.

Goodbye, Fanny.

She walks out briskly.

Fanny   She's gone.

Cellist   Gone for good.

Fanny   All for nothing. Everything for nothing.

Pause.

Cellist   No one ever asked me anything.
About myself, I mean.

She comes forward.

I was the daughter of a parson. All I wanted to do was to play
music but of course there was nowhere for girls to study. My
father died and my brother inherited everything. So I . . .

Fanny   Oh, shut up.

Pause.

Cellist   Is Fanny your real name?

Fanny   No, it was a joke.

Cellist   I don't get it.

Fanny   Never mind.

Cellist   What was your name?

Fanny   I don't know. Something beginning with an E. Or a
P. Or a T.

Cellist   You never remember anything.

Fanny   No. I seem to have forgot myself.

Cellist   Oh dear.

Fanny   Sometimes I have this dream. God says, 'Fanny,
you may have one wish,' so I ask for some holes. Then
whoosh just like that all these holes appear all over me, small
at first but big enough to stick a finger in. I'm delighted.
What a time I'll have with these, I think. I have tripled in
value and tripled again. And then my mouth opens wider
and wider and all the holes get bigger still and bigger till
finally all the holes join up at the edges until I'm just one big

hole. Big enough for God or a giant reader to fuck and then I disappear.

Pause.

I disappear.

Cellist   What a funny dream.

Pause.

Shall I play you something?
What's your favourite?

Fanny *opens her mouth but can't reply.*

Cellist   Don't remember?

Pause.

Then I shall play something for myself.
Something . . . diverting.

Pause.

If a book like that should be read by an innocent wench . . . like me . . . where would it lead?

Where?

She smiles.

She plays and sings a version of 'My Lady Has A Thing Most Rare'. She laughs. She stretches luxuriantly, she slides her hands between her legs. She looks out. She smiles.

Where?

Lights down.

End.

April De Angelis was born in London and studied English at Sussex University. On leaving, she worked as an actor primarily in devised community/women's/educational theatre. In 1986, her first play, *Breathless*, was winner of the Second Wave Playwriting Competition for Young Women and was subsequently produced at the Albany Empire. Other plays include: *Women in Law* (1987) and *Ironmistress* (1988, published by Methuen in *Plays by Women: Eight*) both commissioned by ReSisters Theatre Company; *Crux* (Paines Plough, 1989); *The Life and Times of Fanny Hill* (Red Shift, 1991); *Hush* (Royal Court Theatre, 1992, published by Methuen in *Frontline Intelligence 1*); *Playhouse Creatures* (Sphinx Theatre Company, 1993); *Soft Vengeance* (Graeae Theatre Company, 1993). Radio includes *Visitants*, winner, BBC Young Writers Festival, 1988, and *Outlander*, Writers' Guild Award for Best Children's Radio Drama, 1991. Television includes *Aristophanes* (Channel 4/Bandung Productions, 1995). April was writer in residence for Paines Plough from 1989 to 1990. She is currently under commission to the Royal Court Theatre and Glyndebourne Opera.

Great Expectations

adapted from Charles Dickens
by John Clifford

*for Rebecca and Katie
and their expectations*

Great Expectations was first performed in the Chandler Studio of the RSAMD as part of the Glasgow Mayfest on 10 May 1988. The cast was as follows:

Young Pip, Herbert's Servant, First Man	Bruce Campbell
Pip	Alan Cumming
Magwitch, Herbert Pocket	James Durrell
Joe, Wemmick	Alistair Galbraith
Miss Havisham	Liz Ingram
Biddy, Second Man	Jane MacFarlane
Mr Wopsle, Jaggers	Forbes Masson
Estella	Rachel Ogilvy
Mrs Joe, Molly	Jane Scott Barnett

Keyboards Glas Molland
Cello Jane MacFarlane
Flute Alistair Galbraith

Directed by Ian Brown
Designed by Lucy Weller
Lighting by Mike Lancaster
Movement by Gregory Nash
Music composed by Peter Salem

The production won the 'Spirit of Mayfest' Award for 1988. It was revived in 1989 by the Traverse Theatre and successfully toured Iraq, Egypt, India, Sri Lanka and Bangladesh.

Characters

Pip
Estella
Miss Havisham
Joe
Mrs Joe
Mr Wopsle
Magwitch
Biddy
Jaggers
Wemmick
Molly
Herbert Pocket
Herbert's Servant
Two Men (Debt Collectors)

Minimum requirement: seven actors (four males, three females) as follows:
M1: Pip
M2: Jaggers, Wopsle
M3: Magwitch, Pocket
M4: Joe, Wemmick
F1: Miss Havisham
F2: Estella
F3: Mrs Joe, Molly, Biddy

Part One

Pip *is alone in the dark house. Enter* **Estella**.

Estella   This is the room, Pip.
This is where she lived, remember?

Pip   I don't want to.

Estella   How dark it is. How musty and old.
Coming back here is like exploring a grave.
I believe no light has entered here since before the day we
were born.

Pip   I hate it. Let's go.

Estella   No, Pip. You have to stay.

Pip   The past is something I'd rather forget.

Estella   All you've done is close a door. But you can't wipe
out what there is behind it.
Pip, all our lives we walk in darkness. Not understanding
who we are, where we come from, or where we are bound.
Pip, I am tired of the dark. Tired of not knowing. Of not
understanding. Let's open the doors.
Open the doors and let in the light.

Pip   I'm frightened.

Estella   Don't be afraid. Open them, Pip. Open them
wide.

They open the doors of the house. **Miss Havisham** *stands behind
them. She leads a procession of figures from* **Pip**'*s past:* **Joe, Mrs
Joe, Mr Wopsle**.

Estella   And there she is. Miss Havisham. My mother by
adoption.

Pip   Whose death we mourn.

Estella   Who made this house and formed our memories.

Pip   So very long ago.

Estella   When I was just a girl,
Wandering about this great dark house
Lost and all alone.

Pip   Estella.

Miss Havisham   A bright star.

Estella   Shining in darkness!

Pip   And Mr Wopsle.

Mr Wopsle   Cornchandler. Tailor. Thespian of renown.
Famous throughout the Home Counties!

Pip   And Joe.

Joe   Always the best of friends, eh, Pip?

Pip   And Mrs Joe.

Mrs Joe   Worn down to skin and bone
Bringing you up by hand!

Pip   But who was I? I never really knew.
Life was always a mystery to me.

Mrs Joe   No mystery about you.

Mr Wopsle   You were just a boy.

Mrs Joe   A wretched snivelling boy I brought up by hand.
I don't know why. I'd never do it again.
Never there where you want him. Always thin and miserable
and wretched. And always a running off to the marshes.

Pip   Where the churchyard was
Where the dark flat wilderness was the lonely marsh
Where the low leaden line was the river
Where the small bundle of shivers growing afraid of it all and
beginning to cry
Was Pip.

Magwitch *the convict suddenly appears and grabs* **Pip**.

Magwitch   What's your name, boy?
Quick. Give it mouth.

Pip   Pip, sir.

Magwitch   Where's your mother?

Pip   There, sir.

Magwitch   Where do you say?

Pip   There, sir. Also Georgiana. My mother. And there's my father. Late of this parish. And my brothers. Twelve brothers, sir.

Magwitch   So where do you live? Supposing I lets you live. Which I ain't decided yet.

Pip   With my sister, sir. Mrs Joe Gargery. Wife of the blacksmith, sir.

Magwitch   Blacksmith?

Pip   Yes, sir.

Magwitch   You know what a file is?
You know what wittles is?
Then you bring me a file and you bring me wittles
Or I'll have your heart and liver out.
And see here, boy. I ain't alone. There's a young man with me, boy, and in comparison with that young man I am an angel. This young man has a secret way pecooliar to himself of getting at a young boy, and at his heart, and his liver. A boy may lock his door, and may be warm in bed, may draw the clothes over his head and think himself safe, but this young man will creep his way to him and tear him open. Now what do you say?

Pip   I'll bring you what you want, sir.

Magwitch   And what's that?

Pip   That's a file, sir. And wittles.

Magwitch   And you'll be secret?

Pip   Very secret.

Magwitch   Say the Lord strike me dead if I don't.

Pip   The Lord strike me dead if I don't.

Magwitch   And you'll remember?

Pip   If you'd let me stay upright, sir, perhaps I wouldn't be sick, and I could remember better. Please let me go.

Magwitch   Bring it in the morning then, boy. In the morning!

Pip   Good night, sir.

Magwitch   No chance of that!
I wish I were a frog!
Or an eel!

Pip   And he hugged his shuddering body in both his arms
And limped over the low church wall
And I ran away home without stopping.

He runs back to the forge. He finds **Joe**.

Joe!

Joe   What's wrong, Pip?

Pip   I was frightened, Joe.

Joe   Don't you be frightened, Pip.

Pip   I was down in the graveyard!

Joe   But you're with Joe now, Pip. Your friend, Joe. Us ever the best of friends, eh, Pip.

Pip   Yes, Joe.

Mrs Joe (*off*)   Where's that boy?

Joe   You be careful, Pip. She's after you.
She's on the rampage.

Mrs Joe (*off: louder*)   Where is that boy?

Joe   And the worst of it is, Pip, she's got Tickler with her. You hide here, old chap.

Pip *hides. Enter* **Mrs Joe**.

Mrs Joe   Where is he?

She finds **Pip**.

So there he is. The little wretch.

She beats **Pip**.

Pip   Thank you.

Mrs Joe *gives them their supper: a chunk of bread each.*

Mrs Joe   Here's your supper. Wears me out it does, feeding you. Wears me down to skin and bone. And me so sick and weak. So be grateful. Go on. Be grateful.

Joe *eats. He keeps wanting* **Pip** *to compare slices.* **Pip** *is about to eat, but remembers the convict. And all the while* **Mrs Joe** *cleans and cleans.*

Mrs Joe   Why didn't you marry a Negress slave and be done with it? Tell me that.

Pip *finally manages to hide his slice.*

Joe   That won't do, Pip. Won't do at all.

Mrs Joe   What won't do?

Joe   You'll do yourself a mischief, Pip.
It'll stick somewhere.

Mrs Joe   What'll stick?

Joe   You can't have chewed it at all.

Mrs Joe   Chewed what, you big booby? Chewed what?

Joe   You know, Pip, you and me is always friends, and I'd be the last to tell on you at any time. But such a bolt! Such a great uncommon bolt as that!

Mrs Joe   Been bolting his food, has he? You come along here and be dosed.

She gives **Joe** *and* **Pip** *a dose of revolting medicine.*

Tar. Does you a power of good.
And here's a dose for you and all. You've had a turn. You could do with it.

Pip *and* **Joe** *choke on the revolting medicine. A distant gun goes off.*

Mrs Joe   And there's the guns going off. As if I didn't have enough to do without guns.

Joe   Another convict off.

Pip   What's a convict?

Mrs Joe Convicts are them that gets imprisoned in hulks.

Pip But what are hulks?

Mrs Joe Haven't I enough to do what with scrubbing and toiling and cleaning and wearing myself down to the bone? And me so sick and weak? How should I have time to answer questions?

Pip But what are they?

Mrs Joe Hulks is where people are put because they are bad. Because they rob and murder and steal. Because they are generally wicked. And they always begin by asking questions. Now go to bed the pair of you. Blundering boobies! Go to bed.

Exit **Joe** *and* **Mrs Joe**. **Pip** *gets out of bed and steals food.*

Enter **Magwitch**. *He is hungry and cold.* **Pip** *finds* **Magwitch** *and gives him the food and bread. He eats like a starving man.*

Pip I'm glad you're enjoying your food, sir.

Magwitch Thank 'ee, my boy. I do.
You're not an imp, are you?

Pip No, sir.

Magwitch Not a deceiving imp? You brought no one with you?

Pip Not me, sir.

Magwitch It'd be a harsh thing, and you'd be a fierce young hound, if at your time of life you could help hunt a wretched warmint, hunted as near death and dunghill as this poor wretched warmint is.

Pip I'd never tell on you, sir. Never in all my days. And here's your file. I hopes you gets free, sir. I hopes you gets free.

Magwitch *files at the iron on his leg.*

Magwitch Thank you, boy. Thank you. I won't forget this, boy. I swear I won't forget it.

The scene changes. Enter **Mr Wopsle**, **Joe** *and* **Mrs Joe**. *They have been having a meal.* **Mr Wopsle** *grabs* **Pip**.

Mr Wopsle   Take pigs now. There's a subject for you.
Take pigs. There's plenty to be said about pigs.
See the boy. Now if he'd been born a squeaker –

Mrs Joe   He was, Mr Wopsle. He squeaks all the time.

Mr Wopsle   I meant a four-footed squeaker, Mrs Joe. Not
the other kind. Now may I proceed? Attend. Take heed.
Take the boy; who had the good fortune to be born a boy,
and not a pig. The undeserved good fortune. And had he
been – born a pig – would he have been here? Enjoying
himself? Benefiting from the company of his elders and
betters? Oh no. No indeed. He'd have been sold for
fourpence. And Dunstable the butcher would have crept up
on him as he lay in the straw and he'd have picked him up
and held him under his left arm.
And he'd have whipped out his penknife and cut his throat
and you'd have served him up for our supper. And then he'd
have been a credit to you.

Mrs Joe   Not otherwise.

Magwitch *gets free of his iron; but is pursued.*

Joe   The soldiers caught the convict, and took him back to
the hulk.
We went with them, me and Pip.
We walked for miles, slow like, cause the man was tired.
Poor creatur, he was wearied and spent.
The landing place was way out, way out distant in the
marshes,
Built out of stakes and stones. There was a boat waiting.
He got in, and no one looked at him.
No one seemed surprised or sorry or glad.
No one spoke a word, except a soldier in the stern
And he growled like he was talking to dogs.

The convict is imprisoned.

Pip   And the hulk was black and cribbed and barred.
And it looked to me like it was chained.

A wicked boat it looked, a wicked Noah's Ark.
And I saw them take him in, and my heart
Went out to him. And the torches were flung
Into the water, and they hissed and went dark.

Mr Wopsle   And there's an end to him.
Let it be an awful warning to the young.

Mrs Joe *has a letter*.

Mrs Joe   And here's a letter come.
And me worn down to skin and bone.

Mr Wopsle   Open it, Mrs Joe.

Mrs Joe   If you ask me to, Mr Wopsle.

Mr Wopsle   I ask, Mrs Joe. I beg. I supplicate.
As the poet says.

Mrs Joe   Boy. You're summonsed. Be grateful.
Grateful for them that brings you up by hand.

Joe   But where –

Mrs Joe   Where's what, you noodle?

Joe   Where's he summonsed?

Mr Wopsle   To Miss Havisham's.
Miss Havisham wants the boy to go and play.

Mrs Joe   And he will go. And he will play. Or I'll work
him.
But look at him. Lor a-mussy me, just look at the state of him.
Did you ever see such a dirty boy?

Mrs Joe *cleans* **Pip**.

Mr Wopsle   This'll be the making of him, Mrs Joe.

Mrs Joe   If I ever get the dirt off of him, Mr Wopsle, it will.

Mr Wopsle   Mrs Havisham is very rich. And she wants
him.
Mrs Joe, it could mean money.
I can feel my muse shake and stir his wings.

Joe   Oh dear.

Mrs Joe   Good on you, Mr Wopsle.

Mr Wopsle   I can see the tremulous hand of fate
Swoop down upon the boy and lift him up
Take him from dirt and dust and grime
And mount him on the highest shelf
With the golden cuff links and the fancy ties
With the silver watch chains and the better class of sock
In the great haberdashery of Life.
Now, boy.

Mrs Joe   You behave. Or I'll jigger you.

Joe   Goodbye, Pip. God bless.
When you're a wee bit bigger, Pip, and you're my regular
prentice, what larks then, eh, Pip. What larks.

Exit **Joe**, **Mrs Joe** *and* **Mr Wopsle**. **Pip** *walks nervously to*
Miss Havisham'*s*.

Estella *meets him*.

Estella   This way, boy.

Estella *leads* **Pip** *into the house. They go on a complicated journey*
along dark and spooky corridors.

Estella   Do you know what this house is called, boy?
No you don't. Satis House is its name.
And do you know what that means, boy?
No you don't. It's Latin. It means enough.
It means whoever had this house could want nothing else.
They must have been easily satisfied those days,
Don't you think, boy? No. You don't think.
You're just a boy. Don't loiter.
Dark, isn't it, boy? And empty. And very old.
And cold and full of dust. There's rats in the corners
And who knows what else besides.
Are you frightened, boy? Go in there.

Pip   After you.

Estella   Don't be ridiculous. I'm not going in.

Exit **Estella**. **Pip** *is alone*. **Miss Havisham** *appears*.

Miss Havisham   Play.

Pip *does not want to play*.

Miss Havisham   Play. Play. Play!
Are you sullen and obstinate?

Pip   No, ma'am. I just can't play now. I'm sorry. I'd play if
I could.
But it's all so new here and so strange and fine . . . and
so . . . melancholy.

Miss Havisham   So new to him. So old to me.
So strange to him. So familiar to me.
So melancholy to both of us!
Call Estella.
You can do that. Call Estella. At the door.

Pip   Estella.

Miss Havisham   Louder.

Pip   Estella!

Miss Havisham   Louder.

Pip   Estella!!

Enter **Estella**.

Miss Havisham   Play with the boy, Estella.

Estella   With the boy! Why, he's only a common labouring
boy!

Miss Havisham   Well? You can break his heart.

Estella   What do you play, boy?

Pip   Beggar-my-neighbour.

Miss Havisham   Beggar him.

Estella   I won't play such a common game.

Miss Havisham   Then dance with him. Dance. Dance!

Pip *dances with* **Estella**. *He is clumsy and embarrassed*.

Estella   What coarse hands the boy has.
And what thick boots.

Miss Havisham   Take him out.
Bring him back in a week.

Exit **Miss Havisham**.

Estella   Why don't you cry?

Pip   I don't want to.

Estella   Liar. You are crying inside.
Boy. Little boy.

Exit **Estella**. *Enter* **Joe, Mrs Joe** *and* **Mr Wopsle**.

Mr Wopsle   Well, boy. How did you get on up town?

Pip   Pretty well.

Mrs Joe   Pretty well is no answer.

Mr Wopsle   Now, boy. Miss Havisham. What was she
doing, when you went in to see her?

Pip   Sitting.

Mr Wopsle   Good! This is the way to have him!
And where was she sitting?

Pip   In a coach.

Mr Wopsle   Excellent. Hear that, mum? In a coach. We
are beginning to hold our own.
In a what did you say?

Pip   A coach. A black velvet coach. And Miss Estella whom
I think is her niece handed her cake and wine through the
window. On a gold plate. And I got up behind to eat mine,
because she told me to. I think it was because of the dogs.

Mr Wopsle   Dogs?

Pip   Four immense wolfhounds. And they fought for veal
cutlets out of a silver basket.

Mrs Joe   Is this possible, Mr Wopsle?

Mr Wopsle   She is flighty, ma'am. Very flighty.

Mrs Joe   And what did you play at?

Pip   Flags.

Mrs Joe Flags?

Pip Estella waved a blue flag and I waved a red one and Miss Havisham waved one with little gold stars.

Mr Wopsle See, ma'am. They played with flags.

Mrs Joe But what could it all mean?

Pip And I'm to go back in a week.

Mr Wopsle In a week! Hear that, ma'am? She'll make his fortune for him!

Joe I think she'll give him one of them dogs.

Mr Wopsle Joseph!!

Mrs Joe Noodle! If that's all you can say you're better saying nothing!

Mr Wopsle She'll translate him to a higher sphere.

Mrs Joe As long as she doesn't pamper him.

Mr Wopsle No fear of that, mum. No fear of that.

Mrs Joe And he'd better be grateful.

Exit **Mrs Joe** *and* **Mr Wopsle**.

Pip Joe.

Joe Wonderful, eh, Pip. Just wonderful.

Pip It's all lies, Joe.

Joe What are you telling me, Pip? You don't mean to say it's all untrue?

Pip All of it.

Joe But not all of it, Pip. Not all of it.

Pip Every word, Joe. I'm sorry.

Joe You mean to say there was no black welwet coach? No flags? No veal cutlets?
Oh, come on, Pip, if there weren't any veal cutlets at least there was dogs?

Pip No, Joe.

Joe   A dog?
A puppy?
That's terrible, Pip. That's awful. What possessed you?

Pip   Joe, I wish you'd taught me to dance.

Joe   What's that got to do with anything, Pip, old son?

Pip   And I wish my boots weren't so thick and my hands so coarse.

Joe   What's come over you, Pip, old chap?

Pip   Joe, there was a beautiful young lady there and she said I was common.

Joe   But you're not common, Pip. You're uncommon in some things. I mean, you're uncommon small.

Pip   Joe, that's no comfort.
She told me I was common and I looked at myself and knew. I am common. And that's where the lies come from, somehow.

Joe   Lookee here, Pip, at what is said to you by a true friend.
And this true friend, Pip, this true friend do say: if you can't get to be uncommon through going straight, you'll never get to do it through being crooked. So don't tell any more on 'em lies, Pip, and live well and die happy.
And what larks, eh, Pip. When you're my regular prentice. What larks.

They sing and work happily together. Time passes.

Pip/Joe   Hammer boys round, Old Clem
With a thump and a shout, Old Clem,
With a clink for the stout,
Blow the fire blow the fire,
Burning dryer soaring higher, Old Clem.

After a while, **Miss Havisham** *enters, beating time with her stick.*
Joe *slips away.* **Pip** *sings alone until his voice fades away.* **Miss Havisham** *stands before him.*

Miss Havisham   What do I touch here?

Pip   Your heart.

Miss Havisham   Broken!
Are you ready to play?

Pip   I don't know, ma'am.

Miss Havisham   If you do not wish to play, will you
work?

Pip   If you like, ma'am.

Miss Havisham   Then come. Walk me. Walk me.

Pip *walks* **Miss Havisham**.

Miss Havisham   Look, Pip, where the cobwebs are.
It's a bride cake. Mine.
On this day, Pip, long before you were born,
They brought here this heap of decay.
It and I have worn away together.
The mice have gnawed at it, and sharper teeth than mice
Have gnawed at me.
Call Estella.

Pip   Estella! Estella!

Enter **Estella**.

Miss Havisham   Isn't she beautiful, Pip?
Each day she becomes more beautiful.

She decks **Estella** *with jewels*.

Break their hearts, my pride and hope
Break their hearts and have no mercy.
Will you play now? You and Estella?

Estella   You can kiss me if you like.

Hesitantly **Pip** *comes closer and closer.*
Then **Estella** *slaps him, hard*.

Estella   Little monster.
Cry now, you common little brute.

Pip *cries. Enter* **Joe**. *They are back in the forge*.

Pip   Joe!

Joe   What's wrong, Pip?

Pip   I'm ignorant, Joe.

Joe   Are you, Pip?

Pip   Joe. Why weren't you educated?

Joe   What's that?

Pip   Why didn't you go to school?

Joe   See here, Pip, my father he was given over to drink. And when he was overtook by drink, he hammered away at my mother most unmerciful. That was about the only hammering he ever did, Pip, when he weren't a-hammering at me. He was a blacksmith too, see, Pip, right here in this forge.

Only he never hammered at the forge. He hammered at my mother instead. Consequence, Pip, my mother and me we ran way from home. And then my mother said, 'Joe,' she'd say, 'now, Please God, you shall have some schooling,' and she'd put me to school. But my father were that good in his heart that he couldn't bear to be without us. So he'd come along with the most tremenjous crowd and make such a row at the houses where we was that they used to have no more to do with us and give us up to him. And then he took us home and hammered us. And that, Pip, were a drawback on my learning.

But he was that good at heart he had no objection to my working, Pip. So I set to work and I kep him too, after a while.

Until he took a purple leptic fit and died.

And my mother followed soon after. She was in poor elth and quite broke. But she got her share of peace at last.

And then I was lonely, Pip. All alone out here on the forge. Out here on the edge of the lonesome marshes. And I met your sister.

And your sister, Pip, is a fine figure of a woman. A little sick and weak maybe, Pip, but a fine figure of a woman. You have to admit that. I mean, Pip, a little redness, or a little manner of bone, what does it signify?

Pip   Well –

Joe   Nothing at all, you're right, Pip. Right there. Nothing at all. And another thing. When I got acquainted with her, Pip, she had this miserable little creatur with her, and that were you, Pip.

Pip   Never mind me, Joe.

Joe   But I did, Pip. I did. And when I offered your sister to keep company, I said, 'Bring the poor little child,' I said to her. 'God bless the poor little child,' I said, 'there's room for him at the forge!'
And here we are, Pip. Ever the best of friends. Don't cry, old chap. Here we are. Ever the best of friends. Ain't us, Pip?

They hug. Exit **Joe**. *Enter* **Miss Havisham**.

Miss Havisham   Sing, Pip.

Pip   I don't know how.

Miss Havisham   Sing. Sing!

Pip *starts to sing 'Old Clem' and* **Miss Havisham** *joins in. They walk together.*

Miss Havisham   Pip, you are growing tall.

Pip   I can't help it, ma'am.

Miss Havisham   Who is to be your master?

Pip   Joe Gargery, ma'am, the blacksmith.

Miss Havisham   Then you must be bound.
You are too tall for me.
Take this. It is your reward. Expect no other and expect no more. Goodbye, Pip.

Exit **Miss Havisham**. *Enter* **Mrs Joe** *and* **Mr Wopsle**. *They take the money.*

Mr Wopsle   Five and twenty pounds, mum! Five and twenty pounds she gave the boy! It's no more than you deserve.

Mrs Joe   It's poetry, Mr Wopsle. Real poetry.

Pip *and* **Joe** *work.*

Pip Joe.

Joe Yes, Pip, old chap.

Pip Don't you think I ought to make Miss Havisham a visit?

Joe You told me she said you weren't to go, Pip. Me to the north, she said, you to the south. Keep in sunders.

Pip But, Joe.

Joe Yes, old chap.

Pip Here am I, getting on for a year of my time, and I've not been back in all that while to thank Miss Havisham or show that I remember her.

Joe That's true, Pip.

Pip So you see, Joe –

Joe Unless you was to make her a present, Pip. Turn her out a set of shoes all round.

Pip No, Joe.

Joe You're right, Pip, she ain't got no horses. Still, Pip, you could knock her up a gross of shark-headed screws.

Pip No, Joe.

Joe You could give her a gridiron.

Pip But I don't want to give her a present at all!

Joe What I say, Pip, is, you're right. Don't give her a present at all.

Pip Joe, what I meant was, if you would give me a half-day holiday, I could go uptown and see Miss Est–Havisham.

Joe Which her name ain't Estavisham, Pip.

Pip No, Joe.

Joe Unless she's been rechristened.

Pip It was a slip, Joe.

Joe Ah. A slip.

Pip Joe, can I go?

Joe If you think well of it, Pip. I think well of it.

Enter **Mrs Joe** *and* **Mr Wopsle**.

Mrs Joe And you think we're rich I suppose to waste wages on holidays? Noodle!

Mr Wopsle You're right, ma'am. You're right.
The wages of idleness is sin. As the poet says.

Joe There's surely no harm in half a day off.

Mrs Joe Oh! Did you hear that? Did you hear that?

Mr Wopsle At him, mum. Keep at him.

Mrs Joe To say that to me. A married woman. To be told that by my husband. My own husband. The insult! Mr Wopsle, I have been insulted. By my own husband! And by the boy, Mr Wopsle! Insulted by that ungrateful boy! The boy that I brought up by hand! He'll be the death of me, Mr Wopsle. Me so sick and weak. And it's the ingratitude! The ingratitude that cuts me to the heart! The ingratitude of one brought up by hand! And me so sick and weak! I cannot bear it! I simply cannot bear it! O! O!! O!!!

Mrs Joe *goes on the rampage. Then she bursts into tears.* **Mr Wopsle** *escorts her to the door.*

Mr Wopsle Sad and bereft the lady weeps.
Her cruel husband deprives her of her sleep.

Exit **Mr Wopsle** *and* **Mrs Joe**.

Joe She'll get over it, Pip, don't you worry.
On the Rampage, and then off the Rampage. Such is life.

Exit **Joe**. *Enter* **Miss Havisham**.

Miss Havisham I hope you want nothing. You'll get nothing.

Pip I just wanted to say I am doing well in my apprenticeship and am always much obliged to you.

Miss Havisham You are looking round for Estella? Hey?

Pip I hope she is well.

Miss Havisham   Abroad.
Educating for a lady.
Prettier than ever.
Do you feel you have lost her?

Exit **Miss Havisham**. **Pip** *sadly returns home.*

Joe   Pip, old chap.

Pip   Yes, Joe.

Joe   You're moping, Pip.

Pip   Am I, Joe?

Joe   Don't you mope, Pip, old chap.

Pip   No, Joe.

Joe   There's Biddy, Pip.

Pip   Is there, Joe?

Joe   Who helps about the house sometimes.

Pip   Yes, Joe.

Joe   There's a girl for you, Pip.

Pip   But she's an orphan, Joe.

Joe   Like yourself, Pip.

Pip   But, Joe, her hair always wants brushing.
Her hands always want washing.
And her shoes are always down at heel.

Joe   But, Pip, that don't matter.

Pip   But it does, Joe.

Joe   She's a good girl, Pip. Serviceabubble.

Pip   But she's common, Joe!

Joe   Is she, Pip?

Pip   Yes, Joe. Awful common!
Oh. Good day, Miss Biddy.

Biddy *has entered.*

Biddy   Good day, Pip. Good day, Mr Joe.

Joe　Good day, Biddy. Good day.

Exit **Joe** *and* **Biddy**.

Pip　And I ran from the forge
And the little house at the edge of the marshes
And ran to Miss Havisham's
Where I dared not go in.
I stood and I stared at the great gloomy house
Where nobody came and nobody went
And the weeds grew up between the flagstones
And I thought of who I was and who I might become.
And I heard a gun boom out from the prison hulk
And I knew they were looking for a convict
And I kept imagining they were looking for me.

Enter **Joe** *and* **Biddy**.

Joe　Pip.

Pip　What's wrong, Joe?

Joe　Bad news, Pip. Terrible, terrible news.

Pip　What is it, Joe?

Joe　It's Mrs Joe, Pip. Mrs Joe!
Tell him, Biddy.

Biddy　She's dead, Pip. I went to see her and –

Joe　Murdered, Pip. She was murdered!

Pip　Joe!

Joe　They killed her for the money, Pip. Cause I took a holiday too.
She were all alone and resting. Her being so sick and weak.
She was all alone, Pip and someone crept up . . . and . . .

Pip　Poor Joe.

Joe　They killed her for the money.

Pip　The money Miss Havisham gave me.

Joe　She's worth more 'n money. More 'n any amount of money. She was a fine figure, Pip, say what you like. A fine figure of a woman.

Mourners bring on **Mrs Joe**'s *body.*

Joe   She'll not go on the rampage ever more.

Pip   It's my fault. It's all my fault.

Joe   And what'll we do?

Biddy   I'll look after you, Joe. I've no one.
Will you give me a home, Joe? You and Pip?

Joe   Biddy!

Biddy   Come on now, Joe. Don't fret.

Exit mourners, **Joe** *and* **Biddy**.

Pip   And so we buried her.
And days passed.
And I fell into an apprentice's routine
A grimy curtain fell down over my life
And shut me out from anything save dull endurance.

Biddy *comes on to hang up washing.*

Biddy   What's wrong, Pip?

Pip   Nothing.

Biddy   Let's talk, Pip. Shall we? You and me?
Us both together, Pip, and have a proper talk?

Pip   If you like.

Biddy   Then tell me, Pip. What's wrong?

Pip   Will you be secret?

Biddy   Yes, Pip, I will.

Pip   Do you promise?

Biddy   I promise.

Pip   Biddy, I want to be a gentleman.

Biddy   I wouldn't if I were you.

Pip   Biddy!

Biddy   Don't you think you are happier as you are?

Pip   Biddy, I am not at all happy as I am.

Biddy   I'm sorry to hear that, Pip.
I just want you to do well, and be comfortable.

Pip   Understand, Biddy, once and for all.
I can never be comfortable. Never anything but miserable
unless I lead a very different kind of life from the life that I
lead now.

Biddy   That's a pity.

Pip   You're right, Biddy. It is a pity.
It is a pity, but I can't help it.
If I could have settled down.
If I could have settled down and been half as fond of the forge
now as I was when I was little, it would have been much
better for me.
You and I and Joe would have wanted nothing then.
Joe and I might be partners and I might even have grown up
to keep company with you.
I should have been good enough for you, shouldn't I, Biddy?

Biddy   Yes. I am not over-particular.

Pip   Well, I am, Biddy. I am. And look at me. Dissatisfied,
and uncomfortable . . . and . . . and . . . why should I care
about being coarse if no one had told me so!

Biddy   That was not a very true, and not a very polite thing
to say. Who said it?

Pip   The beautiful young lady at Miss Havisham's and
she's more beautiful than anybody ever was and I admire her
dreadfully and I want to be a gentleman on her account!

Biddy   Do you want to be a gentleman to spite her or to win
her over?

Pip   I don't know.

Biddy   Because, if it is to spite her, I should think – but you
know best – that it might be better done by not caring for her
words.
And if it is to win her over, I should think – but you know best
– that she was not worth winning.

Pip You may be right, Biddy. In fact I know you're right.
But the thing is Biddy, the thing is . . . I admire her
dreadfully.

Biddy I am glad of one thing, and that is that you felt you
could tell me everything, Pip.

Pip Biddy, I will always tell you everything.

Biddy Till you're a gentleman.

Pip And that means for ever, Biddy. That means for ever.

Enter **Joe** *and* **Jaggers**.

Jaggers Is this the boy called Pip?

Joe Yes. He is. And what is it to you?

Jaggers My name is Jaggers. I am a lawyer in London.
And as for the boy, he has great expectations.
Furthermore, he will come into a handsome property.
Furthermore, the possessor of this property wishes to take
him out from his present sphere of life and have him brought
up as a gentleman.
Furthermore, it is a condition of the person from whom I take
my instructions, that the young man always bears the name
of Pip.
Furthermore, it is a condition of the person from whom I take
my instructions that his or her identity remain a profound
secret.
I am empowered only to mention that it is the intention of
the aforesaid person to reveal his or her identity at first hand
by word of mouth to yourself.
When it will be revealed, I cannot say. It may be years hence.
In the meantime, you are distinctly to understand that you
are most positively prohibited from making any inquiry on
this head, or any allusion or reference, however distant, to
any individual whomsoever as the individual, in all the
communications you may have with me.
Is that clear?
Is that clear?
Good.
You will come to London. When?

Pip   I suppose, directly.

Jaggers   You suppose directly. First you will need new clothes. So let us say today week. You'll want some money. Shall I leave you twenty guineas?
You think twenty guineas will be ample?
Here they are.
Well, Joseph Gargery. You look dumbfounded.

Joe   I am!

Jaggers   Is it understood you want nothing for yourself?

Joe   It were understood. And it are understood. And it ever will be understood.

Jaggers   But what if I were instructed to make you a present, as compensation?

Joe   Compensation for what?

Jaggers   For the loss of his services.

Joe   Do you think money can make compensation to me for the loss of the little child – what came to the forge – and ever the best of friends!

Jaggers   I warn you, Joseph Gargery, this is your last chance. If you mean to take a present that I have it in charge to make you, speak out and you shall have it. If on the contrary you mean to say –

Joe   Which I meantersay that if you come into my place bull-baiting and badgering me, come out!
Which I meantersay as such if you're a man, come out!
Which I meantersay that what I say I meantersay!

Jaggers   Well, Mr Pip, the sooner you leave here the better.
Let us make it five days hence. Come straight to my office. Here it is.
But understand I express no opinion on the trust I undertake. I am paid for undertaking it, and I do so.
I do as I am paid. Nothing less, and nothing more.
Now, understand that. Finally. Understand that!

Exit **Jaggers**.

Joe   Well, Pip's a gentleman of fortune. And God bless him in it!

Pip *turns from* **Joe** *and contemplates his good fortune.*

Pip   No more low wet grounds. No more dykes and sluices.
No more grazing cattle. No more dull work.
Farewell all of you. Farewell.
I'm done with you for ever!

He approaches **Joe**.

Five days left, Joe. They'll soon pass.

Joe   Ay. Soon pass.

Enter **Mr Wopsle**.

Mr Wopsle   Dear Boy. Dearest dearest Boy.
I knew you would turn out well. I knew it. I always knew it.
And didn't I always say it? Didn't I? Didn't I?
Always, dearest Boy, always. And may I? May I?
We must render thanks, dear boy, to the gracious Miss H –

Pip   It is a secret, Mr Wopsle.

Mr Wopsle   I know, dear Boy. My lips are sealed.
Observe. Sealed. But may I?
And now, if I may have the privilege . . . Your clothes, sir.
Your new clothes. Your finery. Your splendour.
You did say ready money?
Of course. If I may be so bold.
But try them, dear Boy. Try them on.

Pip *tries on his new clothes.*

Mr Wopsle   Here is a boy on whom the eye of heaven shines
And this th'optician, tailor, sage opines.
As the poet says.

Pip *has finished dressing. He shows off the effect.*

Mr Wopsle   The poet is speechless.
Positively speechless.
Joseph! Come and admire the boy.

And so I take my leave. Farewell, dearest of urchins.
Farewell.

Exit **Mr Wopsle. Pip** *is self-conscious before* **Biddy** *and* **Joe**.

Biddy   You could show your new clothes at the village, Pip.
They'd take it as a compliment.

Pip   But, Biddy, they would make so coarse a business of it I
couldn't bear myself.

Biddy   Well, Pip, if you can't bear yourself . . .

Pip   Biddy . . .

Biddy   Yes, Pip?

Pip   You won't omit any opportunity of helping Joe on, a
little.

Biddy   How helping him on?

Pip   Well, Joe is a dear good fellow, but he is rather
backward in some things.

Biddy   Backward, is he, Pip?

Pip   Yes, Biddy, in his learning, for instance. And his
manners.

Biddy   Won't his manners do then?

Pip   Dear Biddy, they do very well here –

Biddy   Oh, they do very well here?

Pip   Biddy, I am sorry to see this in you. You are envious,
Biddy, and grudging. You are dissatisfied to see my rise in
fortune, and you can't help showing it.
It is a bad side in human nature, and I am sorry to see it.
I did intend, Biddy, to ask you to use any little opportunities
you might have after I was gone of improving poor Joe.
But now I ask you nothing. I am extremely sorry to see this in
you, Biddy. It's a bad side of human nature.

He storms over to **Miss Havisham**'s.

Miss Havisham! Miss Havisham!

Miss Havisham   This is a gay figure, Pip.

Pip I have come into such good fortune since I saw you last, Miss Havisham. And I am so grateful for it, Miss Havisham!

Miss Havisham You are adopted by a rich person?

Pip Yes, Miss Havisham.

Miss Havisham Not named?

Pip No, Miss Havisham.

Miss Havisham And Mr Jaggers is made your guardian?

Pip Yes, Miss Havisham.

Miss Havisham My lawyer, Pip.

Pip I know, Miss Havisham.

Miss Havisham Well, Pip. Be good.

Pip Yes, Miss Havisham.

Miss Havisham Goodbye, Pip.

She stretches out her hand. **Pip** *goes down on one knee and kisses it.*

Exit **Miss Havisham**. **Pip** *finishes his packing. He is miserable.*

Pip I'm glad to go. I'm glad to. I won't be sad.
I won't be. I won't be sad!

He straps and unstraps his valise.

Biddy Your breakfast's ready, Pip.

Pip I don't think I want any breakfast, Biddy.
I'm not hungry.

The three of them look at each other. They don't know what to say.

Well. I suppose I must be going.
Goodbye, Joe.

A miserable, constrained farewell.

Goodbye, Biddy.
Goodbye.

Pip *sets off.* **Joe** *throws a shoe after him.*

Part Two

Pip *struggles through a crowd.*

Pip   And so I came to London.

A sinister **Man** *approaches him.*

Man   Do you want to see a hanging?

Pip   No thank you very much.

Man   I can show you a judge.

Pip   And he did. And there he was. Like a waxwork.
In his robes. Sentencing a man to death.
I ran out and stumbled into Smithfield. They were cutting
the throats of cows. It was all asmear with filth and fat and
foam, and it seemed to stick to me.

He enters **Jaggers**'s *office.*

Is Mr Jaggers in?

Wemmick   No.

Pip   When will he be back?

Wemmick   Presently.
Do wait.

Pip   The room was very small and hot and close.

Wemmick   The clients have the habit of leaning against
the wall.

Pip   It was greasy with shoulders.
There were two dreadful casts on a shelf
Of faces oddly swollen, and twitchy about the nose.
And they seemed to laugh at me.

Enter **Jaggers**. *He is besieged by suppliants.*

Suppliants   Mr Jaggers! A moment please! Half a
moment, Mr Jaggers! Half a quarter of a moment! Mr
Jaggers! Mr Jaggers!

Jaggers Silence!
Have you paid Wemmick? If you've paid him, you've done
all you have to. And don't think. I think for you. And as for
you.
I'm against you.
Get them out, Wemmick. Get rid of them.

Wemmick *drives out the suppliants*.

Jaggers Hands!

Enter **Molly** *with a basin.* **Jaggers** *washes his hands*.

Pip Mr Jaggers.

Jaggers Wait!

He dries his hands.

Now. You.

He starts taking out business cards.

Your address. Your tailor. Your tutor. Your cobbler. Your
cash. You'll go wrong, of course, but that's no fault of mine.
And don't thank me. I do as I am paid. Nothing less: nothing
more. Wemmick!

Enter **Wemmick**.

Take Mr Pip to Barnard's Inn. Hands!

Jaggers *washes hands. Exit* **Jaggers** *and* **Molly**. **Pip** *and*
Wemmick *walk*.

Wemmick You're new here? I was new once. Funny to
think of it.

Pip Is London a very dangerous place?

Wemmick No worse than most.

Pip Is there much bad blood about?

Wemmick Very little, Mr Pip. Very little blood. If they
cut your throat it's because they think they can make a profit
out of it. Here's Barnard's Inn. Good day.

Pip Good day.

Pip *goes as if to shake* **Wemmick**'*s hand*.

Wemmick You're in the habit of shaking hands?

Pip   Yes.

Wemmick   I have so got out of it. Except at the last. Good day.

Exit **Wemmick**. *Enter* **Herbert Pocket**.

Herbert   Pocket. Herbert Pocket. Your tutor. Your lodgings.

Pip   There's not much furniture.

Herbert   Gentlemen don't need furniture. It's not considered essential.

Pip   I see.

Herbert   I did however take the liberty of engaging a servant.
Quite essential. We'd better call him.

He claps his hands.

That's how you call for a servant. Not imperiously – the lower orders do that – but with the absolute certainty, the absolute certainty, that your orders will be obeyed.

Enter a **Servant**. *He is surly and intimidating.*

Herbert   Ah! You see? Absolutely indispensable.

Pause.

Pip   Could he get us something to eat, do you think? I haven't eaten all day.

Herbert   Raspberry or strawberry?

Pip   Sorry?

Herbert   Jam. No one eats anything but jam.

Pip   Raspberry, I think.

Herbert   Don't think, Mr Pip. Gentlemen never think.
Now go up to him and ask. He's your boy.
No, dear boy, not like that. Try to cultivate a manly step. An assured step. No. Not that. A step of authority. Like this. The step of a gentleman of expectations.
There. That's better.

Pip   Um. Er.

Herbert   Remember: absolute certainty.

Pip   Absolute . . . would you . . . would you mind very much . . .

Herbert   No no. My dear Pip. Try this. Boy.

Pip   Boy.

Herbert   Be so good.

Pip   Be so good . . .

Herbert   No. Not like that. Be lordly. Be so good . . .

Pip   Be so good . . .

Herbert   That's it. That's it. Capital. Capital. What was it?

Pip   What was it what?

Herbert   What were we going to ask him to do?

Pip   Give us some jam.

Herbert   Serve us with jam. Gentlemen are not given anything, Pip.
Gentlemen are served. Try again.

Pip   Be so good as to serve us with jam.

Herbert   There's a good fellow.

Pip   There's a good fellow.

Herbert   That's the way. That's the way to treat them.

Servant *serves jam.*

Herbert   Jam – forgive me for saying – is eaten with a fork. Never with the finger. With a fork. And you hold it upside down. Like this.
Good. That's all. Good day.

Exit **Herbert** *and the* **Servant**. **Pip** *returns to the office. Enter* **Wemmick**. *Enter* **Jaggers** *and* **Molly**.

Pip   Mr Jaggers!

Jaggers Wait! Hands!
Mr Wemmick, you are getting slack.

Wemmick Me, sir?

Jaggers I have distinctly prohibited you from allowing
creatures to pester me.

Wemmick Sir.

Jaggers Mr Wemmick, but a moment ago a young
woman pawed at me, blubbering some nonsense about her
child – a wretched little girl about to be imprisoned. She
hadn't paid you, Mr Wemmick. She had no business to be
there.
There were tears, Mr Wemmick. She was leaking like a
cheap pen. In my own office hallway. I won't have it.

Wemmick No, sir.

Jaggers You're not having feelings, are you, Mr
Wemmick?

Wemmick No, sir!

Jaggers I won't have feelings in my office. Is that
understood?

Wemmick Yes, sir.

Jaggers Any more feelings and I'll show you the door.
Now pay Pip his money.

Exit **Jaggers**. **Wemmick** *counts the money.*

Pip It's a lot of money, Mr Wemmick.

Wemmick Some people would think so, sir.

Pip More than I need. There's others need it.

Wemmick People always think they need money, sir.

Pip There is so much distress.

Wemmick Distress is a relative word, sir. There's your
money.

Pip Mr Wemmick.

Wemmick Sir.

Pip   I want to help someone. Anyone. I want to help.

Wemmick   How many bridges are there, sir, over the river?

Pip   Mr Wemmick?

Wemmick   There's London, one. Southwark, two. Blackfriars, three. Waterloo, four. Westminster, five and Vauxhall, six. You've as many as six, you see, sir, to choose from.

Pip   No, Mr Wemmick, I don't see. I don't see at all.

Wemmick   Choose your bridge, sir, and take a walk upon it. Stop at the centre arch. Parcel your money up and pitch it into the Thames. Then you'll know the end of it.
Use it to help, sir, and you'll know the end of it too.
A much less pleasant and profitable end. Good day.

Exit **Wemmick**. *Enter* **Herbert**.

Herbert   Understand, Pip, a gentleman does not work. A gentleman lives off the work of others. A gentleman does not soil his hands. A gentleman may be a brewer, but never brew. He owns those who do. A gentleman may be a banker, but never bank. He owns those who do. A gentleman does not build. He owns the builders. A gentleman does not labour. He owns the labourers. A gentleman does not work the earth. He owns the earth.

Enter **Joe**, *timidly*. **Pip***'s first impulse is to greet him warmly*.

Pip   Joe!

Herbert   You can tell a gentleman from his acquaintances. The acquaintances that befit a labouring boy do not befit a gentleman. Good day.

Exit **Herbert**. **Pip** *takes his advice to heart: and is formal towards* **Joe**.

Pip   Joseph. Mr Gargery. How are you?

Joe   How AIR you, Pip?

Pip   I am glad to see you, Joe. Give me your hat.

Joe *won't give up his hat. He puts it in an insecure place. It keeps falling down.*

Joe   Well well. Well well well well well. WELL WELL.

Pip   Well, Joe.

Joe   You have that growed and that swelled and that gentlefolked.

Pip   Yes, Joe. I have improved, I hope.

Joe   I think you're an honour to king and country. And I hope as that you get your elth in this close spot.

Pip   I think London suits me.

Joe   I wouldn't keep a pig in it myself.

Pip   Wouldn't you, Joe?

Joe   No, sir. Not if I wished him to fatten wholesome and have a meller flavour on him.

Pip   Have you seen much of London, Joe?

Joe   Yes, sir. Some of it. And very architectooraloooral it is, sir.

Pip   Joe, how can you call me sir?

Joe   Me having the intentions and abilities to stay not many minutes more, sir, I will now conclude. Or leastways begin to mention what have led to my having had the present honour.

Pip   Joe!

Joe   See, Pip, I got a message from Miss Havisham. To say she wanted to see me. So I clean myself up, and off I goes to see her. Miss A, sir.

Pip   Miss A, Joe?

Joe   Miss A, sir, or otherways Havisham. Her expression then air as follering: Mr Gargery. You air in correspondence with Mr Pip? I am, I said. Would you tell him then, said she, that which Estella is come home and would be glad to see him.

So here I am, sir. I have now concluded. I wish you well and ever prospering.

Pip   But you're not going, Joe?

Joe   Yes I am.

Pip   But won't you stay and have something to eat?

Joe   No.
Pip, old chap, don't think bad of me. You and me is not two figures to be together in London. You won't see me again here, and not in these clothes. It ain't that I'm proud, Pip, but I want to be right. I'm wrong in these clothes. I'm wrong out of the forge, the kitchen, and off the meshes. Think of me, Pip, in the forge, with me hammer in my hand, or even my pipe. You won't find fault in me then, Pip.
Think of me, there at the old anvil, in the old burnt apron, sticking to the old work. Think of me there. And now God bless, Pip. God bless.

Exit **Joe**. **Pip** *feels sad: his new clothes feel alien to him. Enter* **Miss Havisham** *and* **Estella**. **Estella** *has grown up.* **Pip** *is now in Satis House; and at once tries to appear more confident.*

Miss Havisham   So. You kiss my hand as if I were a queen.

Pip   You are more than that to me, Miss Havisham.
You have made me what I am.
You called me, and I came back to you.

Miss Havisham   Well?

Pip   Estella!
I did not recognise you.

Miss Havisham   Do you find her much changed?

Pip   Very much.

Miss Havisham   Is he changed?

Estella   Perhaps.

Miss Havisham   Less coarse and common?

Estella   A little.

Miss Havisham   Tell him your news.

Estella   I am to go to London. You are to escort me. You will be my page.

Miss Havisham   Aren't you happy, Pip?

Pip   Of course. Delighted.

Miss Havisham   Do you know what love is, Pip?

Pip   I think so.

Miss Havisham   You do not. You know nothing. Ask Estella. I have taught her what love is. Ask Estella.

Estella   Love is blind devotion.
Love is unquestioning self humiliation.
Love is utter submission.
Love is trust and belief against yourself.
Love is giving up heart and soul.
Giving up heart and soul to the smiter.

Miss Havisham   As I did!

Miss Havisham *is distressed.* **Pip** *would comfort her, but* **Estella** *prevents him.*

Estella   Leave her, Pip.

Pip   Leave her?
Do you not feel for her?

Estella   Feel for her, Pip?

Pip   Have you no heart?

Estella   I suppose I have a thing that beats
And if it stops I die. But that is all.
I have no tenderness. I have not bestowed it anywhere:
I do not have any such thing at all.
Believe this, Pip. Believe it at once.
And go!

Exit **Estella** *and* **Miss Havisham**. *Enter* **Herbert**.

Herbert   A gentleman, Pip, does not love. A gentleman bestows his affections. And he does not bestow his affections on your common doxy or whore. He may buy her, of course,

but only under a decent cloak of discretion. His affections are
elsewhere: directed towards purity and the greatest
refinement. Are your affections bestowed, Mr Pip? Are they
well bestowed?

Pip   I think so. With all my heart I think so.

Enter **Estella** *and the Company. Dance music plays.*

Herbert   The Richmond Ball. The Richmond
Subscription Ball.

A dance. **Estella** *flirts.* **Pip** *suffers.*

Estella   Pip. Don't sulk. Meet my new friend.
Bentley Drummle of Gloucestershire.
He has excellent prospects. One day he'll be a duke.
Aren't I honoured?

Pip   No. Not in the least!
I wonder how you can bear him.
He is a brute. A rich ugly brute.

Estella   Moths and all kinds of ugly creatures
Hover over a lighted flame.
Can the flame help it?

Pip   Cannot Estella help it?

Estella   Well. Perhaps. Anything you like.

Pip   Then why do you look at him so?

Estella   Am I not to use my eyes?

Pip   You give him looks and smiles
Such as you never gave to me.

Estella   Do you want me then to deceive and entrap you?

Pip   Do you deceive and entrap him, Estella?

Estella   Yes, him, and many others. As I was taught. I
deceive and entrap them all.
Pip, you foolish boy have I not warned you?

Pip   Love is blind.

Estella   Love is a fancy, Pip. I know nothing of it.

Pip   You are sad.

Estella   Do you think it is a pleasure to be brought up to be admired?
Do you think that in itself is sufficient? Pip, you are so taken up with yourself. Have you noticed nothing?
Do you not know her story? Did you never take the trouble to enquire?
You think she's away, Pip, and safely locked up
There in her dead dark room in the cobwebs and dust.
But I cannot leave her. Nor can she leave me.
She walks through the halls in her shroud like a ghost.
I have to write to her each night,
A long letter, Pip, telling her of my conquests.
And you don't know why. Pip, Pip. You are blind.

Miss Havisham *wanders through the ball like a ghost.*

Estella   She had everything. Her father loved her.
But she was orphaned, Pip, while she was still young.
She was rich, Pip, and very lovely, and all alone.
Satis House was a grand place then, she told me,
Full of laughter and sunlight. At night,
The candles in the parties shone like stars.
As they do here, Pip.
One night she met a man at the Midsummer ball.
A tall man, he was, and handsome and dark.
They danced all night long as they do in the stories
And when dawn came, and it was over, and the candles were tired and pale,
She was still fresh and overflowing with laughter
And could have danced the whole night all over again.
The wedding was fixed. It was to be a grand affair.
The most beautiful wedding that ever was seen.
The dress was bought, the guests were invited
She was putting on the most beautiful silk gown.

Miss Havisham   And then the letter came.

Estella   It was brought by one of his servants.

Miss Havisham *opens the letter and reads it. She lets out a terrible cry.*

Estella   It broke off the wedding. It told her she was worthless
It told her she'd been useful for the money
But marriage was a joke.

Miss Havisham   What do I touch here?

Pip   Your heart.

Miss Havisham   Broken!

Estella   She sat all day in her dress, holding the letter
And that night sent for Jaggers. She had read his name in the papers.

Miss Havisham   Jaggers! Stop the clocks!

Estella   She laid the place to waste.
And then she found me.

Miss Havisham   Find a girl, Jaggers, find a girl. I want a baby.

Jaggers *detaches* **Estella** *from* **Molly**'s *arms and hands her over to* **Miss Havisham**.

Jaggers   Babies can be found. Babies can be bought.
I do as I am paid. I do not approve.
I am not paid to approve.

Estella   You see, Pip, like you, I never knew who I was.
All I remember is a dark room in a dark house.
And a sad lady looking down on me.

Miss Havisham   I want to spare her what happened to me.

Estella   I was brought up to be admired.
You have heard her,
Heard her say it. Brought up to be admired.
To be gawped at, Pip. To be smelt and pawed at.
And why do you think that was?

Pip   I thought it was for yourself.

Estella   Fool. It was for her revenge!

Pip   I know that, and yet I love you.
I love you against hope, against reason, against the deepest
instincts of my soul.
I spend days on end at your door. Always I long to be in your
company, convinced that to be with you will make me the
happiest man in the world,
And yet, when I am with you,
You bring me nothing but misery.

Pip *is left alone with the casts on the shelf. He is now in* **Jaggers**'*s*
office. Enter **Wemmick**.

Wemmick   Looking at the faces, sir?
The faces on the wall?

Pip   Why do their faces twitch so? Why are they so puffed
up?

Wemmick   They were hanged.

Pip   Why were they hanged, Wemmick? What had they
done?

Wemmick   One for coining. One for forging wills. And he
did a bit of murder on the side. But he'd have got off for that.
It was the wills he had to hang for. They could never forgive
him that. Still. You were a good client, weren't you, Artful?
You both were. Good clients. You were the making of us.
That's why we had you cut down straight after the hanging,
and had the casts made. To say thank you.
They gave me these. They usually give me something, old
clients. Before they drop. Unless they're destitute. Mr
Jaggers does ask substantial fees. But then he earns them.
And there's always a little something left over, even if it's just
a brace of pigeons for the pot. Some of 'em puts in a word for
me at the butchers so I'll get a good cut of steak. See this?
Prime steak. Got it off this morning's burglar. You see, sir,
I've got my old father out at Walworth and he likes his bit of
steak. Or it might be something more substantial. A brooch,
perhaps, or a funeral ring. Sometimes it's a pair of trousers,
or a jacket or a tie. It's a good pair I've got on now. Belonged

to a poisoner. He was always very particular about the
clothes he wore. They've done me for years.
Oh, I know for someone like you, sir, with all your riches,
they must seem like nothing at all. But they count for me, sir,
they count for me. They're property, you see. Portable
property. There's one rule in life, sir. I find it prudent to
apply: always get hold of portable property.

Pip   Is that all life is? That we should feast off each other
like vultures?

Wemmick   Don't take on so, sir. It's only work.

Enter **Jaggers**.

Jaggers   Hands!

Enter **Molly** *with basin*.

You admire my servant, Pip?
I'll show you a wrist.
Molly, show the gentleman your wrist.

Molly *backs away*.

Jaggers   Molly! Your wrist!

Molly *shows it*.

Jaggers   There is strength in that wrist, Pip. Animal
strength. The strength of a beast that is torn from its young.
Strength that could kill.
Strength that must be tamed!
Molly, you may go. You have been admired.

Exit **Molly**.

You have something to say, Pip?

Pip   Mr Jaggers, I am now twenty-one years old.

Jaggers   I am aware of that, Pip. And henceforth I shall
treat you differently. I shall call you Mr Pip.

Pip   Mr Jaggers, that is not enough!

Jaggers   What else can you expect?

Pip   Answers, Mr Jaggers.

Jaggers Come come, Mr Pip. Is it reasonable to expect answers when you ask no questions?

Pip I will not ask you who my benefactor is, Mr Jaggers.

Jaggers Quite right, Mr Pip.

Pip But I will ask this: is she —

Jaggers Or he.

Pip Very well, Mr Jaggers. She or he. But when am I to be told? Am I to be told today?

Jaggers No. Ask another.

Pip When will I be told?

Jaggers Later. Ask another.

Pip Mr Jaggers, there is nothing else to ask!

Jaggers Mr Pip, these are questions that you cannot ask me.

Pip But is it likely, Mr Jaggers, that my patron will soon —

Jaggers Soon what? Mr Pip. That isn't a question, you know.

Pip Will soon come to London, or summon me anywhere else?

Jaggers Unlikely.

Pip Will it be years hence, Mr Jaggers?

Jaggers Pip — Mr Pip — you will come to understand that this is a question that could compromise me.
And Pip, when that person discloses I will not need to know. My part in these affairs will have ended.

Pip Mr Jaggers —

Jaggers Don't argue, Pip. Don't protest to me. I do not approve. I am not paid to approve. And that is all I have to say.

Pip If that is all you have to say, —
There can be nothing left for me to ask.

Jaggers One more thing, Mr Pip.

Pip   Yes.

Jaggers   I have a message for you. You are to go to Miss Havisham's.
Hands!
You are amazed, Mr Pip.

Pip   Delighted, Mr Jaggers.

Exit **Jaggers** *and* **Wemmick** *and* **Molly**.
Enter **Estella** *and* **Miss Havisham**. *We are now at Satis House.*
Miss Havisham *adores* **Estella**. **Estella** *tries to detach herself.*

Miss Havisham   Are you tired of me?

Estella   Tired of myself.

Miss Havisham   Liar. You are tired of me.

Estella   I told you I was not tired of you.
I told you I was tired of myself.

Miss Havisham   Stock and stone. Cold cold heart.

Estella   You reproach me for being cold? You?
I am what you made me.

Miss Havisham   Thankless. Hard and thankless.

Estella   What would you have me thank you for?
You have brought me up, to be sure.
But what would you have?
You have given me everything. But I did not ask you to give me everything.
What would you have?

Miss Havisham   Love.

Estella   You have it.

Miss Havisham   I have not.

Estella   Mother by adoption, I have said I owe everything to you.
All I possess is freely yours. All you have given me,
Is at your command to have again.
Beyond that, I have nothing.

Miss Havisham   So proud. So proud!

Estella   Who taught me to be proud? Who praised me when I learnt the lesson?

Miss Havisham   So hard. So hard!

Estella   Who taught me to be hard? Who praised me when I learnt the lesson?

Miss Havisham   But to be proud and hard to me! To be proud and hard to me!

Miss Havisham *thinks she has lost* **Estella** *and mourns.*

Estella   I begin to think I almost understand how this comes about.
You have brought up your adopted daughter to live only in these always darkened rooms,
You have taught her that there was no such thing as daylight,
And now, for reasons of your own, you want her to understand there is daylight after all.
Is it so surprising she should find that hard?
Oh, adopted mother, you talk to me of love. But you have always taught me, from the first dawn of my understanding, always taught me with your utmost energy and might, that love is an enemy, love a destroyer. That I must always turn against it, for it has blighted you, and will as surely blight me. And now you want me to take to it, as if it were daylight. And because I cannot you feel disappointed and angry. But understand this, adopted mother, I am what you made me! Nothing more and nothing less. I am what you made me!

Enter **Pip**.

Miss Havisham   Oh, Pip, Pip.

Pip   You sent for me, Miss Havisham, and I came.
I understood you had news for me.

Estella   I will tell you the news, since, it seems, she cannot. 'The marriage is announced between Miss Estella Havisham of Satis House and Mr Bentley Drummle of Gloucestershire.' That was the announcement, was it not?

Pip   That is not the news I expected to hear.

Estella   Does Miss Estella's marriage surprise you?

Pip   How can you speak of yourself like that? As if you were another person?

Estella   How else can I live?

Pip   Are you doing it for her?

Estella   No. Pip. She would have me stay. But I am weary of this life.
Who would not be? I would willingly change it.
Don't argue with me, Pip. Don't remonstrate.
I know you will talk to me of love. There is no use in talking of that. It is only a form of words, a noise that other people make, and may mean something to them. But not to me, Pip, not to me. Will you not believe me?
Oh, Pip, believe me. Sometimes I may wish it were not so, sometimes I may wish I was as other people are.
And if I were, Pip . . .
And if I could . . .
But it cannot be.
Do not fear I will be a blessing to him, Pip. There is no chance of that.

Exit **Miss Havisham** *and* **Estella**. **Pip** *is at home. It has got very dark. We hear the wind. Someone is approaching.* **Pip** *starts up.*

Pip   There was a wind that night.
A gale of wind
As I lay in my lonely lodgings by the water.
Storm and rain. Storm and rain.
A storm so furious.
That trees were falling in the country
And the sails of windmills were being carried away.
Gloomy accounts came in from every coast
Sad tales of shipwreck. Shipwreck and death.

Pause.

And then I heard a footstep on the stair.

Pause.

Who is it?
Who do you want to see?

Enter the convict.

Magwitch   Mr Pip.

Pip   There is nothing the matter?

Magwitch   Nothing the matter.

Pip   Who are you? What do you want? Have you business
with me?

Magwitch   Yes, Mr Pip. You could say I had business.

Pip *recognises him, and does not know what to say or do.*

Pip   The convict!

Magwitch   My boy. My dear boy.
It was noble what you did for me. Noble.
I ain't never forgotten it.

Pip   Things have changed for me since then. I do not wish
to renew an acquaintance I made so long ago.

Magwitch   It's dissapinting to a man arter having looked
for'ard so distant, and come so far.

Pip   I am sorry.

Magwitch   You're not to blame for that – neither on us is
to blame for that.

Pip   I did not mean to speak harshly.
I wish you well, and happy.

Magwitch   I'm glad to hear you say so, boy.

Pip   Do you want some money? I have plenty to spare.
As you see, I have done well.

Magwitch   You have done well. Might I ask how you have
done well?
How it's come about, since you and me was out there all
alone on the shivering marshes?

Pip   I've come into property.

Magwitch   Might a mere warmint ask what property?

Pip I don't know.

Magwitch Might a mere warmint ask whose property?

Pip I don't know.

Magwitch Might a mere warmint ask who administered
that property?
Someone must have. You must have had a guardian, or such
like.
Might a mere warmint guess his name?
Did it start with a J?
Might a mere warmint guess his name to be Jaggers?
Yes, my boy, it's me wot's done it. It's me wot's made a
gentleman of you.
I've worked and I've prospered and I've done it.
Dear boy, I've done it!

He stretches out his hands. **Pip** *is revolted by his touch.*

You never thought it might be me?

Pip Never! Never!

Magwitch Well, it was me, and single-handed.

Pip There was no one else?

Magwitch Who else could there be?
There's no one else, dear boy. No one else at all.
And I'm your second father.
And as your second father, boy, I'm proud.
See, Pip. Look at this, dear boy. Look.

He takes out a pocket-book full of money.

There's money worth spending in this, dear boy, and there's
more.
More where that came from.
I've come from the old country to see my gentleman
And see him spend money like a gentleman.
That'll be my pleasure. My pleasure'll be fur to see him do it.
And blast you all! Blast all of you that looked down on me
All of you that locked me up and had me chained
I've got a gentleman better than all of you put together!
And I made him myself. I made him myself!

Pip   Stop! Please stop!

Magwitch   Look 'ee here, Pip. Look 'ee here. I forgot myself a minute ago. I been low, Pip. Right low. I didn't make myself a gentleman just to forget myself afore him. I won't be low, dear boy, I won't be low.

Pip   But what are you going to do?

Magwitch   Why stay here, of course, and be with you. Where will you put me?
I must be put somewheres, dear boy. I'm weary.
I've been sea-tossed and sea-washed months and months.

Pip   Go there. Sleep. Go there!

He goes to **Miss Havisham**.

Miss Havisham, you deceived me.

Miss Havisham   I said nothing.

Pip   You let me believe, Miss Havisham. Was that kind?

Miss Havisham   Who am I that I should be kind?

Enter **Jaggers** *and* **Wemmick**.

Pip   Mr Jaggers! Mr Jaggers!

Jaggers   Caution, Mr Pip. Caution is necessary. Don't commit yourself.
Don't commit anyone. You understand, Mr Pip?
Anyone.

Pip   Mr Jaggers –

Jaggers   Don't tell me anything. I am not curious. I want to know nothing.

Pip   Can you at least confirm that what I have been told is true?

Jaggers   Did you say told, Mr Pip? Try 'informed'. 'Told' would seem to imply verbal communication. You can't have verbal communication with a man in New South Wales.

Pip   Can you confirm then that what I have been informed is true?

Jaggers   That's better, Mr Pip. Much better. I can confirm that a certain Abel Magwitch, resident in New South Wales, is your benefactor.

Pip   I thought it was Miss Havisham.

Jaggers   I am not responsible for that.

Pip   What can I do?

Jaggers   Look at the evidence. Take nothing on looks; take everything on evidence. Hands!

Exit **Jaggers**.

Wemmick   Take care, Mr Pip. He was sentenced for life. If they catch him, he'll hang.

Exit **Wemmick**. **Pip** *returns to* **Magwitch**. *He looks at him a while.* **Magwitch** *wakes.*

Magwitch   Boy. Dear boy.

Pip   Why did they sentence you? What have you done?

Magwitch   I been a warmint, dear boy. That's all I've been. That's what I was born. Born a warmint.
First thing I remember is thieving turnips down in Essex. There was a man had been with me, but he'd run off. He'd taken the fire with him, and I was cold.
I had a kind of face on me that scared folk. They'd look at me and say, he's a hard un. Awfully hardened, that un. Lives in jails. And they looked at me through the bars. And some of em talked at me and some of em preached at me and some of em measured my head. Some of em gave me bibles I couldn't read and made speeches at me I couldn't understand. But they never gave me a thing to eat. And what was I to do? I must eat, mustn't I? I'm a-getting low, Pip. I'm sorry. Don't you be feared of me getting low. I'll tell you as it was. Not that there's much to tell, Pip, but in jail and out of jail and then in jail again.
Then I met this man, Compeyson. A talker. A smooth talker. And we done things together. He did the talking and I did the stealing. And the fighting and the necessary. It wasn't much. We swindled folk and passed on false money. We done small

stuff mostly. Once we done this lady in a house. He said he'd
marry her, and he could have too. She laughed at me. It were
nothing much. She gave him jewels, and he took a load of
money.
Then we ran off. And we was took soon after that. I had
Jaggers.
I'd have hung otherwise.
As it was I got life, Pip. Transported for life.
I 'ad a little girl then, new born. Just a tiny little thing she was,
Pip, but big enough to look at me and smile. And I lost her.
Lost her for good. I won't be low, don't be frightened.
I won't be low.

Pip   I am not afraid of that. I just want to see you safe.

Magwitch   Thank 'ee, boy. Thank 'ee.

A knock on the door. They start. Enter **Wemmick**.

Wemmick   There's money on his head, Mr Pip. There's a
profit to be had from his taking.

Pip   What shall I do?

Wemmick   Get him abroad, Mr Pip. They're after him.
I've heard word.
Get his portable property and get him abroad.

Pip   I have heard of a steamer to Hamburg.

Wemmick   Hamburg will do nicely, Mr Pip. But get his
property.
Take him to the steamer, Mr Pip. But not in the open. Not in
the port. Get him down river. But don't hire boat men or
ferry men or any kind of men. Take him out yourself. Row
him. And get his property. Get his portable property.

Exit **Wemmick**.

Pip   And so we took to the water.

Magwitch   Dear boy. Faithful boy. Thank 'ee, thank 'ee!

Pip   In and out among the tiers of shipping, among the
rusty chain cables, frayed hempen hawsers, and bobbing
buoys, in and out, hammers going in shipbuilders' yards,

saws going at timber, clashing engines going at things
unknown, pumps going in leaky ships, capstans going, in and
out –
Until at last we reached the open river.
Where the ships' boys might take their fenders in and where
the festooned sails might fly out to the wind.
You don't seem anxious at all.

Magwitch If you knowed, dear boy, what it is to sit here
alonger my dear boy and have my smoke, arter having been
day by day atwixt four walls, you'd envy me. But you don't
know what it is.

Pip I think I know what freedom is.

Magwitch You don't know it equal to me.
You'd have to have been under lock and key dear boy to
know it equal to me. But I ain't going to be low.

Pip And so the winding river turned and turned,
And the great floating buoys upon it turned and turned
And everything else seemed stranded and still.
If all goes well, you should be safe soon.

Magwitch I hope so.

Pip And think so?

Magwitch See, boy, we drifts by on the river so pleasant
and so soft
We just flows along together. And we can't see what's at the
bottom of the next few hours no more than we can see to the
bottom of this water.
And we can't hold on to the tide of the next few hours no
more than we can hold this water.
And see, Pip, see. It's all run through my fingers and gone.

Pip And then began an anxious time. For as the tide began
to flow more strongly, it flapped at irregular intervals along
the shore.
And each time it did, I would start, and look, and strain my
eyes, and see nothing.
What's that?

Magwitch   Nothing, boy.

Pip   Is that a boat?

Magwitch   It's the steamer, boy. Don't fret. Don't you
fret, my boy.

Pip   And we pulled out towards it,
We were under its shadow when a galley came,
A four-oared galley, most expertly handled.
It fell alongside us, drifting when we drifted, and pulling a
stroke or two when I pulled.

Man in Boat   You have a returned transport there. His
name is Abel Magwitch. I apprehend him and call on you to
assist me.

Pip   And the steamer bore down upon us and we were gone.
I was taken on board the galley and we drifted in the tide.
Every man looking swiftly and eagerly at the water astern.
Magwitch was gone,
And for a while we saw nothing
And then a dark object, drifting towards us with the tide.
They brought him on board.
His right arm was broken and horribly cut and something
had smashed in his chest. He could hardly breathe.
They took all his belongings
And I understood I had lost everything.

Magwitch   Don't fret for me, dear boy. I am content. My
boy can be a gentleman without me.

Pip   In those days it was the custom
To devote a whole day of Court Sessions to the passing of
Sentence
And to finish that day with the Sentence of Death.
On his day there were thirty-two to be sentenced
All crowded close together in a pen.
And a huge congregation had assembled to watch.
The Judge put on his Cap and confronted them,
The thirty-two who were doomed to die,
And he spoke of civic duty and the upholding of law.
He singled out my convict, who had so tried to help me,

As the one the most signally, most rightfully
And most justly deserving to Die.
And then he turned to the others and he sentenced them
One by one to be hung.
There were men, and there were women. Some were old,
And some were no older than children.

Magwitch *is among the convicts.*

Pip   Some sat in stony silence and affected not to know.
Some tried to laugh. Some screamed. Some shivered.
Most wept.
He stood. He was very weak. But he stood,
And he never flinched. He looked the Judge in the eye and
said:

Magwitch   My Lord, I have already heard the sentence of
God.
But I now hear yours.

Magwitch *lies in* **Pip's** *arms. Enter* **Miss Havisham**.
Estella *enters slowly.* **Miss Havisham** *looks up and sees her.*

Miss Havisham   Is this real?

Estella   Oh yes, mother by adoption. This is real.

Miss Havisham   Why are you here?

Estella   I thought you had taught me what suffering was.
But I knew nothing. I knew nothing.
His only care was to hit me
Where the bruises wouldn't show.
He took all my money and he took all my jewels
And I have run from him to you.

Miss Havisham   Daughter, believe me.
I wanted to save you from what happened to me.

Estella   You did worse.

Miss Havisham   Believe me.

Estella   You took away my heart
And instead you gave me a heart of ice.

Miss Havisham   I wanted to save you.

Estella   Better to have left me a natural heart
Better to have left me a heart to be bruised
A heart to be broken.

Miss Havisham   I did what I could. Can you forgive me?

Estella   No.

Miss Havisham   Daughter, I beg you.

Estella   No.

Miss Havisham   Can you not find it in your heart?

Estella   I have no heart!

Miss Havisham *is enveloped in flame. A terrible scream.*

Estella   And a great flaming light sprang up!
And all about her blazed a whirl of fire
A fire that burnt her up as she screamed
Then moaned in agony and distress
And I forgave her then
I pitied and forgave her.
But it was too late. It was too late.

When all is still, the dead **Miss Havisham** *is laid to rest.*

Pip   A change came over him.
From the day the prison door closed upon him.
He wasted and became slowly weaker and worse.
But he never complained. He lay on his back
And looked up at the ceiling
And the light drained away.

Wemmick   Lost his property. You lost his portable
property.
What a fool to lose his property.
What a fool. You couldn't save him,
But you could have saved the property.

Pip   As for me, I lay on the sofa
I lay on the floor.
Anywhere, according to where I sank down
To no purpose. To no power.

And my limbs were heavy and my head was aching
And there were figures threatening me.

Threatening figures shadow **Pip**. *He is ill and delirious.*

What do you want? I don't know you.

First Man   Well, sir, this is a small matter –

Second Man   And we're sure you'll arrange it.

First Man   But the fact is, you're arrested.

Pip   How much is the debt?

First Man   One hundred and twenty-three pound –

Second Man   Fifteen and six.

First Man   Jewellers bill.

Pip   What's to be done.

First Man   You'd better come with me, to my house.

Second Man   I keep a very nice house.

Pip   But I am ill! You see my state. I would come if I could,
but as it is I cannot.

First Man   I think he'll die on the way.

Second Man   Or in the house.

First Man   Either way we lose out.

Second Man   We'd have to pay to get rid of the corpse.

First Man   Whereas if we leave him . . .

Second Man   He'll die here.

First Man   And then we can grab the proceeds.

First *and* **Second Men**   Good thinking!

Pip *has a nightmare.*

Wemmick   Portable property!

Miss Havisham   You see this heart?

Jaggers   I'll show you a wrist.

Estella   Coarse common boy!

Mrs Joe   Ungrateful wretch!

Joe   Don't you fret, Pip, old son, don't you fret. You're safe
with Joe. Joe's here now. And when you're better, Pip, old
son, what larks, eh. What larks.

Pip   Joe! It is you.

Joe   Who else could it be, Pip, old chap. Who else could it
be.

Pip   I've seen so many faces, Joe, leering at me and
laughing at me and snarling at me. So many faces, but they
all changed into you, somehow.

Joe   See here, Pip, we heard from Mr Jaggers you was ill.
And Biddy said to me, she said you'd be looked after by
strangers, and you and me being friends, she said, a visit from
me might not prove unacceptabobble. 'Go to him', says
Biddy, 'without loss of time.' And so I did, Pip, old chap,
hoping as how that suits you.

Pip   There's no one, Joe. No one makes me happier than
you.

Pip *and* **Joe** *walk together. Time passes.* **Pip** *gets better.*

See, Joe, I can walk quite strongly now. Look, I'll walk back
by myself.

Joe   Which do not over do it, Pip. But I'll be happy to see
you able, sir.

Pip   Oh, Joe. I'm glad I've been ill. It has been a
memorable time for me.

Joe   Likeways for me, sir.

Pip   We have had a time together Joe, that I can never
forget.
There were days once, I know, that I did for a while forget;
but I never shall forget these.

Joe   Pip, there has been larks. And, dear sir, what have
been between us – have been.
Will you be as well in the morning?

Pip   Yes, Joe.

Joe   And always getting stronger?

Pip   Yes, Joe, steadily. Dear Joe.

Joe   Good night.

Pip   And in the morning he was gone.
On the table was a letter.

Joe   'Not wishful to intrude I have departured for you are
well again dear Pip and will do better without Joe. P.S. Ever
the best of friends.'

Pip   And beside the letter was a receipt for the debt.
Joe had paid it all.
I'll go back to the forge and thank him.
And I will go to Biddy and I will take her by the hand, and
I'll say,
Dear Biddy, I have been so foolish, but now I repent.
Will you take me, I'll say. Will you take me?
And perhaps I'll work in the forge, next to Joe, and we'll all
be together again.
I'll say, Biddy, will you forgive me? Biddy, will you take me?

He sees **Biddy**, *arm-in-arm with* **Joe**, *and at first can say nothing at
all.*

Biddy! How smart you are!

Biddy   Yes, Pip.

Pip   And Joe, how smart you are!

Joe   Yes. Dear Pip.

Biddy   It's my wedding day, and I'm married to Joe!

Pip   And there and then, another poor dream was smashed
to pieces.
The child in me was dead and gone for ever.

Enter **Estella**. *She is older.*

And here I found you, lost in the dark house,
And you said:

Estella   Pip, do you still know me? I have greatly changed.

Pip   My heart has not changed.

Estella   Shall we walk?

They walk, not quite sure what to say.

Pip   And your husband?

Estella   He died. He was drunk. He fell off his horse.

They laugh, as at the very beginning. **Estella** *breaks off.*

Pip   And I knew I understood you not at all.
I went to Jaggers.

Jaggers   Mr Pip.

Pip   Mr Jaggers, there is one more thing.

Jaggers   Is there, Mr Pip?

Pip   Mr Jaggers, you have not told me enough.

Jaggers   Mr Pip, you are becoming a cross-examiner.

Pip   Mr Jaggers, you have not told me who Estella is.

Jaggers   And why should that concern you, Mr Pip?

Pip   Mr Jaggers, I beg you. I know you care nothing for
broken dreams,
But I have lived all my life among them.
I have loved Estella dearly and long,
And have lost her. And everything that touches her
Touches me. Touches my heart.
I beg you, Mr Jaggers. Be open with me.

Jaggers   I will put a case to you, Mr Pip.
But understand that I make no admissions.
I put it to you, Mr Pip, that there was once a lawyer
No connection with anyone living or dead.
Who entered his profession with the highest of hopes
Because he wanted to do good in the world.
Remember that I make no admissions.
And this lawyer, Mr Pip, with all his high hopes,
Entered into an atmosphere of evil.
Day after day, Mr Pip, he went about his work and saw evil.
And all he saw of children, Pip, from the minute they were
born,
From the minute they were brought into this evil world,
Was that they were brought there to be destroyed.
Day after day, Mr Pip, he saw them being tried.
He saw them being tried at the criminal bar.
Day after day he saw them brought out to be whipped.
Brought out to be imprisoned, transported, neglected, cast out.

Qualified for nothing but the hangman.
Growing up for nothing but to be hanged.
And I have seen it too, Pip. I saw it then and I see it still.
I put it to you, Mr Pip, that he came upon a child,
Estella, Pip. A pretty little girl, whose mother was his servant,
and whose father had been sentenced to transportation for
life.
And I put the case again, Mr Pip, that he knew
Of a rich eccentric old lady who wanted a child.
Oh, Pip, I put it to you.
I wanted to save one. Just one.
And Pip don't talk to me of broken dreams

Pip   All the doors are open now
And the wind blows through the empty house.

Estella   What will happen to the house
When the sunlight breaks in upon it?
What will happen to the house
The old dirty unloved house?
Will she still walk down all the dark passages
Will she walk and trail her shroud in the dust?
Will she still walk down all the dark corridors
Hugging her grief to her breast?

Pip   Will the convict walk and rattle his chains?

Estella   Will she walk? Will she walk?
Oh, Pip, we have been bent and broken by suffering
All of us bent and broken.
Have we been twisted into a better shape?
I will take a child, Pip, a little girl
And she will run laughing down the passages.
She will raise great clouds of dust
For the sunlight that streams through the windows.
I will take a child and I will keep her safe
And preserve her from what happened to me.
Oh, Pip, take my hand before we part for ever.

Exit **Estella**. **Pip** *is alone, as at the beginning*.

John Clifford has written over forty scripts – including original plays, translations and adaptations – for theatre, radio, television, film, opera and puppets, which have been performed all over the world. Plays include *Losing Venice*, *Inés de Castro* and *Light in the Village* (all Traverse Theatre, Edinburgh) and *Visões de febre* (Lisbon, 1995). Translations and adaptations include Calderón's *Schism in England* (National Theatre), Tirso de Molina's *Heaven Bent, Hell Bound* (ATC), *Romeo and Juliet* (TAG), *La Vie de Bohème* and *Wuthering Heights* (both Pitlochry), and as yet unperformed versions of *Celestina*, Liliane Atlan's *Un opéra pour Térézin* and Calderón's *La vida es sueño*. *Inés de Castro* has been turned into an opera by James MacMillan, premiered by Scottish Opera at the Edinburgh International Festival, 1996. His latest play, *War in America*, is being written for the Royal Lyceum Theatre, Edinburgh. John combines playwriting with childcare and lecturing. He lives with his partner and daughters in Edinburgh.

The Mill on the Floss

adapted from George Eliot
by Helen Edmundson

Author's Note

This play was written to be performed on a stage with two levels. It could, however, be performed on a single-level stage, as long as the space would allow for simultaneous action in two areas, and an alternative method of 'ducking the witch' could be found.

Although the play is split into scenes, this is more for the benefit of director and actor in rehearsal. Wherever possible, the action of each scene should flow into the next (indeed, this is sometimes demanded by the text). Care should be taken, however, where identical characters are used in consecutive scenes, to delineate any changes of place or movement of time.

H.E.

The Mill on the Floss was first performed by Shared
Experience Theatre Company in association with the
Wolsey Theatre, Ipswich, on 17 March 1994. The cast was as
follows:

Mr Tulliver, Dr Kenn	Simeon Andrews
First Maggie	Shirley Henderson
Bob Jakin, Phillip Wakem,	
Uncle Pullet	Michael Matus
Second Maggie, Aunt Glegg	Buddug Morgan
Tom Tulliver, Wakem	Ian Puleston-Davies
Stephen Guest, Mr Stelling,	
Uncle Glegg	Simon Robson
Mrs Tulliver, Lucy Deane	Clara Salaman
Third Maggie, Aunt Pullet	Helen Schlesinger

Directed by Nancy Meckler *and* Polly Teale
Designed by Bunny Christie
Music composed by Peter Salem
Lighting by Chris Davey
Movement by Liz Ranken

Scene One

Music.

Lights up on **First Maggie**. *She is standing still on the bank, book in hand, staring at the river. The air is full of the sound of the water rushing through the mill wheel. Above the noise we hear a woman's voice (her mother) calling:*

Maggie. Maggie.

But **Maggie** *does not respond. Instead, she sits cross-legged, and begins to read her book. On the upper platform, dimly lit, the characters of the play gather as a crowd.*

Maggie '. . . bringing those things called witches or conjurors to justice; this is, first to know if a woman be a witch, throw her into a pond; and if she be a witch she will swim, and it is not in her own power to prevent it . . .'

The crowd, suddenly brightly lit, come to life, as **Maggie** *repeats the words of the book. They gather threateningly around a woman (similar to* **Maggie** *with long dark hair), haul her aloft and duck her. As she goes under water,* **Maggie** *turns and sees her and, as if she too is under water, struggles to reach her. The woman is hauled out and ducked a second time.* **Maggie** *fights her way towards her but the woman drowns before her eyes.* **Maggie** *screams –*

Maggie No.

The crowd fall silent and stare down at her.

Then they break. **Mr Tulliver**, **Mrs Tulliver** *and* **Mr Stelling** *descend and take their places for the next scene. The rest leave.* **Maggie** *goes back to her book.*

Scene Two

Mr *and* **Mrs Tulliver** *and* **Mr Stelling** *sit in the parlour at Dorlcote Mill.*

Mr Tulliver   What I want . . . What I want is to give my
son, Tom, a good eddication; an eddication as 'll be a bread
to him. All the learnin' my father ever paid for was a bit o'
birch at one end and the alphabet at the other. Not that a
man can't be an excellent miller and farmer and a shrewd
sensible fellow into the bargain, without much help from the
schoolmaster . . .

Mr Stelling   Oh, I don't doubt it.

Mr Tulliver   But that's just it. I don't want Tom to follow
me into the Mill. I want him to be a bit of a scholard, so as he
might be up to the tricks o' these fellows as talk fine and write
with a flourish. It'ud be a help to me wi' these lawsuits and
arbitrations.

Mr Stelling   Ah. You wish him to be a lawyer.

Mr Tulliver   A lawyer? Nay, I'll not make a downright
lawyer o' the lad. I should be sorry for him to be a raskill.

Mrs Tulliver   Mr Tulliver isn't fond of the lawyers.

Mr Tulliver   No, more of an engineer, or an auctioneer
and vallyer; one of them smartish businesses as are all profits
and no outlay, only for a big watch-chain and a high stool.

Mr Stelling   You are talking to the right man, sir.

Mr Tulliver   I am?

Mr Stelling   I dare say I could prepare your boy for any
one of those commendable occupations. Why, you need only
say to me, 'I wish my son to know arithmetic,' and he would
know it.

Mr Tulliver   What's that? 'I wish my son to know
'rithmetic.'

Mr Stelling   Or you may say, 'I wish my son to draw,' and
he would draw. Of course, I would start with Euclid and the
Eton Grammar. He would soon have a thorough grasp of
etymology and be perfectly *au fait* with his declensions and
conjugations.

Mrs Tulliver   But would you give him seconds o'
pudding? For he's such a boy for pudding as never was. Both
my children can eat as much victuals as most, thank God.

Mr Tulliver   Hush now, Bessy. There's other things to
think on besides pudding. That's the fault I have to find with
her; if she see a stick i' the road, she's allays thinkin' she can't
step over it. You'd stop me hiring a good waggoner 'cause
he'd got a mole on his face.

Mrs Tulliver   Dear heart! When did I iver make
objection to a man because he'd got a mole on his face? Or
anywhere out of sight, for that matter? I'm sure I'm rether
fond o' the moles.

Mr Tulliver   No, no, Bessy. I didn't mean justly the mole;
I meant . . . but niver mind. It's puzzlin' work, talking. No,
what I'm afraid on is as Tom hasn't got the right sort o'
brains for a smart fellow.

Mr Stelling   Is the boy stupid?

Mrs Tulliver   No.

Mr Tulliver   No. But I doubt he's a bit slowish. He takes
after your family, Bessy.

Mrs Tulliver   Yes, that he does.

Mr Tulliver   He's got a notion o' things out o' door, an a
sort o' common-sense, as he'd lay hold o' things by the right
handle. But he can't abide the books, and spells all wrong,
they tell me. You never hear him say cute things like the little
wench. The little 'un takes after my side; she's twice as cute as
Tom.

Mr Stelling   Is that right?

Mr Tulliver   Oh yes. Too cute for a woman, I'm afraid.
It's no mischief much while she's a little 'un, but an over-cute
woman's no better nor a long-tailed sheep – she'll fetch none
the bigger price for that.

Mrs Tulliver   Yes, it is a mischief, for it all runs to
naughtiness. How to keep her in a clean pinafore two hours
together passes my cunning. I don't know where she is now

and it's pretty nigh tea-time. (*She goes to the window and looks out.*) I thought so – sitting at the edge of the water with her book. She'll tumble in and drown some day. (*Rapping on the window.*) Maggie. Maggie.

Mr Tulliver (*quietly to* **Mr Stelling**)   It's the wonderful'st thing as I picked the mother from her sisters 'o purpose, 'cause she was a bit weak, like. That's the worse wi' the crossing of breeds: you can never justly calkilate what'll come on't.

Maggie *enters, dropping her bonnet on the floor and staring at the visitor.*

Mrs Tulliver   Oh dear, oh dear, Maggie, what are you thinkin' of, to throw your bonnet down there?

Mr Tulliver   Now then, Maggie. This is the Reverend Mr Stelling. He has come to discuss your brother's edication.

Maggie   Am I to have an education?

Mr Tulliver   What did I tell you? Cute as can be.

Mr Stelling   From what I've been hearing, you have no need of one. I see you have been reading.

Maggie   Yes, sir.

Mr Tulliver   She reads straight off as if she knowed it all beforehand.

Mr Stelling   Come here then, little miss and show me your book. (*She goes to him.*) Here are some pictures – can you tell me what they mean?

Maggie   I can tell you what they all mean. That's a horrible picture, isn't it? But I can't help looking at it. That woman in the water is a witch – well, they've put her in to find out whether she's a witch or not, and if she swims she's a witch, and if she's drowned, and killed, you know, she's innocent and not a witch, just a poor silly woman. But what good would it do her when she was drowned? I suppose she'd go to heaven and God would make it up to her. And this dreadful blacksmith with his arms akimbo, laughing – he's ugly, isn't he? – I'll tell you what he is. He's the devil really.

The devil takes the shape of wicked men, mostly blacksmiths because if people saw he was the devil and he roared at them, they'd run away and he couldn't make 'em do what he wanted.

Mr Stelling   Well!

Mrs Tulliver   God bless us.

Mr Tulliver   Why, what book is it the wench has got hold on?

Mr Stelling   *The History of the Devil*, by Daniel Defoe. Not quite the right book for a little girl.

Mr Tulliver   Did you ever hear the like on't? It's a pity but what she'd been the lad. She'd a been a match for the lawyers, she would.

Mr Stelling   She certainly has a way with words.

Mr Tulliver   Now, what about Tom? You can knock him into shape?

Maggie   Father, is it a long way off where Tom is to go?

Mr Tulliver   What? Worrying already that you won't have your brother? She fair worships him, you know?

Mr Stelling   O, a long, long way off. You must borrow the seven-leagued boots to reach him.

Maggie   That's nonsense.

Mrs Tulliver   Maggie! But is it so far off as I couldn't wash and mend him?

Mr Stelling   About fifteen miles, that's all.

Mrs Tulliver   Too far for the linen, I doubt.

Mr Stelling   I would suggest that you take some time to think it over, Mr Tulliver, but I have had other propositions from interested parties and I can only accommodate one boy – two at the most.

Mr Tulliver   Interested parties, eh?

Mr Stelling   One of them is a neighbour of yours. You may know him; a lawyer by the name of Wakem.

Mr Tulliver   Wakem? Wakem?

Mrs Tulliver   Mr Tulliver isn't fond o' Mr Wakem.

Mr Tulliver   I've just gone into arbitration with a client o' Wakem's.

Mr Stelling   I'm sorry, I didn't realise . . .

Mr Tulliver   Don't you be sorry. I'll cut his comb for him. I'll show him there are other folk as know how to handle the law. They can't try telling me that this errigation nonsense upstream won't stop my mill. If you've got a mill, you must have water to turn it. Water's a very particular thing. You can't pick it up with a pitchfork but you can steal it all the same, eh, Maggie? And Wakem's just the sort of raskill to side with a thief.

Mrs Tulliver   Dear heart, I'm sure Mr Stelling hasn't the time for this.

Mr Tulliver (*thoughtful*)   So, Wakem's going to send his lad to you.

Mr Stelling   Merely a passing remark . . . nothing's settled.

Mrs Tulliver   You won't make any hasty decisions, Mr Tulliver? After all, there's no hurry. Tom only returns from the 'cademy tomorrow and he'll want to enjoy the summer.

Mr Tulliver   All the more reason to get him to a proper school. He's learnt nothing at that 'cademy but how to pull potatoes and black boots.

Mrs Tulliver   Pehraps I should kill a couple of fowl, and have the aunts and uncles to dinner. You would want to hear what they have to say?

Mr Tulliver   You may kill every fowl i' the yard, if you like, Bessy, but I shall ask neither aunt nor uncle what I'm to do wi' my own lad. No. I'm decided. You shall have him, sir, if you'll take him.

Mrs Tulliver   Dear heart!

Mr Tulliver   What's good enough for Wakem, is good enough for me.

Scene Three

The following day. At Dorlcote Mill. A great crying and screaming is heard as **Maggie** *is dragged into the parlour by her mother, kicking and wriggling all the while.* **Mrs Tulliver** *tries in vain to brush her daughter's hair.*

Mrs Tulliver   Maggie, Maggie, be quiet now. Stop this at once. It's far too wet for little girls to go riding in open gigs in their best bonnets. You'll see Tom as soon as your father has fetched him. Hold still now. Hold still. Don't you want to look pretty for Tom?

Maggie *suddenly rushes out of her grasp and plunges her head into a pail of water.*

As her head goes under, we hear the strange deaf but booming noise that she would hear. She brings her head up, but the noise continues.

Mrs Tulliver (*above the noise*)   Maggie, Maggie, what is to become of you if you are so naughty? No one will love you any more. Oh, look at your clean pinafore! Folks 'ull think I've done something wicked to have such a child. It's a judgement on me.

During this speech, **Maggie** *has run to the upper platform, which is now her attic.*

Lost in her deaf rage. She picks up her fetish — the trunk of a large wooden doll and begins to beat and grind it and hurl it against the wall, until gradually the noise subsides and she calms. She pets the doll and kisses it better.

Down below, **Bob Jakin** *has entered, with a large barrel of flour.* **Maggie** *sees him and runs down the steps. She spins round and round —*

Maggie   Tom's coming home. Tom's coming home. Bob, Tom's coming home today.

Bob   I know that.

Maggie Can I come into the mill?

Bob No, you can't.

Maggie Why?

Bob Because if the maister saw me dallyin' with you instead 'o doin' my work, he'd whip me good an' proper like he did for not frightenin' the birds.

Maggie Bob? How old are you?

Bob Thirteen.

Maggie I'm nine.

Bob I know that.

Maggie Can you read?

Bob No. I'm no reader, I aren't.

Maggie Do you want me to teach you?

Bob No thank you, if it's all the same to you.

Maggie But don't you want to know things? There are countries full of creatures called elephants and civet cats and sun-fish, instead of horses and cows, you know. Don't you want to read about them?

Bob I'll go an' see 'em wi' me own eyes, I will. I'm going to work on the ships and see the whole world as soon as I's growed enough.

Maggie So am I. But I'll read about things first.

Bob Tell your brother there's a rattin' tonight. He can come with me. I know the chap as owns the ferrets. He's the biggest rot-catcher anywhere, he is. I'd sooner be a rot-catcher nor anything, I would.

Maggie I thought you wanted to work on the ships.

Bob I'm goin' to do both, I am. I'm goin' to hev white ferrets wi' pink eyes and catch my own rots, an' put a rot in a cage wi' a ferret, an' see 'em fight.

Maggie That's cruel.

Bob So? It's only rots.

Maggie   What if the rot . . . rat you catch has babies, waiting for it to come home?

Bob   All the better.

Maggie   But they're our fellow-creatures, Bob. We ought to care about them.

Bob   You can talk. You'll catch it from your brother when he sees his rebbits are all dead.

Maggie   Dead? (*Tremulously.*) What? The lop-eared one and the spotted doe?

Bob   As dead as moles.

Maggie (*bursting into tears*)   But Tom told us to take care of them.

Bob   Told you.

Maggie   He told me to be sure and remember them every day but how could I when they didn't come into my head? He'll be so angry. What am I going to do? What am I going to do?

Bob   You could hide, miss. That's what I'd do. (*He goes.*)

Maggie *begins to panic. She takes large gasping breaths. She runs about the yard in desperation.*

Maggie   Oh, it's cruel, it's cruel. Oh, please don't let the rabbits be dead. No. No. No. Oh, please let them be very well and make me have fed them and make Tom be pleased with me. Oh, please, please.

Music. **Tom** *is born in aloft on his father's shoulders, wearing a laurel wreath. He is surrounded by a cheering crowd. He leaps down and goes straight to* **Maggie** *and clasps her in his arms as if she is the most precious thing in his life.* **Maggie** *is thrilled.*

The music stops. The crowd goes. **Tom**, *just a boy now, is standing before* **Maggie**.

Tom   Hello, Maggie.

Maggie (*hurling herself around his neck and kissing him*)   Tom, Tom . . . (**Tom** *allows this but keeps his arms by his side*.) Mother wouldn't let me go to meet you. But I wanted to. I really did.

Tom   What happened to your hair?

Maggie   I'm sick of it.

Tom *suddenly runs and jumps high to touch the branch of a tree.* **Maggie** *copies him.*

Tom   Guess what I've got in my pockets.

Maggie   Is it marbles?

Tom   Marbles? No. I've swapped all my marbles with the little ones.

Maggie   What then?

Tom   Guess.

Maggie   How am I supposed to guess?

Tom   Don't be a spitfire or I won't tell you.

Maggie   Oh, please tell me. I won't be a spitfire, Tom, I promise. Please.

Tom   All right. It's two new fish-lines. One for me and one for you. I wouldn't go halves on the toffee and gingerbread on purpose to save the money and Gibson and Spouncer fought with me because I wouldn't.

Maggie   Oh, Tom!

Tom   We'll go fishing tomorrow at the round pool and you can catch one yourself and put the worms on and everything. (**Maggie** *throws her arms around his neck*.) Wasn't I a good brother, now, to buy you a line all to yourself?

Maggie   Yes, very, very, very good. I do love you Tom.

Tom   And the boys fought with me because I wouldn't give in about the toffee.

Maggie   I wish you wouldn't fight at your school. Did they hurt you?

Tom Of course not. I gave Spouncer a black eye. That's what he got for wanting to leather me. Come on.

Maggie Where are we going?

Tom To look at the rabbits.

Music. A terrible sickening dread fills **Maggie***'s heart.*

Maggie Tom, how much money did you give for your rabbits?

Tom Two half-crowns and a sixpence.

Maggie I think I've got more than that in my steel purse upstairs. I'll ask mother to give it you.

Tom What for? I don't need your money.

Maggie To buy some more rabbits with.

Tom Rabbits? I don't want any more.

Maggie But they're all dead.

Pause.

Tom You forgot to feed them. And Bob Jakin forgot. I'll kill him. I'll have him turned off our land. And I don't love you, Maggie. And you won't be coming fishing with me.

Maggie Tom, I couldn't help it, I forgot. I'm very, very sorry.

Tom You're a stupid girl and I don't love you.

Maggie Oh, please forgive me, Tom, please. I'd forgive you if you forgot anything.

Tom Now you just listen to me, Maggie: aren't I a good brother to you?

Maggie Yes. And I do love you so much, Tom.

Tom But you're a naughty girl. Last holidays you licked the paint off my lozenge-box and the holidays before that you pushed your head through my kite all for nothing.

Maggie (*beginning to hear the boom of a deaf rage*) I couldn't help it.

Tom   Yes you could, you could if you'd minded what you were doing.

Maggie   I couldn't . . .

Tom   You're a naughty girl and you're not coming fishing with me. Now, go away.

Maggie*'s rage is now very loud. She runs to the attic and throws herself on the ground, sobbing. Down below,* **Bob Jakin** *enters. Above* **Maggie***'s rage we hear –*

Tom   You let my rabbits die.

Bob   I did not.

Tom   That's a lie.

Tom *launches into him. They fight ferociously as* **Maggie***'s deaf rage reaches a peak.* **Mr Tulliver** *enters.*

Mr Tulliver   What's this? What's this? Fighting already?

He pulls them apart. **Bob** *runs off.*

Tom   He killed my rabbits. Him and Maggie. They killed them.

Mr Tulliver   Killed them?

Tom   I told them to feed them and they didn't.

Mr Tulliver   Well, they'd happen ha' died, if they'd been fed. They're nesh things, them lop-eared rabbits. I told you that. Things out o' natur never thrive. Where's your little sister?

Tom   I don't know.

Mr Tulliver   But she was with you. You've been naughty to her, haven't you?

Tom   No, Father. I only told her about the rabbits.

Mr Tulliver   She'll be in the attic, I doubt. You go and fetch her down and bring her for her tea. And be good to her, d'you hear? Else I'll let you know better.

He leaves. **Tom** *shuffles about, trying to overcome his absolute unwillingness to go and be nice to* **Maggie**. *Slowly, he climbs to the attic.*

Maggie, *who has been crouching in a corner, perks up when she hears the footsteps, and waits in trepidation, to see who it will be.* **Tom** *reaches the top of the steps and stops.*

Tom   Maggie, you're to come down for your tea.

She rushes to him and clings around his neck and sobs –

Maggie   Oh, Tom, Tom, please forgive me. I can't bear it, I'm so sorry and I'll always be good and remember things, I will. Please love me, Tom. Please. Please.

She caresses him and kisses his ears.

Tom   All right. All right. Don't cry, Magsie. Don't cry.

They cuddle and hug each other.

Scene Four

Music.

Maggie *and* **Tom** *are sitting on the upper platform, as if at the edge of the pool, fishing. Each sits very straight and quiet (which is agony for* **Maggie**) *with their new rods dangling in the water.*

Pause.

Maggie   What if there aren't any fish?

Tom   Shh. The round pool is full of fish. Everyone knows that. There was a big flood once when the round pool was made. Father told me. The animals all drowned and boats went all over the fields and everything. When I'm a man, I'll make a boat with a wooden house on the top of it, like Noah's Ark. And if a flood came, I wouldn't mind and I'd take you in.

Maggie   What would we eat?

Tom   Rabbits. I'd hit 'em on the head as they swam by.

Cut to: the parlour at the mill. **Mrs Tulliver** *is ministering to* **Aunt** *and* **Uncle Glegg**.

Aunt Glegg *is sitting very straight in her chair and tapping her watch.*

Mrs Glegg Half-past five. Whatever time it might be by other people's clocks and watches, it has gone half-past five by mine.

Mrs Tulliver Oh dear, I'm sure Sister Pullet will be here in time, sister. The tea won't be ready till half-past six.

Mrs Glegg I detest this nonsense of having your tea at half-past six, when you might have it at six. That was never the way in our family.

Mrs Tulliver Why, Jane, what can I do? Mr Tulliver doesn't like his tea before seven, but I put it half an hour earlier for you.

Mrs Glegg And where are those children of yours? Don't they come and greet their Aunt Glegg?

Mrs Tulliver They're fishing at the round pool.

Mrs Glegg Fishing! What kind of work is fishing for a gell? I'm sure I never went fishing.

Mrs Tulliver I'd rather have her with her brother and sure of where she is, for she gets up to such mischief. I'm sure the child's half an idiot in some things; I send her upstairs to fetch something and she forgets what she's gone for, an' sits on the floor i' the sunshine plaiting her hair and singing like a Bedlam creatur. You've no idea the trouble I have.

Mrs Glegg Well, that niver ran i' our family, thank God, no more nor a brown skin as makes her look like a gypsy. She's a Tulliver through and through. There's no Dodson there. Eh, Mr Glegg?

Mr Glegg If you say so, dear.

Cut to: the round pool.

Maggie Tom? In my book it says they used to put women under water and if they swam they were witches and were killed and if they drowned and died they weren't witches. But that isn't right, is it?

Tom   Yes it is. Nasty old witches deserve to die.

Cut to: the parlour.

Aunt Pullet *enters, crying copiously, supported by* **Uncle Pullet**.

Mrs Glegg   Now then Sophy, you're late. What's the matter with you?

Mrs Pullet (*eventually*)   She's gone. Died the day before yesterday, an' her legs was as thick as my body. They'd tapped her no end o' times and the water – they say you might ha' swum in it.

Mrs Glegg   Well, it's a mercy she's gone then, whoever she may be.

Mrs Pullet   It's old Mrs Sutton o' the Twentylands.

Mrs Glegg   She's no kin o' yours, then, nor much acquaintance as I iver heared of.

Mrs Pullet   She's so much acquaintance as I've seen her legs when they was like bladders.

Mrs Tulliver   Now, you sit here, dear. There.

She exits.

Mrs Glegg   Sophy, I wonder at you, fretting and injuring your health about people as don't belong to you. That was never the way in our family.

Mrs Tulliver (*entering with a large, frilly doll – Lucy*)   And look who's here to complete our little gathering.

Mrs Glegg   Ah, Lucy. And how are you? Don't you come and kiss your Aunt Glegg? Whatever is the matter now, Sophy?

Mrs Pullet   I can't look at her without thinking of our poor dead Sister Deane. To think she should ha' gone so young.

Mrs Tulliver   But she doesn't look a bit like her mother. I'm sure she's more like me, for Sister Deane was sallow.

Mrs Glegg   But she knows how to hold her tongue like her mother did.

Mrs Tulliver   Oh yes. It's no trouble having her visit. I can sit her on a stool for hours together and not hear a peep from her. Such a pretty little thing.

Mrs Pullet   I think I'm ready to take my bonnet off, Pullet. Did you see as the cap-box was put out?

He hands the box to his wife, who ceremoniously removes her bonnet while her sisters look on.

Mrs Tulliver   What a bonnet. I'll try it on later, if I may.

Mrs Pullet   Pullet payed for it. He said I was to have the best bonnet at Garam Church . . .

Mr Pullet   Let the next best be whose it would.

Mrs Pullet (*on the verge of tears*)   And to think I may never wear it twice; who knows?

Cut to: the round pool.

Tom   Look, look, Maggie. You've caught one. Oh, Magsie, you little duck! You little duck!

The fish is hauled in. **Maggie** *is overcome with joy.* **Tom** *gives it a hefty whack on the ground in order to kill it and hands it to* **Maggie** *at the very moment she notices* **Lucy** –

Maggie   *Lucy!*

She throws the fish and it lands with a slap in the middle of the parlour, causing a great flurry of panic.

Mrs Glegg   God bless us!

Tom *and* **Maggie** *descend.*

Maggie   Lucy! I didn't know you were coming today. We caught a fish.

Mrs Glegg   Heyday! (*Silence falls.*) Do little boys and gells come into a room without taking notice o' their uncles and aunts? That wasn't the way when I was a little gell.

Mrs Tulliver   Go and speak to your aunts and uncles, my dears. And don't touch Lucy, your hands aren't clean.

Maggie *and* **Tom** *sidle towards* **Aunt Glegg**.

Mrs Glegg (*loudly, as if they are deaf*)   Well, and how do you do? And I hope you're good children, are you?

She takes hold of their hands, very tightly and they are forced to kiss her.

Look up, Tom, look up. Put your hair behind your ears, Maggie, and keep your frock on your shoulders.

Mrs Pullet   Well, my dears, you grow wonderful fast. I doubt they'll outgrow their strength, Bessy. I think the gell has too much hair. It isn't good for her health. It's that as makes her so brown, I shouldn't wonder.

Mr Tulliver *enters just in time to hear this remark*.

Mr Tulliver   There's nothing wrong with the child. She's healthy enough. There's red wheat as well as white, for that matter, and some like the dark grain best. But I've told Bessy to have the child's hair cut, so it lies smooth.

Mr Glegg   Afternoon, neighbour Tulliver.

Mr Tulliver   Afternoon to you all.

Mrs Tulliver (*quietly to* **Maggie**)   Go and brush your hair – do, for shame. I told you to be back early to change, you know I did.

Mr Tulliver   I see you're all here.

Mrs Glegg   We were all invited, weren't we?

Mr Tulliver   Well, little Lucy, is your father not with you then?

Mrs Tulliver   Busy at Guest and Co., I'm afraid.

Mr Tulliver   That's a shame now, isn't it? I would have liked your father to hear what I've got to say.

Mrs Glegg   And we won't do, I suppose?

Maggie *beckons* **Tom** *to the attic. He goes*.

Mr Tulliver   You'll do well enough. And now's as good a time as any.

Mrs Tulliver   Can't it wait until after tea, dear heart?

Mr Tulliver   You wanted me to tell'em, Bessy, so I'll tell
'em and eat the better for't. I've settled to send Tom to a Mr
Stelling, a parson, down at King's Lorton. Parsons make the
best schoolmasters and this fellow is the sort o' man I want.

Cut to: the attic.

Tom   There's no time to play at anything before tea.

Maggie *takes a pair of scissors out of her pocket.*

Tom   What are they for?

She answers by seizing a handful of her hair and cutting it.

Oh no, Maggie. You'll catch it now. (*Snip.*) Oh no, you'd
better not cut off any more.

Maggie   I don't care. Do the back. Do the back.

Tom, *giggling now, takes the scissors and snips the back. He looks at
her and collapses in laughter, rolling around and clutching his stomach.*

Tom   You should see what you look like. Look at yourself
in the glass. You look like the idiot we throw our nut shells to
at school.

Maggie (*hearing the boom of a deaf rage*)   I do not.

Tom   You do, you do. Idiot. You'll have to come
downstairs now. Oh no . . .

Maggie (*stamping and pushing him*)   Don't laugh at me.

Tom   Now then, spitfire. What did you cut it for, then? I'm
going for my tea.

Maggie   Don't go, Tom, please.

Tom   Idiot.

He runs downstairs. **Maggie**'s *deaf rage has risen. She goes to the
mirror and peers at herself and sobs and grabs her fetish and hurls it
against the wall.*

Cut to: the parlour.

Mrs Pullet   I hear Lawyer Wakem is sending his son – the
deformed boy, to a clergyman.

Mr Tulliver   The very same. Wakem's as big a scoundrel as Old Harry ever made, but he knows the length of every man's foot. Tell me who's Wakem's butcher, and I'll tell you where to get your meat.

Mrs Glegg   It 'ud be a fine deal better for some people if they let the lawyers alone.

Mr Glegg   You'll have to pay a swinging half-yearly bill, then, Tulliver?

Mr Tulliver   A cool hundred a year, that's all. But it's an investment, you know. Tom's eddication 'ull be so much capital to him. Eh, Tom?

Mr Glegg   Ay, there's something in that. 'What land is gone and money's spent, Then learning is most excellent.' but us that have got no learning had better keep our money, eh neighbour Pullet?

Mrs Glegg   Mr Clegg, I wonder at you. It's very unbecoming in a man o' your age and belongings to be making a joke when you see your own kin going headlongs to ruin.

At this moment, **Maggie** *appears in the doorway.*

Mrs Tulliver *see her and utters a little cry.*

Mr Glegg   Heyday! What little girl's this? I don't think I know her. It must be a little gypsy child from the common.

Mr Tulliver (*laughing*)   Why, she's gone and cut her hair off herself. Did you ever know such a little hussy as it is?

Mr Pullet   Why, little miss, you've made yourself look very funny.

Mrs Glegg   Fie, for shame. Little gells as cut their own hair should be whipped and fed on bread and water.

Mrs Pullet   She's certainly like a gypsy now. I doubt it'll stand in her way i' life to be so brown.

Mrs Tulliver   She's a naughty child, as'll break her mother's heart.

Maggie *begins to cry. Her father goes to her.*

Mr Tulliver   Come, come, my wench, never mind. You was i' the right to cut it off if it plagued you. Give over crying now.

Mrs Glegg   Spoiling the child like that will be the ruin of her. Just as bringin' the boy up above his fortin' will be the ruin of him.

Mr Tulliver (*flaring up*)   I don't need you to tell me how to raise my own youngsters.

Maggie *goes to* **Tom** *for comfort. He pulls her hair*.

Tom   Idiot.

Maggie *runs out*.

Mrs Glegg   O, I say nothing. My advice has never been asked for and I don't give it.

Mrs Tulliver   It'll be the first time then. It's the only thing you're over-ready at giving.

Mrs Glegg   I've been over-ready at lending, then. There's folks I've lent money to as perhaps I shall repent o' lending money to kin.

Mrs Tulliver   Sister, can I get you some almonds and raisins?

Mrs Glegg   Bessy, I'm sorry for you. It's poor work talking o' almonds and raisins.

Mrs Pullet   Lors, sister Glegg, don't be so quarrelsome. It's very bad among sisters.

Mrs Glegg   Indeed it is bad, when one sister invites another to her house o' purpose to quarrel with her.

Mr Tulliver   I should never want to quarrel with any woman if she kept her place.

Mrs Glegg   My place! You wouldn't have the chance to stand there abusing me, if there hadn't been them in our family who married worse than they might ha' done.

Mr Tulliver   My family's as good as yours, and better, for it hasn't got a damned ill-tempered woman in it.

Mrs Glegg   Well. I don't know whether you think it's a fine thing to sit by and hear me swore at, Mr Glegg, but I'm not going to stay a minute longer in this house. You may take the gig home. I will walk.

She leaves.

Mr Glegg (*following*)   Dear heart, dear heart. It's almost dark.

Mrs Tulliver   Mr Tulliver, how could you talk so?

Mr Tulliver   Let her go. And the sooner the better. We'll eat our tea now, Bessy. Some of us are hungry as have done a day's work. Go and fetch your sister from the attic, Tom.

Tom *runs up the stairs, calling 'Maggie'.*

Mrs Tulliver   Sister Pullet, do you think you should go after her and try to pacify her?

Mrs Pullet   I don't know what could pacify her in such a mood.

Mr Tulliver   Leave her, I say. She won't be trying to domineer over me again, in a hurry.

Tom (*returning*)   She isn't there.

Mrs Tulliver   Where is she then?

Mrs Pullet *bursts into tears.*

Scene Five

Somewhere on the road to the common, **Maggie** *is running. It is starting to get dark. A* **Man** *enters in front of her. She sees him and stops. He looks like a gypsy. He approaches.*

Man   Have you got a copper, to give a poor man?

Maggie   I haven't got any money.

Man   What? Nothing at all?

Maggie   My uncle Pullet usually gives me sixpence, but he didn't this time. I've got my silver thimble. You can have that. (*She hands it to him.*)

Man   Thank you kindly. And where are you off to, pretty lady?

Maggie   To the gypsies on the common. I've run away.

Man   Have you now? That's interesting.

Maggie   Everyone says I'm a gypsy really. I'm going to live with them and I think they'll make me their queen when they find out how much I know. I'm going to teach them how to read. (*The* **Man** *starts to laugh.*) I'm not an idiot. I just cut my hair.

Man   Oh, no, I'm sure you're not an idiot, your Majesty. And you know which way to go, do you? To find the gypsies.

Maggie   Yes . . . well, I thought I did.

Man   Give me your hand, then, and I'll take you to 'em. I'm going that way myself and I'm sure they'll be very grateful to me for bringing them their queen. (*He holds out his hand to her.*) Your Majesty . . . (**Maggie** *hesitates.*) Your Majesty . . .

Maggie *is about to take his hand, but as she looks at him the lights grow dark and there is a strange red glow around him and he gradually takes the shape of the* **Blacksmith** *who is the devil, and his leathern apron and his arms akimbo and a great laugh. He grabs her and she screams and doesn't stop screaming until* **Mr Tulliver** *has entered and taken her in his arms and the devil has gone.*

Maggie (*sobbing*)   Father.

Mr Tulliver   You mustn't think o' running away from father. What 'ud father do without his little wench?

Maggie   Father . . . I saw the devil.

Mr Tulliver   I know, I know. But father 'll take your part, Maggie. Always remember that. Father 'll take your part.

He carries her back to the parlour and sits down and rocks her. **Tom** *and* **Mrs Tulliver** *gather round.*

She's sleeping now.

Mrs Tulliver   She must have been running for hours.

Mr Tulliver Now you listen to me, both of you; I won't have a single word said to her about this, d'you understand? No teasing and no harsh words. Eh, Tom?

Tom Yes, Father.

Mr Tulliver I want you to be good to your sister. For she feels things. And she loves you very much.

Tom Father? You wouldn't want me to go to school with Wakem's son, would you?

Mr Tulliver It doesn't matter much. The lad's a poor mismade creatur. Takes after his dead mother in the face. Don't you learn anything bad of him, that's all.

Scene Six

Music.

Maggie *and* **Tom** *are holding hands, staring at the river. The air is full of the sound of the water rushing through the mill wheel.*

After a moment, **Maggie** *turns to* **Tom** *and kisses him.*

Tom *takes his place at his desk in the schoolroom.* **Maggie** *sits cross-legged and reads her book.* **Mr Stelling** *enters.* **Tom** *is gazing dreamily towards* **Maggie**.

Mr Stelling '. . . sunt etiam volucrum . . .' Yes? Sunt etiam volucrum . . . (*Suddenly rapping the desk with his stick.*) Tulliver.

Tom Sir?

Mr Stelling Go on please. (**Tom** *cannot begin.*) This is not good enough. Not good enough at all. What are you thinking about, Tulliver?

Tom I . . . I don't know, sir.

Mr Stelling You feel no interest in what you are doing, sir. Inability to understand is one thing, but plain indifference is quite another. I will not tolerate it. Now. Let us try again – Sunt etiam volucrum . . .

There are tears gathering in **Tom**'s *eyes. He scratches the side of his face in a vain attempt to hide them.*

Tom   Sunt etiam volucrum . . . ut ostrea . . .

Mr Stelling   No.

Tom   Ut . . .

Mr Stelling   No. (*Losing patience.*) Sunt etiam volucrum ceu passer, hirundo . . .

Tom   Sunt etiam volucrum ceu passer hirundo. Sunt etiam volucrum ceu passer hirundo.

Mr Stelling *goes.* **Tom** *charges about the stage. He is angry and frustrated. He runs to the garden and picks up a stick and beats everything in sight.*

Phillip *enters and sits down with a sketchpad and pencil. He begins to draw.*

Tom *watches him suspiciously for several moments, until his curiosity gets the better of him and he approaches.*

Tom (*looking at* **Phillip**'s *drawings*)   That's a donkey with paniers. And that's a spaniel. I wish I could draw like that. I'm going to learn drawing this half.

Phillip   You can do it without learning. I never learnt. You just have to look carefully at things and draw them again and again.

Pause.

Tom   I hate Latin, do you?

Phillip   I don't really care about it.

Tom   But have you got into the Propria quae maribus yet?

Phillip   I've finished all the grammar.

Tom   So you won't have the same lessons as me?

Phillip   No. But I'll help you, if you like. I'd be glad to.

Tom (*after taking this in*)   I don't see why we have to learn Latin anyway.

Phillip   It's part of a gentleman's education. You can study what you like eventually and forget your Latin. That's what most people do.

Tom   That's what I'll do. But I won't study. I'll buy a horse and ride round my land like my father does.

Phillip   Do you like Greek history? I do. I would like to have been a Greek and fought the Persians and then have come home and written tragedies or have been listened to by everybody for my wisdom, like Socrates, and died a grand death.

Tom   Were the Greeks fighters? Are there stories like Attila the Hun in the Greeks?

Phillip   Yes. Lots.

Tom   But are they all in Greek?

Phillip   I've got them in English too. You can read them.

Tom   I don't like reading.

Phillip   I'll tell you them, then. As many as you want.

Pause.

Tom   Do you love your father?

Phillip (*blushing slightly*)   Yes, don't you love yours?

Scene Seven

In the garden, a week later. **Tom** *runs in and throws himself on the ground.* **Phillip** *enters, wielding a stick.*

Tom   Come on! What happens now?

Phillip   Now Odysseus takes the burning pike and thrusts it into the Cyclops' eye.

Tom   No he doesn't.

Phillip   Yes he does. And the Cyclops roars with pain.

Tom   But I'm a big giant and you're just a tiny little man.

Phillip   Yes, but you're asleep because I've plied you with wine.

Tom   I wouldn't have drunk it.

Phillip   You did drink it, and then I escape with my men because you're blind.

Tom   No you don't.

Phillip   Yes I do.

Tom (*sitting up*)   I don't want to do this story any more.

Phillip   All right. It was you who asked for it.

Pause.

Tom (*suddenly making a grab for the stick*)   Right, I'm Odysseus now, and you're the Cyclops.

Phillip *topples to the ground.* **Tom** *goes to help him.*

Phillip   Get away! You big lumbering idiot.

Tom   If I'm a lumbering idiot, you're an imp – a mean little imp and if you weren't no better than a girl, I'd hit you. And I'm an honest man's son and your father's a rogue. Everybody says so.

Phillip (*tearful*)   Well you're no better than a cart-horse, Tulliver. You're not fit to talk to a cart-horse.

He leaves. **Tom** *is angry and upset. Suddenly* **Maggie** *is there.*

Tom   Maggie! How long can you stay? Till Christmas?

Maggie   Two weeks.

Tom   Yes!

He grabs her round the waist and they dance round and round until they are dizzy. **Phillip** *is watching with curiosity from the shadows.* **Maggie** *catches sight of him. He goes.*

Maggie   There was somebody there, then.

Tom   A creature with a hump? That's Wakem; the lawyer's son. And you're not to talk to him or go anywhere near him because he's mean and crafty. Now mind you don't. Has my father beaten his father yet?

Maggie   I don't know. But he talks a lot about it and goes red in the face.

Tom   We'll show him.

Maggie (*looking about*)   Look at all these books. I'd love to have this many books.

Tom   You couldn't read one of them. They're in Latin.

Maggie   I can read the back of that one. *History of the Decline and Fall of the Roman Empire*.

Tom   Well, what does that mean? You don't know.

Maggie   I could soon find out.

Tom   How?

Maggie   I could open it. (*She picks up another.*)

Tom   You can't understand that one.

Maggie (*opening it and trying to read*)   'Nomen non creskens genittivo . . .'

Tom   'Creskens genittivo! Creskens genittivo!' It's 'Crescens genitivo.'

Maggie   So? I could do it if I'd learnt what you'd learnt.

Tom   No you couldn't. Girls can't do Latin. 'Creskens genittivo!'

Maggie   I could work it out.

Tom   No you couldn't.

Mr Stelling *enters*. **Phillip** *hovers behind him*.

Mr Stelling   Ah. Here you both are. Impressing her with your learning, are you, Tulliver?

Maggie   Mr Stelling? Couldn't I do Latin and all Tom's lessons if you were to teach me?

Tom   Girls can't do Latin, can they, sir?

Mr Stelling   Well . . . They can pick up a little of everything, I daresay. They've got a great deal of superficial cleverness; but they couldn't go far into anything. They're quick and shallow. Come along now. Roast beef for dinner.

Which would you rather decline, Tulliver – roast beef, or the Latin for it?

Tom (*hesitating*)   Roast beef, sir.

Mr Stelling (*chuckling*)   Roast beef, eh? Roast beef.

He goes.

Tom   Ha, ha, Miss Maggie. It's not so good to be quick after all. Ha, ha, Miss Maggie.

Maggie   Shut up.

Tom   Ha, ha, Miss Maggie. Ha, ha, Miss Maggie.

She closes her ears. A deaf rage has begun. **Tom** *goes.*

Scene Eight

Phillip *stands in the middle of the schoolroom and begins to sing.* **Maggie** *gradually comes out of her rage and listens to him. She is enchanted. She moves nearer. He stops.*

Maggie   Don't.

Phillip   What?

Maggie   Stop.

Phillip   Maggie?

Maggie   Yes.

Phillip   I'm Phillip.

Maggie   It's beautiful.

Phillip   I like to sing.

Maggie   At Christmas, angels come and sing outside our window. Tom says it's just the parish choir but I know it's angels.

Phillip   I'm sure it is. You don't look like Tulliver's sister.

Maggie   I'm dark. Like a . . . like my father. Do you know Latin?

Phillip   Yes. And Greek. You would if you were taught.

Maggie   Will you teach me?

Phillip   Won't you be going to school?

Maggie   I'll go to boarding school with my cousin Lucy. But we won't do Latin. I think it's sewing mostly.

Phillip   I'll teach you what I can. You have dark eyes. They're not like other eyes. They seem as if they are trying to speak . . .

Maggie   What do they say?

Phillip   They are trying to speak kindly. I don't like other people to look at me, but I like you to look at me.

Maggie   I will always look at you. I am so, so sorry for you. (**Phillip** *turns away.* **Maggie** *realises her mistake.*) But you are very clever, and you can sing like an angel. I wish you were my brother as well as Tom. You would stay at home with me when Tom went out and you would teach me everything.

Phillip   You'll go away soon and forget about me. And when you're grown up, you'll see me and you won't take any notice of me.

Maggie   I won't forget you. I never forget anything and I think about everybody when I'm away from them. (*Pause.*) Would you like me to kiss you, as I kiss Tom? I will if you like.

Phillip   Yes, very much: nobody kisses me.

Maggie *puts an arm around his neck and kisses him earnestly.*

Maggie   I will always remember you, and kiss you when I see you again, even if it's a very long time.

Maggie *glances round and finds* **Tom** *looking at her from the doorway. He goes. The lights dim.*

The crowds have gathered on the upper platform. They repeat some of the actions used in ducking the witch.

Scene Nine

In **Maggie**'s *room at boarding school.* **Lucy** *enters. (She is real now, but dressed identically to the doll.)*

She combs **Maggie**'s *hair and dresses it in a grown-up style. The two girls sit together and begin to sew.*

Tom *enters. He is dressed as a man now, in tails and stand-up collar. He looks very serious and pale.*

Tom   Maggie. Lucy.

Maggie   Tom. What are you doing here?

She runs and kisses him but he hardly responds.

Tom   Maggie, we're to go home immediately.

Maggie   What's wrong?

Tom   Father has lost the lawsuit. We are ruined.

Maggie   Lost . . . (**Lucy** *takes her arm.*)

Tom   Father is very ill. The news has . . . He has had a sort of seizure, I think.

Maggie   Is he . . . ?

Tom   Mother says he has been asking for you.

Lucy   I'll get your things. Shall I come with you?

Tom   No, Lucy. Thank you. I think it would better if just Maggie and I . . . (*He is overcome.* **Maggie** *hugs him.*)

Lucy   If there's anything I can do to help, you will tell me, won't you? Anything at all.

She goes, leaving brother and sister alone.

Scene Ten

Music.

At the mill. As **Maggie** *and* **Tom** *enter the parlour, they see the* **Bailiff** *walking about the room, picking up objects, and examining them.*

Bailiff   Good day to you.

Tom   Good day. (*Pause.*) Where is my mother? Mrs
Tulliver?

Bailiff   I don't rightly know. She left me here ten minutes
since.

Maggie (*whispering to* **Tom**)   Who is that?

Tom *begins looking for his mother.*

Tom   Mother! Mother!

Maggie   Who is that, Tom? That's not Dr Turnbull.

Tom   It's the bailiff. Mother!

*They hear the sound of someone sobbing and go towards it. It is coming
from a wardrobe.* **Mrs Tulliver** *is inside, sitting amongst her linen
and 'chany', quite distraught.*

Mrs Tulliver   Oh, my boy, my boy. To think as I should
live to see this day. We're ruined. Everything is to be sold up.
We shall be beggars, we must go to the workhouse. To think
as your father should ha' married me to bring me to this.

Maggie   Mother, what's happening? Where is my father?

Mrs Tulliver   To think o' these cloths as I spun myself,
and I marked 'em so as nobody ever saw such marking – and
they're all to be sold and go into strange people's houses and
I meant 'em for you. I wanted you to have all this pattern.
Maggie could have had the large check, it never looks good
when the dishes are on it.

Tom   But surely my aunts won't let them be sold, Mother.
Haven't you sent to them?

Mrs Tulliver   Yes. Directly they put the bailies in. But I
know they'll none of them take my chany for they all found
fault with 'em when I bought 'em 'cause o' the small gold
sprig between the flowers. And I bought 'em wi' my own
money as I'd saved ever since I was turned fifteen and the
silver teapot too. (**Maggie** *begins to hear the boom of a deaf rage.*)
And I did say to him times and times, 'Whativer you do,
don't go to law.' And I've had to sit by while my own fortin's

been spent. You'll have niver a penny, my boy, but it isn't your poor mother's fault.

Tom   Don't fret, Mother. I'll get money. I'll get a situation of some sort.

Mrs Tulliver   Bless you, my boy. I shouldn't ha' minded so much if we could have kept the things with my name on.

Maggie   Stop it. How can you talk like that? As if you only cared for things with your name on? Don't you care for my father? Tom . . . Tom, you shouldn't let anyone find fault with my father. Where is he? Where?

She runs to find him. **Tom** *and her mother follow.*

Mr Tulliver *is lying silently on a bed.* **Maggie** *falls on her knees beside him.*

Mrs Tulliver   Dr Turnbull says it was a stroke, brought on by the . . . the shock. He fell from his horse. They can't say how long it may be before he recovers. Perhaps he may never . . .

Tom   Don't, Mother.

Mrs Tulliver   But he has roused himself a couple o' times. He's asked for you, Maggie. So there's hope, they say.

Maggie   Father . . . Father, it's Maggie. I'm here now. I won't leave you. I will never leave you.

Scene Eleven

In the parlour. **Aunt** *and* **Uncle Glegg**, **Aunt** *and* **Uncle Pullet**, **Mrs Tulliver**, **Maggie** *and* **Tom** *have gathered,* **Mrs Tulliver**, *half-deranged by the thought of losing her possessions, is intent on laying out a tea party on the floor.*

Mrs Tulliver   Now, sister, you must sit here, and Sophy, you must sit here and then Lucy . . . Lucy goes there . . .

Tom   Lucy isn't here, Mother.

Mrs Tulliver   Not here? But there's a cup for her. Oh . . . oh . . . well then, I shall go there and . . . no . . .

Mrs Glegg   Bankrupt. There's never been such disgrace in the family, I'm sure.

Mrs Pullet (*sobbing*)   I doubt he's got the water on his brain. It's much if he ever gets up again.

Mrs Glegg   You must bring your mind to your circumstances, Bessy, and be thinking whether you shall get so much as a flock bed to lie on and a stool to sit on. And if you do, it'll be because your friends have bought 'em. You're dependent upon us for everything now.

Mrs Pullet   And if he does he'll most like be childish, as Mr Carr was, poor man. They fed him with a spoon as if he'd been a babby.

Mrs Glegg   Sophy! You do talk of people's complaints till it's quite indecent.

Mrs Tulliver   Shall I be mother? Yes, I think I will. What a very fine pourer this teapot is. Very fine. Everyone always says so.

Tom   Mother, don't worry about the tea.

Mrs Tulliver   But we're having a party, Tom. Now, who takes sugar?

Mr Pullet   Yes please.

Mrs Glegg   Heyday. I didn't come here for tea, sugar or no sugar. If we aren't come for one to hear what the other 'ull do to save a sister from the parish, I shall go home.

Mrs Pullet   Well, I was here yesterday and looked at all Bessy's linen and things and told her I'd buy in the spotted table-cloths. But I can't take the teapot, for what would I do with two silver teapots?

Mrs Tulliver   Table-cloth. Did somebody say table-cloth? I've a great many table-cloths. This isn't my best one by any means.

Mrs Glegg   Bessy, do be quiet! What use is it talking o' table-cloths when the roof above your head is to be sold?

Mrs Tulliver   Sold?

Mrs Glegg   Yes, sold. The mill, the land, the whole lot. Sold.

Mrs Tulliver   Now, who would like milk? I shall pass my chany jug round. What a pretty pattern, don't you think?

Mrs Pullet (*sobbing*)   They shall have to go to the workhouse.

Mrs Glegg   There was never any of our family in the workhouse, and never will be. We must settle on what's to become of 'em.

Mr Glegg   Well, young sir, now's the time to let us see the good of your learning – 'When land is gone and money's spent, Then learning . . .'

Mrs Glegg   Now's the time to bear the fruits of his father's disgrace and bring his mind to fare hard and to work hard. And his sister too, must make up her mind to be humble and work.

Mrs Pullet   They'll be no servants to wait on her any more.

Tom (*seeing* **Maggie** *is about to speak*)   Be quiet, Maggie. Aunt, if it is a disgrace to the family that we should be sold up, and I do feel the disgrace, wouldn't it be better to prevent it altogether? If you and Aunt Pullet think of leaving any money to me and Maggie, wouldn't it be better to give it now, and save my mother from parting with her furniture?

Pause.

Mr Glegg   Ay, ay. What young man is this, then?

Tom   I could work and pay the interest you would lose.

Mr Glegg   Well done, Tom! Well done.

Mrs Glegg   Yes, Mr Glegg. It's pleasant work for you to be giving my money away, I'm sure. My money, as I've saved myself and it's to go and be squandered on them as have had the same chance as me, only they've been wicked and wasteful.

Maggie *is going into a deaf rage.*

Mrs Pullet   La, Jane, how fiery you are. I'm sure you'll have the blood in your head and have to be cupped.

Mrs Tulliver (*offering tea*)   This one is yours, and this one is yours and . . . Oh dear, I'm getting muddled . . . and . . .

Tom   Mother . . .

Mrs Glegg   Take it away. You're a disgrace making tea when . . . it's a disgrace . . . Disgraceful.

Maggie   Why do you come here, then? Interfering and shouting and . . . Keep away from us and don't come finding fault with my father. He's better than any of you, he's kind. Tom and I don't ever want to have any of your money. We'd rather not have it. We'll do without you.

Pause. **Mrs Tulliver** *sits down abruptly.* **Tom** *looks angry.*

Mrs Glegg   I've said over and over again – years ago I've said – 'Mark my words, that child 'ull come to no good: there isn't a bit of our family in her.'

Scene Twelve

The following day. **Maggie** *is in the parlour.* **Tom** *enters, looking thoroughly miserable. He ignores* **Maggie**.

Maggie   Did you speak to Uncle Deane? Will he find you a situation?

Tom   I don't know.

Maggie   But did he speak kindly?

Tom   I don't care about him speaking kindly, I just want a job. All that wasted time with Latin and . . . he says I've had all the rough work taken out of me. He makes out I'm good for nothing. He doesn't even seem to think I'm fit to work on a wharf or in a warehouse. But I am. I'll do it. He says I must learn bookkeeping and calculation.

Maggie   If only I was Lucy Bertram in Walter Scott's novel. She was taught bookkeeping by double entry, after the Italian method. Then I could teach you.

Tom   Teach. Yes. You teach, that's always the tone you take.

Maggie   I was only joking, Tom.

Tom   But it's always the same. You're always setting yourself up above me and everyone else. You shouldn't have spoken to my aunts like that. You shouldn't speak to anyone like that. You should leave it to me to take care of my mother and you and not put yourself forward. I can judge things better than you. It's time you started to learn that.

Maggie (*fighting a deaf rage*)   I don't put myself above you. You often think I'm being conceited when I don't mean to be. I know you behave better than me. I know. But I don't see why you have to be so harsh.

Tom   I'm always kind to you and I always will be but you must listen to what I say and act on it.

Music.

Maggie *runs to the attic. She is sobbing and the rage is booming in her ears. Gradually, she calms and goes to the mirror. She looks at herself, trying perhaps, to see herself the way others see her. She feels the weight of* **Tom**'s *words and knows she will have to change. Life isn't how she thought it was. She was wrong.*

Gradually a new **Maggie** *looks back at her — a more subdued, introspective* **Maggie**, *with her hair tied back, who steps out from the mirror and takes the* **First Maggie** *in her arms and comforts her.*

Second Maggie   Don't look for love, Maggie. There is no love in life, and no happiness.

They cry together.

Scene Thirteen

Music.

Second Maggie, **Tom** *and* **Mrs Tulliver** *huddle round* **Mr Tulliver**'s *sick-bed. The bailiff begins to auction the furniture and all* **Mrs Tulliver**'s *household goods. Each item is named and*

*followed by a cry of 'sold', at which the Tullivers shudder. Then the
item is placed at the back of the stage. As more items are sold the cry of
'sold' becomes louder and the shudder more pronounced. Eventually, all
that is left in the parlour is the family Bible. A large dust sheet is
thrown over everything at the back.*

Scene Fourteen

Mr Wakem *is standing in the parlour, looking about with interest.*
Mrs Tulliver *enters. She is shaky and a little confused.*

Mrs Tulliver   Yes? Can I help you? The sale is over . . .
quite over. Yes, over, as you can tell, and I don't see how you
can have any right now to be standing with your boots on
in . . .

Wakem   My parlour? My name is Wakem. I'm the new
owner of the mill.

Mrs Tulliver   You have . . . bought . . .

Wakem   You must be Mrs Tulliver.

Mrs Tulliver   Yes. I'm . . . perhaps you remember me –
Miss Elizabeth Dodson as was . . . Father was close friends
with Squire Darleigh, and we allays went to the dances there
– the Miss Dodsons. Perhaps you remember . . . perhaps we
danced . . .

Wakem   I believe your husband is still poorly, madam.

Mrs Tulliver   Yes, sir.

Wakem   Should he recover his health, I think it only fair
that I offer him the position of manager. That way you and
your family may stay on here. He must be made to
understand, however, that he would be answerable to me. I
will wait two weeks for your answer. I trust that appears
reasonable. Good day.

Mrs Tulliver   Reasonable . . . yes, thank you . . .

He leaves. **Mrs Tulliver** *leaves.*

Tom *enters, shortly followed by* **Maggie**. *The empty room is appalling. They are silent for several moments, just looking at the places where things once stood.*

Maggie   Is this all? Where are the books? There's only your old school books here. I thought Uncle Glegg was going to buy the books.

Tom   Don't start, Maggie . . .

Maggie   I won't. (*With strange resignation.*) I won't.

Scene Fifteen

Tom *and* **Maggie** *help* **Mr Tulliver** *into the parlour. He is still very weak. He looks about him at the emptiness.* **Mrs Tulliver** *cannot look at him, so strong is her anger.*

Mr Tulliver   Ah . . . they've sold me up then . . . they've sold me up. Am I a bankrupt? I see. (*Silence.*) I see now.

Mrs Tulliver *starts to cry.*

Mr Tulliver   Poor Bessy. Don't bear me any ill will . . . we promised one another for better or worse.

Mrs Tulliver   But I never thought it'ud be as worse as this.

Tom   Don't, Mother.

Mrs Tulliver   No, that's right; tell me not to speak . . . that's been the way all my life.

Mr Tulliver   Let her be. What do you mean, Bessy?

Mrs Tulliver   It's all Wakem's. He says you may stay here and manage the business and have thirty shillings a week and a horse to ride to market.

Pause.

Mr Tulliver   It's all Wakem's then? This world's too many for me.

Mrs Tulliver   I want to stay here.

Tom   Father, I don't think you should submit to be under
Wakem. My Uncle Deane has found me a situation – I'll get
a pound a week and you can do something else when you're
well.

Pause.

Mr Tulliver   Fetch the old Bible. And a pen. (**Tom** *and*
Maggie *obey*.) You've got a right to say as I've brought you
into trouble, Bessy. But there'll be the same grave made for us
and we mustn't be bearing one another any ill will.

Tom   What am I to write, Father?

Mr Tulliver   Write as your father, Edward Tulliver, took
service under John Wakem, the man as had ruined him,
because I wanted to make my wife what amends I could and
I wanted to die in the old place . . .

Tom   No, Father . . .

Mr Tulliver   But then write as I don't forgive Wakem,
and for all I'll serve him honest, I wish evil may befall him. I
wish he might be punished with shame till his own son 'ud
like to forget him. Then write as you'll remember what
Wakem's done to your father and you'll make him and his
feel it, if ever the day comes. Make 'em feel it. And sign your
name, Thomas Tulliver.

Maggie   Father, you shouldn't make Tom write that.

Tom   Be quiet, Maggie. I shall write it.

Scene Sixteen

Music. **Maggie** *is sitting outside the mill. It is a beautiful summer's
day. The birds are singing, the water rushing. She is trying to learn
Latin from one of* **Tom**'*s old school books, but her heart isn't in it. She
is deeply sad. She gazes out at the fields.* **First Maggie** *appears,
dressed as she was when a child, with her gypsy's hair. She runs and
jumps. She takes* **Maggie**'*s book from her and makes it a butterfly.*
Maggie *smiles but then takes the book back again and goes on with the
grammar.* **First Maggie** *goes.*

Bob Jakin *enters. He is wearing an oil-skin cap and a plush blue waistcoat and carries a pack. He stops in front of her.*

Bob   Sarvant, Miss Maggie.

Maggie   Bob. Bob Jakin.

Bob   Ay, ay, Bob Jakin it must be if there was so many Bob's as let you loose i' the mill and showed you where the spiders lived.

Maggie   How well you look. Will you come in?

Bob   No thank you, miss. I'll not stop long.

Tom *arrives home from work.*

Maggie   Tom, look. It's Bob Jakin.

Bob   Mr Tom.

Tom (*unsmilingly*)   Hello, Bob. What can I do for you?

Bob   Why, nothing, Mr Tom. I've had a bit o' luck lately; I doused a fire at Torry's mill and a genleman came and told me I was a sperrited chap – but I knowed that – but then he gen me ten sovreigns an' that war summat new. Look . . . (*He takes a bag from his pocket.*) There's nine left and I'd like for you to have 'em. They mayn't go fur, but they'll help – if it's true the master's broke.

Pause. **Maggie** *is close to tears.*

Tom   I can't take them. I would be taking your fortune, and they wouldn't do me much good either.

Bob   Wouldn't they? Don't say so 'cause you think I want 'em. I aren't a poor chap.

Tom   No. I don't want to take anything from anybody. But don't think I feel your kindness less because I say no. Let me shake hands with you. (*They do so.*)

Bob   I'll keep 'em then. But you will have summat, now. (*He produces a pile of books bound with string.*) I bought these for you, miss, special-like. They're cram-full o' print. And there's one or two wi' pictures. You will take them, won't you? For they're a weight to carry.

Maggie (*taking them*)   I never knew you were so good, Bob. I don't think anyone ever did such a kind thing for me before.

Bob   I can't believe that, miss. Well, I shall be off.

Tom   Yes. Thank you again, Bob.

Bob   Be seeing you. (*He goes.*)

Pause. **Maggie** *recovers herself.*

Maggie   He seems happy.

Tom   Yes. He does.

Maggie   How were things at the wharf today?

Tom   All right.

He leaves. **Maggie** *puts the books down and sits with her head in her hands.*

First Maggie *appears and runs to the books.*

First Maggie   Are there any with stories in? (*No reply.*) Are there any with stories in?

Second Maggie   I don't want stories.

First Maggie   This one's full of hymns.

Second Maggie   I want to know why.

First Maggie   Why what?

Second Maggie   Why this? This awful . . . miserable, hopeless life. What I would give to change places with Bob, even for a day! Just to walk about and smile and love the world as I used to. I can't bear this. I can't bear it.

First Maggie   We could go. We could dress up as a boy and work on the barges.

Second Maggie   Don't . . .

First Maggie   We could run away.

Second Maggie   To the gypsies?

First Maggie   We could go and find a great man – Walter Scott. We could tell him how miserable we are and show him how well we can read and how much Latin we've learnt . . .

Second Maggie   Be quiet.

First Maggie   And he'd understand that we're special and do something for us . . .

Second Maggie   I said, be quiet.

First Maggie   Why should we be good all the time? It's mother and father's fault. They don't know anything and they don't want to know. And Tom's the worst of all, he tries to make us feel stupid all the time but he's the one who's stupid, he's . . .

Second Maggie   Shut up, shut up, shut up. (*She puts her hand over* **First Maggie**'s *mouth.*) Such wicked thoughts. What kind of demon is inside me, to have such thoughts?

Pause.

First Maggie   Are there any with stories in?

Second Maggie (*taking up the books*)   *Economy of Human Life. Gregory's Letters. The Imitation of Christ* by Thomas à Kempis. I've heard that name. He was a monk, I think.

First Maggie   Let's see. (*She opens it.*) Someone's put marks at the edge of the pages. 'Know that love of thyself doth hurt thee more than anything in the world . . . if thou seekest to enjoy thy own will and pleasure, thou shalt never be quiet or free from care: for in everything somewhat will be wanting and in every place there will be some that will cross thee . . .

Music. **Maggie** *feels a strange thrill of awe.*

Thou oughtest therefore to call to mind the more heavy sufferings of others, that thou mayest the easier bear thy little adversities.'

Second Maggie   Read that again.

First Maggie   'Thou oughtest therefore . . .'

Second Maggie   No. The first part.

First Maggie   'Know that love of thyself doth hurt thee more than anything in the world . . .'

Second Maggie   Give it to me. (*She takes it and turns the page*.) 'I have often said unto thee, and now again I say the same, forsake thyself, resign thyself, and thou shalt enjoy much inward peace and tranquility. Then shall all vain imaginations, evil perturbations . . . evil perturbations and superfluous cares fly away; then shall immoderate fear leave thee, and inordinate love shall die.'

A great light fills the stage and **Maggie** *falls on her knees*.

Thank you . . . thank you.

First Maggie *looks into the light and sees the figure of Thomas à Kempis*.

Scene Seventeen

In the mill. **Maggie** *is on her knees, scrubbing the floor. As she works, she sings a hymn.*

Tom *enters*.

Tom   Maggie. (*She doesn't stop*.) Maggie. You went to the drapers in St Oggs. You asked for plain sewing work.

Maggie   Yes.

Tom   I don't want my sister dong such things. If you have to do some sewing, ask about amongst our aunts. Don't go into St Oggs parading our situation to the world.

Maggie   I do it to help pay the debts.

Tom   I'm aware of that.

Maggie   I see how hard you work, how you save. I wanted there to be more money in the tin box when father counted it.

Tom   Listen to me: I'll take care the debts are paid. There's no need for you to lower youself.

Maggie   But . . . I'm sorry, Tom. I didn't realise it would make you angry. (*She begins to scrub again*.)

Tom   Mother tells me you have started sleeping on the floor.

Maggie   When I feel I deserve to.

Tom   Deserve to?

Maggie   For a penance.

Tom   This is so typical of you. It's excessive. I want it to stop. I want you to start going out and . . .

Maggie   I do go out.

Tom   Yes, you walk in the Red Deeps where no one sees you. We are not so poor that . . .

Maggie   It has nothing to do with our poverty. It has to do with my soul, something you would not . . .

Tom   What?

Maggie   Forgive me, Tom. I will obtain the sewing more quietly in future.

There is the sound of voices in the yard. **Tom** *looks to see who it is.*

Tom   Wakem. There's someone with him.

He leaves. **Maggie** *goes to the window and looks out. She sees a man in the yard. He looks towards her. She immediately recognizes* **Phillip**. *He raises his hat to her. She darts away from the window.*

Maggie   Phillip!

Music. **First Maggie** *enters.*

First Maggie   My Phillip?

She runs to the window and looks out. She waves to **Phillip**. **Second Maggie** *pulls her away.*

First Maggie   I want to see him. I've missed him. He can tell me all about the world like he used to do. (*She goes to the mirror.*) 'You have dark eyes . . .'

Second Maggie (*turning the mirror to the wall*)   Don't.

Scene Eighteen

Maggie *is walking in the Red Deeps.* **Phillip** *appears. He raises his hat, then holds out his hand to her. She takes it.*

Maggie You startled me. I never meet anyone here.

Phillip Forgive me. I needed to see you. I've been watching your house for days to see if you would come out. I followed you.

Maggie I'm glad. I wished very much to have an opportunity of speaking to you. Shall we walk?

They do so. It is as if they are in a dream.

I like the light here. And the Scotch firs. It is so different from the other scenery about.

Phillip Yes. I remember coming here once, as a child.

Maggie I was frightened to come. The Red Deeps . . . I thought all kinds of devils and wild beasts lurked here. (*Pause.*) I have often thought of you.

Phillip Not so often as I have thought of you.

Maggie I wasn't sure you would remember me.

Phillip *takes a miniature case from his pocket and hands it to her.*

Phillip It's a picture I painted of you on the last day of your visit. In the study . . .

Maggie I remember my hair like that, and that pink frock. I really was like a gypsy. I suppose I still am. Am I how you expected me to be?

Phillip No. You are very much more beautiful.

Pause.

Maggie Phillip, you must go now and we must not see each other again. I wish we could be friends . . . I wish it could have been good and right for us, but it is not. I have lost everything I loved when I was little; the old books went, and Tom is different and my father – it is like death. But that is how it must be. I wanted you to know that if I behave as if I had forgotten you, it is not out of pride or – any bad feeling.

Phillip I know what there is to keep us apart, Maggie. I would always want to obey my father but I will not, cannot obey a wish of his that I do not feel to be right.

Maggie   I don't know . . . I have sometimes thought that I
shouldn't have to give up anything and I've gone on thinking
that until it seems I have no duty at all. But that is an evil
state of mind. I would rather do without anything than make
my father's life harder. He is not at all happy.

Phillip   Neither am I. I am not happy.

Maggie   I am very sorry that you say that. I have a guide
now, Phillip – Thomas à Kempis. Perhaps you have read
him. His words are the only ones that make sense to me. I
have been so much happier since I gave up thinking about
what is easy and pleasant and being discontented because I
couldn't have my own way. Our life is determined for us and
it makes the mind very free when we give up wishing and
only think of bearing what is laid upon us.

Phillip   For goodness sake, Maggie. I can't give up
wishing. How can we give up wishing and longing while we
are thoroughly alive? (*Pause.*) I'm sorry. I have no friend . . .
no one who cares enough about me. If I could only see you
now and then and you would let me talk to you and show me
that you cared for me and that we may always be friends in
our hearts – then I might come to be glad of my life.

Maggie   Oh, Phillip . . .

Phillip   If there is enmity between those who belong to us
we ought to try to mend it with our friendship. You must see
that.

Pause.

Maggie   I can't say either yes or no. I must wait and seek
for guidance.

Phillip   Let me see you here once more. If you can't tell me
when, I will come as often as I can until I do see you.

Maggie   Do so, then. (*Pause. They smile.*) How were you so
sure that I would be the same Maggie?

Phillip   I never doubted you would be the same. I don't
know why I was so sure; I think there must be stores laid up in
our natures that our understandings can make no inventory

of. It's like music; there are certain strains which change my whole attitude of mind. If the effect would last I might be capable of heroisms.

Maggie   I know what you mean – or at least, I used to. I never hear music now except the organ at church.

Phillip   You can have very little that is beautiful in your life. (*Taking a book from his pocket.*) Have this. I've finished with it.

Maggie   I've given up books. Except Thomas à Kempis and The Christian Year and the Bible. (*He offers it again.*) Don't, Phillip.

She walks on quickly.

Phillip   Maggie, don't go without saying goodbye. I can't go on any farther, I think.

Maggie   Of course. Goodbye. What a beautiful thing it seems that God made your heart so that you could care about a strange little girl you only knew for a few weeks. I think you cared more for me than Tom did.

Phillip   You would never love me so well as you love your brother.

Maggie   Perhaps not . . . but then, the first thing I remember in my life is standing with Tom by the side of the Floss, while he held my hand; everything before that is dark to me.

Phillip   I kept that little girl in my heart for five years; didn't I earn some part in her too?

Scene Nineteen

Music. **Maggie** *is in the attic, sewing.* **First Maggie** *appears and heads towards the door.*

Second Maggie   Where are you going?

First Maggie   To the Red Deeps.

Second Maggie   We can't go.

First Maggie   Phillip will be waiting. It's five days now. We should be good to Phillip and make him happy. He was always good to us.

Second Maggie   No.

She starts sewing again. **First Maggie** *sits beside her. Then she moves to the door again.*

Where are you going?

First Maggie   To the Red Deeps.

Second Maggie   We can't go.

First Maggie   But what harm would it do? No one would know.

Second Maggie   It would mean concealment.

First Maggie   But . . .

Second Maggie   No. (*She starts sewing.* **First Maggie** *goes to the door.*) Where are you going?

First Maggie   To the Red Deeps. (*She holds out her hand.*)

Second Maggie (*with sudden resolution*)   Very well.

They go. **Phillip** *is there. His face lights up when he sees her.*

Phillip   Maggie . . .

Maggie   This is the last time, Phillip. I don't like to conceal anything from my family. I won't do it. I know their feelings are wrong and unchristian but it makes no difference. We must part.

Pause.

Phillip   Then stay with me for a while and let us talk together. Will you take my hand? (*She does so. They walk.*)

Phillip   I have begun another painting of you. In oils, this time. You will look like a spirit creeping from one of the fir-trees.

Maggie   Phillip, did you mean it when you said you are unhappy and that your life means nothing to you?

Phillip   Yes.

Maggie But why? You have so much . . . your painting, your music, your books. You can travel . . .

Phillip Oh yes, I have a great number of interests. I flit from one to the other at will. I daresay that would be enough for me if I were like other men. But I am not, am I? The society at St Oggs sickens me. I am sure it is sickened by me. My life sickens me.

Maggie I understand what you mean. Sometimes it seems to me that life is very hard and unbearable. But, Phillip, I think we are only like children, and someone who is wiser is taking care of us.

Phillip Ah yes. You have your guide to show you the way.

Maggie Yes I do. Are you mocking me, Phillip?

Phillip No. I only wonder how long you can go on with this.

Maggie I have found great peace this last year – even joy in subduing my will.

Phillip No you haven't.

Maggie I have resigned myself. I bear everything . . .

Phillip You are not resigned. You are only trying to stupefy yourself. It is stupefaction to shut up all the avenues by which you might engage in life.

Maggie I don't want to engage in life.

Phillip You were so full of life when you were a child. I thought you would be a brilliant woman – all wit and imagination. And it flashes out in your face still – there! But then you draw that veil across.

Maggie Why do you speak so bitterly to me?

Phillip Because I care. I can't bear to see you go on with this self-torture.

Maggie I will have strength given me.

Phillip   No one is given strength to do what is unnatural. You will be thrown into the world someday and then all your needs will assault you like a savage appetite.

Maggie   How dare you shake me in this way? You are a tempter.

Phillip   No, I am not. But love gives insight. Maggie.

Pause. **Maggie** *is confused and shocked.*

Do you really want to get up every day for the rest of your life and have no company but that of your parents, nothing to do but to read your Bible? Day after day. Think about it. (*Pause.*) I suppose you will never agree to see me now. (*Pause.*) What if I came to walk here sometimes, and met you by chance? You would not have agreed to meet me. There would be no concealment in that.

She looks at him. There is some relief in her eyes, but she says nothing. **Phillip** *goes, feeling he has cause for hope.*

The crowd has gathered above. They repeat some of the gestures used in testing the witch.

Maggie *falls to her knees, and begins to pray.* **First Maggie** *enters and tries to interrupt her prayer.* **Second Maggie** *moves away and keeps praying.* **First Maggie** *follows her –* **Second Maggie** *moves. This goes on for some time until she cannot go on with her prayer. She turns to* **First Maggie** *and embraces her.*

Second Maggie   Go then.

First Maggie *runs to* **Phillip** *who is waiting in the Red Deeps. She throws her arms around him. They laugh.*

Phillip   Maggie, you promised you would kiss me when you met me again. Do you remember? You haven't kept your promise yet.

She kisses him. It is the same simple, childish kiss. **Phillip** *looks lovingly at* **Second Maggie***, as he and* **First Maggie** *walk away together, hand in hand. Music.*

Aunt Pullet *steps out of the crowd above and slowly begins to descend.*

Mrs Pullet   Do you know who Lucy was standing next to in church today? Do you know? That poor bent boy – Lawyer Wakem's son. Dear, dear! To think o' the property he's like to have. Phillip, I think his name is – Phillip Wakem. And they say he's very strange and lonely, poor Phillip. I doubt he's going out of his mind, for we never come along the road but he's a-scrambling out o' the trees at the Red Deeps.

Maggie *has blushed deeply. She looks up at* **Tom** *and finds his eyes upon her.*

Scene Twenty

In the Red Deeps. **Phillip** *is singing,* **Maggie** *listens. He finishes.*

Phillip   I have made you sad.

Maggie   It's so beautiful.

Phillip   You inspire me. What is it, Maggie? Don't you like being the tenth Muse?

Maggie   Phillip, I never felt I was right in giving way about seeing you. Though this year has been so precious to me. But now the fear comes upon me strongly again that it will lead to evil.

Phillip   But no evil has come of it.

Maggie   I have started to think about the world again . . . I have impatient thoughts. I grow weary of my home and that cuts me to the heart . . .

Phillip   I love you, Maggie. (*Pause.*) Forgive me. Forget I ever said that.

Maggie   I had not thought of it.

Phillip   You think I am a presumptuous fool.

Maggie   Oh, Phillip. How can you think I have such feelings? I would be grateful for any love. But . . . I had never thought of your being my lover. It seemed so far off, a dream, that I should ever have one.

Phillip   Do you love me?

Maggie   I think I could hardly love anyone better. There is nothing but what I love you for.

Phillip   Then my life will be filled with hope, Maggie. We do belong to each other, always?

Maggie   Yes. I should like us never to part. I should like to make your life very happy.

Phillip   I am waiting for something else – I wonder whether it will come.

She kisses him – a grown-up kiss, this time. **Tom** *appears from the shadows.*

Tom   Do you call this acting the part of a man and a gentleman, sir?

Maggie   Tom . . .

Phillip   What do you mean?

First Maggie *enters and watches in horror.*

Tom   Mean? I'll tell you what I mean. I mean taking advantage of a young girl's foolishness, daring to trifle with the respectability of a family that has an honest name to support.

Phillip   I deny that. I could never trifle with your sister's happiness. I honour her more than you ever could; I would give up my life for her.

Tom   Don't try your high-flown nonsense with me. Do you pretend you have any right to make professions of love to her, when neither her father nor your father would ever consent to a marriage? That's your crooked notion of honour, is it?

Second Maggie   Tom, stop it . . .

Phillip   Is it manly of you to talk in this way to me? You are incapable of understanding what I feel for your sister. I feel so much for her that I could even desire a friendship with you.

Tom   I should be sorry to understand your feelings. You understand me: if you make the least attempt to come near her, or to keep the slightest hold on her mind, I won't be put off by your puny miserable body, I'll thrash you – I'll hold you up to public scorn. Who wouldn't laugh at the idea of your being lover to a fine girl?

First Maggie *has gone into a deaf rage.*

Second Maggie (*turning away*)   Tom, stop it . . . stop it, please.

Phillip   Stay, Maggie. Let your sister speak. If she says she is bound to give me up, I shall abide by her wishes to the slightest word.

Tom   Well, Maggie? It seems you have a choice; either you swear now, solemnly, that you will have no further communication with this . . . man, or I tell my father everything. Choose.

Second Maggie   No, Tom! Please don't tell my father, he couldn't bear it.

Tom   You should have thought of that before. Choose.

Second Maggie   Phillip . . . ?

Phillip   It's all right, Maggie.

Second Maggie   I will do as you say.

Tom   Swear.

Second Maggie   I . . . I swear I will never meet with Phillip again without your knowledge.

Tom   Or have any communication with him.

Second Maggie   Or have any communication with him.

Phillip   It is enough, Maggie. It is enough. But my feelings will not change.

Tom   Come away, Maggie.

Phillip   I wish you to hold yourself entirely free. Trust me; believe I want only what is good for you.

Tom   Come away, Maggie.

He seizes her right wrist and pulls her. She puts out her left hand.
Phillip *clasps it for an instant and then turns away and leaves.* **First**
Maggie *runs to the attic.* **Tom** *drags* **Maggie** *home.*

Maggie   Don't suppose I think you are right or that I bow
to your will. I despise the way that you spoke to him. I detest
your insulting allusions to his . . .

Tom   Deformity?

Maggie   You have been reproaching other people all your
life. You are always so sure you are right. And I'll tell you
why; because your mind isn't large enough to see that there is
anything better than your own conduct and your own petty
aims.

Tom   If your conduct is so much better, why have you
needed to be deceitful? I know what I have aimed at in my
conduct, and I've succeeded. I have worked, denied myself
everything to pay my father's debts so that he may hold up
his head before he dies. What good has your conduct brought
to him or anyone else?

Maggie   I know I've been wrong. But I also know that I
have sometimes been wrong because I have feelings which
you would be the better for. If you did anything wrong, I
would be sorry for the pain it caused you. But you have
always enjoyed punishing me. Even when I was a little girl
you would let me go crying to bed without forgiving me. You
have no pity. You have no sense of your own sins. You thank
God for nothing but your own virtues. But there are feelings
in this world which throw your shining virtues into darkness.

Tom   How have your precious feelings led you to serve
either me or my father? By disobeying and deceiving us, by
ridiculous flights into one extreme after another. I have a
different way of showing my affection.

Maggie   Yes: because you are a man, and have power, and
can do something in the world.

Tom   Then if you can do nothing, submit to those that can.

Maggie   I will submit to what I feel to be right. I will even submit to what is unreasonable from my father. But I will not submit to it from you.

Pause.

Tom   Very well. You need say no more to show me what a gulf there is between us. Let us remember that in future and be silent.

Maggie *goes to the attic.* **First Maggie** *has been beating her fetish and is crying quietly now.* **Second Maggie** *sits down and bursts into tears. It is almost a physical pain.*

Second Maggie   Phillip . . . poor Phillip.

They cry together. **Second Maggie** *recovers and becomes thoughtful. She rises and walks to the mirror. Slowly, she turns it round and looks at herself. She sees that she has been mistaken. She has gained no lasting stand on serene heights above worldly temptations and conflict. She is down again in the thick of strife with her own and others' passions. There is more struggle for her and she knows she must change.*

Gradually, a new **Maggie** *looks back, a prouder, more worldly* **Maggie** *with a coronet of black hair. She steps from the mirror and takes the hands of her two former selves.*

Third Maggie   Perhaps it is for the best.

Scene Twenty-One

In the parlour at the mill. **Mrs Tulliver** *is sewing.* **Mr Tulliver** *is sitting by the fire, brooding.* **Tom** *is standing nearby.* **Third Maggie** *enters just as he goes and sits beside his parents.*

Tom   Father, how much money have we got in the tin-box?

Mr Tulliver   One hundred and ninety-three pounds. You've brought less of late.

Tom   So how much more do we need to pay the creditors?

Mr Tulliver   You know how much; there's a little more than three hundred wanting.

Tom   And what would you say if I told you I have three
hundred pounds in the bank?

Pause.

Mrs Tulliver (*throwing her arms around him*)   Oh, my boy,
my boy. I knew you'd make iverything right again when you
got a man.

Mr Tulliver   Three hundred pounds?

Tom   Yes, Father. I've been sending out bits of cargo to
foreign ports. It was Bob Jakin's idea. I borrowed the capital
from my Uncle Glegg.

Maggie   Well done, Tom.

He ignores her. **Mr Tulliver**, *meanwhile, begins to sob.* **Tom** *puts
a hand on his shoulder.*

Mr Tulliver   Bessy, you must kiss me now. The lad has
made you amends. You'll see a bit o' comfort again. (*She does
so.*) I wish you'd brought me the money to look at, Tom. I
should ha' felt surer.

Tom   You shall see it tomorrow, Father. I have appointed
the creditors to meet at the Golden Lion in St Oggs.

Mr Tulliver   Ah, I'll get from under Wakem's thumb
now, though I must leave the old place. Tom, my lad, you'll
make a speech to 'em. I'll tell 'em it's you as got the best part
o' the money. You'll prosper in the world, my lad, and if
you're ever rich enough – mind this – try and get the old mill
again.

Tom   I will.

Mr Tulliver   Shake hands wi' me, my lad. It's a great
thing when a man can be proud as he's got a good son. I've
had that luck.

Tom *does so.* **Maggie** *is desperate to show her affection but* **Tom**
glances coldly at her and she daren't approach him.

Scene Twenty-Two

Music. The air is filled with the sound of water rushing through the mill wheel. **Maggie** *is on the bank, staring at the river. Her mother calls to her.*

Mrs Tulliver   Maggie. Maggie, your father's coming into the yard. I'll fetch the best glasses from upstairs. Be sure and bring the cake through.

Mr Tulliver *enters the mill-yard, at the same time as* **Mr Wakem**. *Both carry riding whips.*

Wakem   Tulliver. I've just been up to the Far Close. What a fool's trick you did, spreading those hard lumps on it. I told you what would happen.

Mr Tulliver   Get somebody else to farm for you then, as'll ask you to teach him.

Wakem   You've been drinking, I suppose.

Mr Tulliver   I'll tell you where I've been; I've been telling my creditors I've the money to pay 'em. Telling how my son has restored the name of Tulliver. And I want no drinking to tell you as I'll serve no longer under a scoundrel.

Wakem   Very well! You may leave my premises tomorrow. Now hold your insolent tongue and let me pass.

Mr Tulliver   I shan't let you pass. I shall tell you what I think of you first. You're too big a raskill to get hanged . . . you're . . .

Wakem   Let me pass you insolent brute.

He attempts to push past **Mr Tulliver**, *who raises his whip and rushes at him. He grabs* **Wakem** *by the arm and, twisting it, pulls him to the ground and begins to flog him.* **Wakem** *cries out.*

Maggie *has, in slow motion, begun to register what is happening. She rushes to her father.*

Maggie   No . . .

She takes hold of his whipping arm. He continues to bring the whip down. She takes hold of the end of the whip, but still he continues, sending her reeling across the stage with every lash. She manages to fight her way towards him. Suddenly the strength drains from him and he collapses into her arms.

Mrs Tulliver *runs on.*

Wakem   Help me to my horse. He's broken my damned arm. You'll suffer for this, sir. Your daughter is a witness to this assault.

Mr Tulliver   Go and show your back and tell 'em I thrashed you. I've made things a bit more even i' the world. Go.

Mrs Tulliver *helps* **Wakem** *off.* **Mr Tulliver** *collapses further.*

Maggie   Father . . . We must get you inside. (*Calling.*) Help us!

Mr Tulliver   Leave me . . . leave me be. I shan't get up again.

Mrs Tulliver *runs to them, shortly followed by* **Tom**.

Mr Tulliver   Tom, this world's been too many for me . . . But you've done what you could to make things even. Look after your mother . . . and the little wench. Kiss me, Maggie . . . don't you fret, my wench . . . there'll come somebody as'll love you and take your part. Come, Bessy . . . I had my turn – I beat him.

Maggie   But, Father . . . you forgive him . . . you forgive everyone now, don't you?

Mr Tulliver   No, my wench. I don't forgive him. What's forgiving to do? I can't love a raskill . . .

He dies.

Maggie   Father.

Music. **First** *and* **Second Maggie***s enter.* **Second Maggie** *helps her father to his feet. He takes* **First Maggie** *in his arms and they leave.* **Mrs Tulliver** *and* **Tom** *follow, leaving* **Third Maggie** *alone in her grief.*

Scene Twenty-Three

At Uncle Deane's house.

Music. **Lucy** *is standing in the drawing-room. It is a summer's day and the room is full of sunshine which streams in through the open french windows.*

She is arranging a vase of flowers, which stands on a piano, and singing quietly. **Maggie** *enters, carrying a case. She smiles when she sees* **Lucy** *and steals up behind her.*

Maggie   Lucy.

Lucy   Maggie! Maggie, what are you doing here?

Maggie   I took an earlier coach.

Lucy   But how did you get from the turnpike?

Maggie   I walked.

Lucy   It's such a long way.

Maggie   It's no distance at all. Not for my long legs. And anyway, I wanted to gaze about at all the familiar hills.

Lucy   But Aunty and I had it all planned: she was going to ride in the carriage and I was going to trot along behind on my new pony. It was going to be a splendid welcoming party.

Maggie   I'm very glad I avoided it then. I'd far rather creep in by the back door.

Lucy   Now then, Miss Tulliver, stand farther away so I can inspect you properly.

Maggie   There's not much to see.

Lucy   What witchery is it in you, that makes you look best in shabby clothes? If I wore such a thing, no one would notice me.

Maggie   This happens to be my best frock.

Lucy   Well, you must have a new one, though it suits you so well. It's the charity ball in two weeks' time.

Maggie   I haven't any money for new dresses. I want to get a better situation so I'm saving up for more lessons.

Lucy   Now, Maggie. Are you really going to seek another situation?

Maggie   Yes.

Lucy   You look sad now, just speaking of it.

Maggie   Don't mind me. I've been in my cage too long. Being unhappy can become a bad habit.

Lucy   Well, in that case I must put you under a regime of pleasure. There will be absolutely nothing sad or dull in the whole of your visit. I mean to fill your room with all my favourite prints and the loveliest flowers from the garden.

Maggie   Oh, Lucy. (*She hugs her.*) I really think you enjoy other people's happiness more than your own.

Lucy   It's easy for me to be happy.

Maggie   I often get angry at the sight of happy people and then I hate myself for it.

Lucy   What nonsense.

Maggie   I think I get worse as I get older. More selfish.

Lucy   I don't believe a word of it. You must banish all such gloomy thoughts. We're having a party tomorrow, for you and Aunty and Tom.

Maggie   Have you seen Tom?

Lucy   He used to visit a lot but he's been quite a stranger of late.

Maggie   I write to him at Bob's but he seldom replies.

The doorbell rings.

Lucy   I hope this is who I think it is.

Maggie   And who would that be, I wonder?

Lucy   Wait and see. (*Taking her hands and kissing her.*) Maggie.

Maggie   Run along now, or you'll have me in tears.

Lucy *goes.* **Maggie** *tries to recover herself. Memories flooding back and* **Lucy**'s *kindness to her have brought on a rush of tears. She goes to the windows and looks out.*

Music. **Stephen** *enters. He watches her for a moment. She turns and sees him. Their gazes lock.*

Stephen   Excuse me. I didn't realise there was anyone in here . . . Miss Deane . . .

Maggie   I am Maggie Tulliver. Lucy's cousin.

Stephen   Are you now? Stephen Guest. How do you do?

Maggie   Very well, thank you.

Stephen   But surely you can't be Miss Tulliver . . .

Maggie   I assure you, I am. Or I was when I last looked.

Lucy (*who has entered and is standing in the doorway, laughing*) Now then, Stephen; how does it feel to be on the end of a laugh for once?

Stephen   I see. Lucy, you really are . . .

Lucy   What?

Stephen   Forgive me, Miss Tulliver. This designing cousin of yours quite deceived me. She told me you had light hair and blue eyes.

Lucy   Not at all – it was you who said so. He thought you would be a smaller version of your mother.

Stephen   I wish I could always be so mistaken, and find reality so much more beautiful than my preconceptions.

Maggie   Now you have proved yourself equal to the occasion, Mr Guest, and said what you feel you ought to say under the circumstances.

Stephen   I hope you will allow that even phrases of compliment have their turn to be true. A man is occasionally grateful when he says 'Thank you'.

Maggie   I hope you will allow that compliments are nothing but expressions of indifference.

Lucy   Dear Maggie, you always claim you are too fond of feeling admired.

Maggie   I am. But compliments will never make me feel so.

Stephen   I will never pay you a compliment again, Miss Tulliver.

Maggie   Thank you. That will be proof of your respect.

Pause. Everyone is embarrassed by this absurd exchange.

Lucy   Maggie has arrived early. Isn't that splendid? She walked from the turnpike.

Stephen   Where have you come from, Miss Tulliver?

Maggie   From a girls' school near Luckreth.

Stephen   You are a governess?

Maggie   No, nothing so grand. I mended the pupils' clothes.

Lucy   Maggie's plain sewing is quite exquisite. I think I must beg your help altering my dress for the charity ball.

Stephen   Lucy is very much involved in preparations for this ball. I confess I am beginning to feel neglected.

Lucy   Poor Stephen. You will have to be patient.

Stephen   I shall be glad when the idiotic thing is done with. So will most of the chaps I know. Even Dr Kenn said the other day that he didn't like this plan of making vanity do the work of charity.

Lucy   He said that? I thought he approved of what we do.

Stephen   I'm sure he approves of you.

Lucy   Dr Kenn is the new vicar at St Oggs, Maggie. I know you will like him.

Stephen   I think him a fine fellow. He gives half his income to charity.

Maggie   That is indeed noble. I never heard of anyone doing such a thing.

Stephen   He's the only man I've ever met, who seems to have anything of the real apostle in him. (**Maggie**'s *honest, open gaze has enchanted him. He sets out to break the spell.*) I only hope he doesn't think of standing for Parliament one day, or he shall find himself my adversary.

Lucy   Do you really think of doing that?

Stephen   Decidedly. My father's heart is set on it and gifts like mine, you know, involve great responsibilities, don't you think, Miss Tulliver?

Maggie   Oh yes. Such fluency and self-possession should not be wasted entirely on private occasions.

Stephen   You are very perceptive. You have discovered already that I am talkative and impudent.

Maggie *walks to the window.*

Maggie   I can hear the Floss from here. You are so lucky to have the river at the bottom of your garden.

Lucy   Maggie and Tom used to live at Dorlcote Mill.

Stephen   Ah yes . . . your brother works for my father, I think.

Maggie   Yes. Do you know Tom?

Stephen   I'm afraid I haven't had the pleasure. (**Maggie** *looks disappointed.*) I wonder, Miss Tulliver, if you would like us all to go for a row on the river, during your stay? I would be happy to oblige.

Lucy   Oh, Maggie! Stephen is an excellent oarsman.

Maggie   Thank you. It is a long time since I was on the river. There is nothing I would like better.

Scene Twenty-Four

In **Maggie**'*s bedroom.* **Maggie** *puts her case down, but is too agitated to unpack. She sits and then stands again and begins to pace the room. Her eyes and cheeks glow, her hands are clasped.* **Second Maggie** *appears and watches.*

Second Maggie   We should go to bed.

Second Maggie *kneels and prays*. **Third Maggie** *begins to unpack, but* **First Maggie** *enters, dancing and joyful.*

Third Maggie   I feel as if I've walked into a book. Into a dream. Everything is so beautiful here; the very air seems charged with delight . . . and love . . . I had given up believing such places exist.

Second Maggie   We should go to bed.

Third Maggie (*sharply*)   What are you doing here?

First *and* **Second Maggie***s leave*. **Lucy** *enters*.

Lucy   Maggie, tell me what you think of him.

Maggie   Oh, I think you should humiliate him a little. A lover should not be so at ease. He ought to tremble more.

Lucy   Tremble at me! You think he is conceited.

Maggie   A little over-confident.

Lucy   Sometimes, when he's away, I think he can't possibly love me, but I never doubt it when he's with me again. We're not engaged, you know.

Maggie   Ah. So if I disapprove of him, you can give him up.

Lucy   You don't disapprove, do you? You don't dislike him?

Maggie   Lucy. Am I in the habit of seeing such charming people, that I should be very difficult to please?

Lucy *is delighted. They embrace.*

Lucy   You know, one of the things I most admire in him is that he makes a greater friend of Phillip Wakem than anyone. (*There is a change in* **Maggie**'s *face*.) I'm sorry. Does it hurt you to hear the name?

Maggie   No. no. I've liked Phillip Wakem since I was a little girl. He was very good to me.

Lucy   So you won't mind if he visits? He and Stephen have the only decent voices in St Oggs. Our musical evenings would suffer without him. Oh, please. I remember what a wild state of joy you used to be in when the singers came round. We can have all the songs you used to love.

Maggie   I don't know . . . I would have to ask Tom. I couldn't see him without his leave.

Lucy   Is Tom such a tyrant as that?

Maggie   Lucy, I promised Tom, solemnly, that I would not speak to Phillip again without his consent.

Lucy   But I've never heard anything so unreasonable. (*Pause.*) You have secrets from me, and I have none from you.

Maggie   I would like to tell you about Phillip. I have needed to tell someone.

Scene Twenty-Five

In **Tom**'s *room at* **Bob Jakin**'s. **Tom** *and* **Maggie** *stand in tense silence.*

Maggie   Tom? Please say something. I only ask because Lucy wishes it. I would only see him in the presence of other people.

Tom   Do you really pretend what I say would make a difference? You will do exactly what you want in the end.

Maggie   That is unfair.

Tom   As you told me, very bluntly, after father's death, you wish to be independent.

Maggie   Is that so hard to understand?

Tom   I wished my sister to be a lady and I would always have taken care of you as my father desired.

Maggie   Dear Tom, I know that you would do a great deal for me . . . but you don't seem to realise how differently we feel about things.

Tom   Oh, I realise only too well – when you can entertain the idea of Phillip Wakem as a lover, a husband, after all that . . . I realise how differently we feel.

Maggie   I know there could never be any question of our marrying. Not as things stand. I am not totally unaware of what is right and wrong.

Tom   But you do not have the strength to resist what is wrong.

Maggie   That is not true.

Tom   Isn't it? (**Maggie** *begins to cry.* **Tom** *softens.*) I don't want to overstrain matters, Maggie. I think, all things considered, it would be best for you to see Phillip Wakem if Lucy wishes it. But if you begin to think of him as anything more than a friend, you will lose me forever.

First Maggie *enters, running to* **Tom** *and flinging her arms around him.*

First Maggie   Oh, Tom, I do love you, so much. I won't be naughty I promise I won't. Please be good to me, Tom.

Tom (*smiling and allowing her to kiss him*)   All right, Magsie. All right.

First Maggie *leaves.*

Third Maggie   I may turn out better than you expect.

Tom   I hope you will.

Maggie   And may I come one day and make tea for you, and meet Bob's new wife?

Tom   Yes. Off you go now. Be a good girl. (*She kisses him and goes to the door.*) Maggie.

Maggie   Yes.

Tom   There may be a chance that I will get the mill back. I have persuaded Guest and Co. to purchase it and allow me to manage it.

Maggie   That's wonderful news. (*Taking his hands.*) Come and have dinner tonight, with me and Lucy. She would love to see you.

Tom   I am sure there are other people Lucy would much rather see. And besides, I have too much to do.

She goes. **Tom** *is upset and angry with himself for not being able to respond to her kindess.*

Scene Twenty-Six

In the drawing-room at **Lucy***'s.* **Stephen** *is just finishing a song.* **Lucy** *and* **Maggie** *lay down their knitting and sewing to applaud.*

Lucy   Bravo! Bravo! Hasn't he a splendid voice?

Maggie   Neither of us can be judges of that. You are not impartial, and I think any barrel-organ splendid.

Stephen   I suppose you would prefer a tenor, Miss Tulliver, warbling sentimental love and constancy.

Maggie   Not at all. I enjoy all music. Even the loud variety.

Stephen   I think that decidedly vicious. I put a great deal of effort into that ditty.

Maggie   There was certainly a quantity of air involved.

Lucy   Really! You two are quite incorrigible.

Maggie   Please sing another song, Mr Guest. I enjoyed it enormously.

Stephen   That sounds dangerously close to a compliment.

Their eyes meet. Both look away. It is compromising to feel the effect they have on one another.

Lucy *and* **Stephen** *go. It is evening.* **Maggie** *takes up her knitting again. She is using scarlet wool. Music.* **Second Maggie** *enters and hovers behind her.*

Third Maggie   I don't know why you're here; I'm doing nothing you could disapprove of.

She carries on knitting. **Second Maggie** *watches her.* **Stephen** *enters. He looks sheepish. He is carrying a book under his arm.* **Maggie** *rises.*

Stephen You are surprised to see me again, Miss Tulliver. I wanted to come into the town and I got our man to row me, so I thought I would bring this music for your cousin.

Maggie But Lucy is not in this evening. She said . . . do you remember? She has gone to a meeting about the ball.

Stephen Ah . . . Well . . . will you give this to her?

Maggie Yes.

She sits again and goes on knitting. He sits on the chair next to hers — something he has never done before. He watches her intently for quite some time.

Stephen That is coming on well. (*Pause.*) We shall have a splendid sunset, I think. Will you go out and see it?

Maggie I don't know. If I'm not playing cards with Uncle.

Pause.

Stephen Do you like sitting alone?

Maggie Would it be quite civil to say yes?

Stephen (*delighted with the look he has received*) It was rather a dangerous question for an intruder to ask.

Pause.

Maggie I wish Lucy had not been obliged to go out. We lose our music.

Stephen We shall have a new voice tomorrow night. Will you tell your cousin that our friend Phillip Wakem has come back from his trip? I saw him as I went home.

Second Maggie *stands.* **Third Maggie** *starts and stands. The ball of scarlet wool falls from her lap and runs across the room.*

She goes to retrieve it, but **Stephen** *gets there first. He picks it up and winds it back towards her. They find themselves very close, their hands almost touching. He hands her the ball.*

Music. **Maggie**, *looking into* **Stephen**'s *eyes, throws the ball again. He retrieves it and hands it back to her. She throws it again but before he can retrieve it,* **Second Maggie** *puts her foot on the wool and* **Third Maggie** *runs and picks it up. All three turn away from each other.*

Stephen   You'll tell your cousin?

Maggie   Yes.

Stephen   That I brought the music, I mean?

Maggie   Yes.

Stephen   And about Phillip?

Maggie   Yes. Good evening.

He goes. **Maggie** *turns back to her chair.* **Second Maggie** *is sitting there and she holds out her arms and embraces her, as* **Maggie** *bursts into tears.*

Second Maggie   Oh, Phillip, Phillip. I wish we were together again, so quietly in the Red Deeps. So quietly . . .

Stephen (*from outside*)   For God's sake, Guest; what are you doing?

Scene Twenty-Seven

In the drawing-room. **Maggie** *is there.* **Lucy** *enters with* **Phillip**. *He looks nervous but* **Maggie** *advances towards him with outheld hand and tears in her eyes.*

Phillip (*taking her hand*)   You look very well.

Maggie   Lucy is my fairy godmother. She does nothing but indulge me all day long.

She smiles at **Lucy**, *who goes.*

I told my brother I wished to see you. I asked him to release me from the promise and he consented.

Phillip   Then we can at least be friends? Does Lucy know?

Maggie   Yes, I confided in her.

Phillip　I'm glad.

Pause.

Maggie　I can't tell you how terrible I felt . . .

Phillip　You don't need to say it.

Maggie　Oh, Phillip. We must talk together as much as we can before I go away again.

Phillip　Is that inevitable?

Maggie　I won't be dependent on Tom. I can't be. Staying here would only unfit me for the life I must lead.

Phillip　Do you not see another alternative, Maggie?

Maggie　Not as things are. I begin to think I will never find much happiness in loving. There is always pain mingled with it. I wish I could make a world outside it, as men do.

Phillip　I thought you had stopped thinking like that. I thought I had cured you of it.

Maggie　Yes. Yes, you are right. I wish I could have you always beside me, to guide me and teach me. So many things you told me have come true.

The thought of **Stephen** *has shot into her head. It shows.*

Phillip　What is the matter, Maggie? Has something happened?

Maggie　No. Nothing. Nothing. You used to say I would feel the effect of my starved life, as you called it, and I do. I am too eager in my enjoyment of . . . luxuries. Tell me of you, Phillip.

Phillip　I still paint and draw a great deal. I have a studio now, at the top of my father's house. It is very private.

Maggie　I had an attic once. It was the only place I could be really myself.

Phillip　Maggie, I could be beside you always. If you wished me to be.

Scene Twenty-Eight

In the drawing-room. **Stephen** *and* **Phillip** *come to the end of a duet.*
Maggie *and* **Lucy** *are enraptured.*

Lucy   More, more! Something spirited again. Maggie
always says she likes a great rush of sound.

Stephen   You sang exceptionally, Phil.

Lucy   You did.

Stephen   You are an enviable fellow, a true artist. When I
sing, my mind wanders dreadfully. But then that has been
observed in men of a great administrative capacity, I believe
– a tendancy to predominance of the reflective powers.
Haven't you observed that, Miss Tulliver?

Maggie   I have observed a tendancy to predominance.

Phillip *notices the look exchanged.*

Lucy   Come, come. Music, more music. We can discuss
each other's qualities another time.

Phillip *begins to sing 'I Love Thee Still'. The others listen.*
Maggie *becomes embarrassed. She goes to get her wool, but*
Stephen *anticipates her want and passes it to her.*

Maggie (*not looking at him*)   Thank you.

Stephen   Is there not a draught here? Would you like to
move nearer to the fire ?

Maggie   No thank you.

Their eyes meet. **Phillip** *has witnessed all. He stops singing and looks
down. Then continues, but his heart has sunk.*

Lucy, **Phillip** *and* **Stephen** *leave. The lights change.* **First**
Maggie *enters, in a state of high excitement, carrying a black brocade
dress. She helps* **Third Maggie** *to put it on.* **Third Maggie** *looks
at herself in the mirror.*

First Maggie   It's beautiful, beautiful.

Second Maggie *enters.*

Second Maggie   Why are you dressed like that?

Third Maggie For the charity ball.

Second Maggie (*grabbing her and trying to tear it from her*) Take it off.

Third Maggie It's an old dress of Aunt Pullet's.

Second Maggie Take it off.

Third Maggie There will be ladies in shining new silks. I have to wear something. (*She pushes her away.*)

First Maggie (*holding out her hand*) Your Majesty . . .

Second Maggie Take it off.

Third Maggie No.

She turns away as the grand music of the ball begins and the stage is filled with people dancing. **First Maggie** *dances alone.* **Second Maggie** *dances with* **Dr Kenn.** **Stephen** *and* **Lucy** *dance together. A man approaches* **Maggie** *and bows but she declines to dance and he withdraws.*

Lucy Why doesn't Maggie dance? She has had so many offers. You must go and ask her. She would dance with you.

Stephen I'm not at all sure she would.

Phillip *enters the upper platform which has become the gallery. He watches* **Maggie.**

She glances up and sees him just as **Stephen** *appears by her side.*

Stephen Maggie.

Maggie Where is Lucy?

Stephen Will you dance with me?

Maggie No. No, I'm sorry.

Stephen Are you angry with me? What have I done? Do look at me.

Maggie Please go away.

She glances again at the gallery. **Stephen** *follows her eyes and sees* **Phillip.** *He realises there must be something between them. He goes up to the gallery.*

Stephen Are you studying for a portrait, Phil?

Phillip   I have been studying expression.

Stephen   Miss Tulliver's? It's rather of the moody order tonight. I have been snubbed as usual. I seldom have the honour to please her.

Phillip   What a hypocrite you are.

Both men stand and face each other. **Phillip** *leaves.* **Stephen** *runs down the steps and sweeps* **Maggie** *off her feet into the waltz. She manages to keep up with him, clumsily at first, but then the music and lights change, and the other dancers become shadows and* **Stephen** *and* **Maggie** *glide perfectly in each other's arms. They stop.*

Maggie   We must go back in. We will be missed.

Stephen *says nothing, but holds out his hand to her. Slowly she takes it. He suddenly showers her hand and arm with kisses. She snatches her hand away.*

Maggie   How dare you? What right have I given you to insult me? (*She runs from him. He follows her, shocked.*) Leave me alone. (*He goes.*)

She runs into **Dr Kenn**.

Father . . .

Doctor   Miss Tulliver, you are finding our party fatiguing, I'm afraid.

Maggie   Yes.

Doctor   I hope I am going to have you as a permanent parishioner now.

Maggie   No. I will go to a new situation.

Doctor   I was hoping you would remain among your friends.

Maggie (*with great emphasis*)   I must go.

Doctor   I understand. But that will not prevent our meeting again, I hope – if I can be of service to you.

Scene Twenty-Nine

In the drawing-room. **Third Maggie** *stands very still.*

First Maggie *enters and runs about, panicking as she did about the rabbits.*

First Maggie   Oh, please don't let it be true. Please, please . . .

Third Maggie *takes, almost rips, the ball dress off.* **First Maggie** *helps her into her old dress.* **Lucy** *enters.*

Lucy   Maggie, you can't go away. Not now.

Maggie   I have to. Please don't try to dissuade me. I had the offer of a situation yesterday.

Lucy   But what about Phillip . . . I thought everything was going to be so happy – you and Phillip, Stephen and I . . .

Maggie   I have to consider Tom's feelings.

Lucy   But I could talk to him.

Maggie   No. Thank you.

Lucy   Maggie, is it that you don't love Phillip enough to marry him? Tell me . . .

Pause.

Maggie   I would choose to marry Phillip. I think it would be the best and highest lot for me. But I must go. Don't press me to stay, dear Lucy. Please.

Lucy *goes.* **Phillip** *enters.*

Phillip   Maggie, I have told my father everything. He will not stand between us.

Maggie   Phillip, I am going away at the end of the week.

Pause.

Phillip   So the future will never join onto the past. That book is quite closed?

Maggie   No. That book will never be closed. I desire no
future that will break the ties of the past. But there is my
brother – I could do nothing that would divide me from him.

Phillip   Maggie, look at me. Is that the only reason that
would keep us apart forever? The only reason?

Maggie   The only reason.

Scene Thirty

In the mill. **Tom** *and* **Maggie, Mrs Tulliver, Aunt** *and*
Uncle Glegg *enter. They look about them.* **Mrs Tulliver** *and*
Maggie *strip the dust sheets from the old furniture.*

Mrs Tulliver   What news, eh, Sister? What news! I never
thought I'd be back in the old place, again.

Mr Glegg   Why, you're a big man now, Tom and carry all
before you. You'll buy the place from Mr Guest one day and
have it for your own, I'll be bound. You won't stop half-way
up the hill.

Mrs Glegg   But I hope he'll bear it in mind as it's his
mother's family as he owes it to. There was never failures, nor
wastefulness in our family.

Mr Glegg   But who would ha' thought Wakem 'ud sell?
Eh?

Mrs Glegg   Well, Bessy, I shall give my nephy some
serviceable sheets and I hope he'll lie down in 'em and think
of his aunt. Though I must say, it's fine work to be dividing
my linen before I die.

Mrs Tulliver   I'm sure it was no wish o' mine, Sister, as I
should lie awake o' nights thinking o' my best-bleached linen
all over the county.

Mrs Glegg   But I shan't be giving Maggie any more o' my
dresses, if she's to go into service when she might stay here
and keep me company, if you didn't want her.

Mr Glegg   Nonsense, nonsense. Don't let us hear o' you
taking a place again, Maggie. Why, you must ha' picked up
half a dozen sweethearts at the ball. In't there one of 'em the
right sort of article? Eh? Eh?

Mrs Glegg   Mr Glegg, if you're going to be undelicate, let
me know.

They go. **Tom** *and* **Maggie** *remain.*

Tom   Magsie, come and live with me and mother. It's not
too late to change your mind.

Maggie   Oh, Tom . . . (*She hugs him.*) Thank you for saying
that. But I have to go.

Tom *turns and goes.*

Scene Thirty-One

Maggie *is standing by the Floss, staring at the water. We can hear it
lapping against the banks.* **Stephen** *approaches.* **Maggie** *sees his
reflection and immediately darts away.*

Stephen   You are angry with me for coming.

Maggie   I did not think you would wish to insult me further
by forcing an interview on me in this way. Kindly let me
return to the house.

Stephen   Of course, it is of no consequence what a man has
to suffer. It is only your woman's dignity which you care
about. As if it were not enough that I am caught up in this,
that I'm mad with love for you, but you must treat me like a
coarse brute who would willingly offend you. And when, if I
had my own choice, I should ask you to take my hand, my
fortune, my whole life and do what you want with them. I
know I forgot myself. I hate myself for having done it but I
repented immediately. The worst pain I could have is to
have pained you. I would give the world to recall the error.

Maggie   You must not say these things. I must not hear
them.

Stephen   Look at me: see what a hunted devil I am. I have been riding thirty miles every day to get away from the thought of you.

Maggie   I don't think any evil of you. I do forgive you. But please go away.

Stephen   I can't go away from you.

Maggie   It is wicked . . . base . . . think of Lucy . . .

Stephen   I do think of her. If I did not . . .

Maggie   And I have other ties.

Stephen   You are engaged to Phillip Wakem? Is it so?

Maggie   I consider myself engaged to him. I don't mean to marry anyone else.

Pause.

Stephen   Tell me then, that you don't care for me. Tell me that you love someone better. Tell me and I'll go. (*She can't answer.*) Come out in the boat with me, Maggie.

Maggie   I can't. It is out of the question.

Stephen   Do you remember, you said how you yearned to be on the river? We will not be long together. Let us have these last moments.

He takes her hand. She does not resist. Music. He leads her, like someone blind, to the boat. He arranges the cushions and opens a parasol above her head. They are afloat. **Stephen** *rows and the air is filled with the rhythmic sound of the oars and birds in flight. Everything is very slow and languid. Occasionally,* **Stephen** *utters a quiet exclamation of love. Then he lays down the oars and sits back. The boat glides.*

The music changes. They sky grows dark. Suddenly **Maggie** *sits up in alarm and looks about.*

Maggie   Are we past Luckreth? We should have stopped there.

Stephen (*in a dreamy absent tone*)   Yes – a long way.

Maggie   Oh, my God . . . we won't get home for hours.
Oh, God, help me . . . Lucy . . .

Stephen   Maggie, let us never go home again until we are
married. Look . . . the tide has carried us away because we
belong to each other. It will take us to Torby, we can get a
carriage to York and then to Scotland and never stop until
we are bound together.

Maggie   Let me go! How could you do this? You knew we
had come too far. How could you bring me to this?

Stephen   I didn't notice that we had passed Luckreth until
it was too late. You clearly don't love me enough. If you did,
nothing else would matter. I will stop the boat and try to get
you out. I'll tell Lucy I was mad and you shall be clear of me
forever.

Maggie   No. I'm sorry . . . I'm . . . I have been as weak as
you. I would always care what happened to you.

Stephen   Oh, Maggie, my darling, my dearest love . . .
marry me, just say the word.

Maggie   No . . . no, I would rather die than fall into that
temptation.

Stephen   It would be wrong to deny our love. Do you not
see how strong it is? How can we go back to those others,
knowing how we feel about each other?

Maggie   Oh, Stephen, please, please don't urge me; help
me . . . help me because I love you.

*He takes her in his arms and kisses her. Her resolution cracks. She sinks
into the temptation and lets go.*

Stephen   You are mine, now. Lie back my darling, rest. I
will row to Torby. Everything is all right now, Maggie.
Everything is all right.

Maggie *closes her eyes and sleeps. But she dreams. We hear snatches
of her past —* **Tom** *saying he will build an ark and take her in,* **Phillip**
saying they will always belong to each other, **Lucy** *saying how much
she loves* **Stephen,** **Mr Tulliver** *saying he will always take her
part. We see* **First Maggie** *with her butterfly book. We see* **Second**

Maggie *falling on her knees to pray and the great light of Thomas à Kempis. Then we see* **Lucy** *and* **Tom** *and* **Phillip** *in a boat, rowing towards the light.* **Maggie** *calls to them but they don't see or hear her and are gone.* **Maggie** *wakens and cries out* –

Maggie Wait!

Scene Thirty-Two

In a room at an inn in Torby. **Maggie** *is very still and silent.* **Stephen** *is trying to ignore the signs.*

Stephen Are you warmer now, my darling? I am sorry you have had to bear so much discomfort. The landlord will have a chaise for us within the hour, and we will leave for Scotland. That will seem rest to you after this.

Maggie I am not going.

Stephen What?

Maggie I am not going.

Stephen Maggie . . . The whole thing is done.

Maggie No. Too much is done – more than we can ever undo. But I will go no farther. I couldn't choose before. Now, I can.

Stephen Maggie, forgive me, I'm sorry for what I did but please don't blight our lives . . . (*She stands.*) No, wait. Sit down, think what you are doing.

Maggie We must part at once.

Stephen Why are you doing this? Do you wish to drive me mad?

Maggie I will not begin any future, even for you, with a deliberate consent to what ought not to have been. That is all. We must part now.

Stephen We will not part. You will kill me. You will make me desperate, I won't know what I do.

Pause.

Maggie   Stephen . . . Stephen, think how you felt about this two weeks ago. You felt that you owed yourself to another. So did I.

Stephen   I am not engaged to Lucy. If her feelings had been withdrawn, I should have felt no right to assert a claim on her . . .

Maggie   That is not . . .

Stephen   You are not absolutely pledged to Phillip.

Maggie   That is not how you felt before. We have raised feelings and expectations in other minds. They are real ties.

Stephen   But our love is stronger. We have proved that. It is right, natural that we should marry.

Maggie   No. If life were quite easy and simple, as it might have been in paradise . . . I mean, if life did not make duties for us before love comes, then love would be a sign that two people belong together. But I know now that isn't true. There are things we must renounce in life; some of us must renounce love.

Stephen   Good God, Maggie . . . I would commit crimes for you and you can stand there balancing and choosing . . . I though you loved me. How could I have been so stupid?

Maggie   Do you think this is easy for me? I am only clinging to the one thing I can see clearly – that I must not, cannot seek my own happiness by sacrificing others. I would be haunted by the suffering I had caused. Our love would be poisoned. Don't you see? (*She starts to cry.*)

Stephen   Maggie, please, listen to me. They would not thank us for our constancy without our love. It would be hateful, horrible to me to ever think of your being the wife of a man you didn't love. We have both been rescued from a mistake. (*He is holding her.*) Listen to me, my darling, if you love me you are mine. There is nothing in the past that can change that. It is the first time either of us have loved with our whole heart and soul.

Maggie (*suddenly calm and brave*)   No. Not with my whole heart and soul. There are things inside me you know nothing of. There are memories and affections and longings after perfect goodness. They would never leave me for long. They would come back and be pain to me; repentance.

First *and* **Second Maggie**s *have entered and are close to her.*

Maggie   I have caused sorrow already. I know – I feel it. I will not cause more. It has never been my will to marry you. If I could wake back again into the time before this, I would choose to be true to my . . . to myself.

Pause.

Stephen   Do you really think you can go back now without marrying me? Do you not know what will be said?

Maggie   Yes, I do. But they will believe me . . .

Stephen   You are raving. You see nothing as it really is.

Maggie   Lucy will believe me, she will forgive you and, and some good will come by clinging to the right. Dear, dear Stephen, let me go. My whole soul has never consented. It does not consent now.

Silence.

Stephen   Go then. (*She goes to touch him. He shrinks from her.*) Leave me.

First *and* **Second Maggie**s *help* **Maggie** *away. She is almost collapsing with despair.*

First Maggie   Where shall we go?

Third Maggie   Anywhere.

Second Maggie   Home.

Scene Thirty-Three

The crowd gather above, in threatening silence. Actions of the witch ducking are echoed. They wait. Slowly, **Maggie** *enters. She looks tired and sad and shabby.*

Her every step is watched. She halts.

As the lights increase we see that **Tom** *is there and* **Mrs Tulliver** *and* **Bob Jakin**. **Maggie** *moves towards* **Tom**.

Maggie   Tom, I have come back to you. I have come home for refuge.

Tom   You will find no home with me. If you are in want, I will provide for you. But you shall not come under my roof. It is enough I have to bear your disgrace. (*He turns his back on her.*)

Maggie   I am perhaps not so guilty as you believe me to be. Let me explain.

He leaves.

Maggie *turns away, crushed. Her mother steps over to her.*

Mrs Tulliver   My child. I'll stand with you. You've got a mother.

Bob Jakin *steps over to her.*

Bob   Come and stay wi' me, the both o' you.

Maggie   Bob, you're too kind. You haven't the room.

Bob   Don't speak so, Miss. If there's anything I can do for you, I should look upon it as a day's earnings.

He gets her a chair and sits her down. **Dr Kenn** *enters.*

Doctor   Miss Tulliver, may we talk together – in private.

Everyone else leaves.

Maggie   I will tell you everything.

Doctor   You may if you wish, but there is no need. I have been made acquainted with the contents of a letter from Mr Stephen Guest.

Maggie   Oh . . . where is he?

Doctor   Abroad. He has written to his father of all that passed. He has vindicated you to the utmost.

Maggie   He does not deserve all the blame.

Pause.

Doctor   Allow me to help you.

Maggie   I must stay here and work. I must atone in some way to Lucy – and to others. Have you seen Lucy?

Doctor   Yes. I'm afraid she hasn't spoken since the news came.

Maggie   And Phillip . . . Phillip Wakem?

Doctor   I don't know. If you wish, I will call on Mr Wakem.

Maggie   Thank you. Yes.

Doctor   Miss Tulliver, you are inexperienced in the ways of the world . . .

Maggie   I know I shall be insulted. I shall be thought worse than I am. I begin to see that.

Doctor   Those who are the most incapable of a conscientious struggle, are precisely those who will shrink from you, because they will not believe in yours. I feel you should consider taking a situation at a distance from here.

Maggie   No. I cannot do that. I have no heart to begin a strange life. I would have nothing to cling to. And I will not go away because people say false things of me. They shall learn to retract them.

Doctor   Very well. No doubt you would be condemned, whatever you decided to do. I will try to find you a position somewhere in St Oggs.

Maggie   Thank you. I will not want much. I can go on lodging here. Bob is a kind and good friend.

Doctor   There are dark days ahead, Miss Tulliver. I shall bear you constantly in mind.

Scene Thirty-Four

In **Maggie**'*s room at* **Bob**'*s.* **Mrs Tulliver** *enters. She looks shocked and pale.*

Maggie   Mother, what is it?

Mrs Tulliver   Oh, nothing, dear. I've just been outside . . . People are . . . (*She starts to cry.* **Maggie** *feels sick with* *guilt*.) Oh dear! Oh dear! What trouble. It's all gone from bad to worse just when the luck seemed on the turn.

Maggie   Oh, my poor, poor mother. I was always naughty to you and now you might have been happy if it wasn't for me.

Mrs Tulliver   Eh dear, I must put up wi' my children – I shall never have no more. And there's nothing much else to be fond on for my furniture went long ago. But you'd got to be very good once; I can't think how it's turned out the wrong way so.

Maggie   Mother, you must go back to the mill. Back to Tom.

Mrs Tulliver   But I can't leave you.

Maggie   You must. I cannot bear inflicting this misery on you. At least it will be better if you are away from St Oggs. I will be all right now. I am quite used to it. Please say you'll go.

Mrs Tulliver *stands and embraces* **Maggie** *and then goes.*

Scene Thirty-Five

In **Phillip**'s *studio.* **Dr Kenn** *waits for* **Phillip** *to speak.*

Phillip   Tell her . . . Tell her I believe in her. I know she tried to keep faith to me, and to all. Tell her I knew there was something stronger in her than her love for him. Tell her no anguish I have had to bear has been too heavy a price for the new life which I have entered in loving her. I never expected happiness, you see; she has reconciled me to my life. She has been to my affections what light and colour are to my eyes, what music is to the inward ear. Tell her I shall not go away. The place where she is, is the one where my mind must live.

God comfort you, my loving, large-souled Maggie. If everyone else has misconceived you, remember that you have never been doubted by him whose heart recognized you ten years ago.

Scene Thirty-Six

In **Maggie**'s *room at* **Bob**'s. *It is a stormy night. There is the sound of torrential rain and wind.* **Maggie** *is sitting in semi-darkness.* **Dr Kenn** *is there.*

Maggie   He said that?

Doctor   Yes.

She nods her head. She is close to tears.

My efforts to find you a situation have failed. I must confess, in all my twenty years as a parish priest, I have never come across such blind obstinacy. I must reluctantly advise that you reconsider the possibility of going . . .

Maggie   Where? Yes. Thank you. I will think about it.

Doctor   I will come again soon. It's a bad night.

Maggie   Yes. It is.

He goes. Music. **First** *and* **Second Maggie**s *enter.* **Second Maggie** *carries a candle which she sets down.*

Third Maggie   So I must be alone. I must go out among strangers, who will not care for me or understand me . . . I must begin again. But I am so unspeakably weary.

Slowly, she takes an unopened letter from her pocket.

Second Maggie   Don't open it.

Third Maggie   I think I must.

Second Maggie   Why? What good can it do? You know what it will say.

Third Maggie   I don't know. I owe it to him to read it. I left him so broken, so . . .

First Maggie *takes it and opens it and hands it back to her.*

Third Maggie *reads, silently. The others wait.*

Oh, Stephen . . .

First Maggie   What does he say?

Third Maggie   'Maggie, call me back to you. This time has only deepened the certainty that I can never care for life without you. Write me one word – say 'Come!' In two days I would be with you. Maggie, have you forgotten what it was to be together? To be within reach of a look? To be within hearing of each other's voice?' Forgotten? Forgotten? There is not a night goes by when I do not see his face, turning to me full of love and hope; when I do not let my imagination fly and my heart leap with the thought of the happiness we might have had.

Second Maggie   A poisoned happiness.

Third Maggie   Oh, God, I miss him so much!

Second Maggie (*to* **First Maggie**, *who is heading across the room*)   Where are you going?

First Maggie   To get paper and a pen.

Second Maggie   No. We shall not write. Thomas à Kempis said, 'I have received the cross. I have received it from Thy hand; I will bear it and bear it till death, as Thou hast laid it upon me.'

Third Maggie   I think of the lonely future I must face . . . with what? Our faith . . . And he is there and he wants me, and I could lean on him for strength. There would be joy where there is sadness.

First Maggie   Poor Stephen. He needs us.

Third Maggie   Fetch the pen and paper.

Second Maggie   No. 'I will bear it and bear it till death.'

Third Maggie (*shouting*)   I want him.

They have reached deadlock. **Third Maggie** *turns away.* **Lucy** *enters. The shock of being truly unhappy for the first time has had a marked effect on her. The light has gone from her eyes.* **Third Maggie** *turns and sees her.*

Lucy   I stole away. My maid brought me in the carriage.

Maggie (*with a sob*)   God bless you for coming, Lucy.

Lucy   Please don't cry. Don't grieve.

Maggie   I didn't mean to deceive you. It was because I thought it would all be overcome.

Lucy   I know. I know you never meant to make me unhappy. It is a trouble that has come on us all. You have more to bear than I have . . . and you gave him up, when . . . it must have been very hard for you.

Maggie   He struggled too. He wanted to be true to you. He will come back to you. Forgive him, he will be happy then.

Lucy   I must go. I am fearful of the storm. When I am strong and well I will come and see you often. (*She starts to go.*)

Maggie   I pray to God that I will never be the cause of sorrow to you any more.

Lucy   Maggie, you are better than I. I can't . . .

She goes. **Maggie** *is still for a moment and then takes* **Stephen**'s *letter to the candle.*

Maggie   Forgive me, Stephen. It will pass away. You will come back to her.

She burns it.

'I will bear it and bear it till death.' But how long must I wait before death comes? How will I go on? What if I must face other trials as hard as this?

She falls on her knees to pray. **Second** *and* **First Maggie**s *kneel on either side of her. Music.* **Second Maggie** *keeps repeating,* '*I will bear it and bear it till death.*'

Amidst the sound of the wind and rain, there is now the sound of rushing water.

Behind them, the crowd have gathered.

First Maggie (*looking down*)   Water! We're in water.

Third Maggie   It's the flood.

There is a sudden horrific cry from the crowd as the flood sweeps into the town.

Second Maggie   We must get to the boats.

Everyone is swept forward and then back, as a great tidal wave hits.

Furniture is swept about the stage, people struggle to cling to their possessions. Others fight for their lives.

The three **Maggie**s *emerge from the chaos in a boat. All three row frantically, their hair streaming and wet.*

First Maggie   We must get to the mill.

All Three   Mother. Tom.

Third Maggie   Oh, God, where are we? Which is the way home?

They keep rowing with all their strength.

Second Maggie   Keep going.

Third Maggie   There's something coming towards us. It's part of a house. It's too big . . .

There is a huge thundering sound as it passes close to them. The boat rocks. They go on.

First Maggie   Look for the roof of the mill. There's the tops of the firs.

Second Maggie   There!

They have reached the mill.

Third Maggie *(crying above the noise)*   Tom, where are you? Mother? It's Maggie.

Tom *(from the attic)*   Who is it? Have you brought a boat?

Third Maggie   It's Maggie. Where's mother?

Tom   Not here.

He starts to climb down to her. **First Maggie** *is held up to help him. He descends safely to the boat.*

You're alone.

First Maggie   Yes, Tom. God has taken care of me to bring me to you. Is there anyone else?

Tom   No.

Tom *takes an oar and they begin to row. Their eyes are locked. He is in awe of her courage. He cannot think how to say it.*

Magsie!

There is the thundering sound of something heading towards them. A voice that sounds like their father cries out in the darkness. 'Get out of the current.' **Tom** *tries to respond but it is too late.*

It is coming, Maggie!

They let go of the oars and all four cling together.

They are hit. They are broken apart. **Second** *and* **Third Maggie**s *are swept away.* **Tom** *and* **First Maggie** *struggle to stay together, choking as the water rises above them.* **Maggie** *is hauled up to the platform by the crowd. She screams.* **Tom** *fights his way towards her under the water. She is ducked. (As the woman was in Scene One.)*

We hear the sound of the deaf rage.

As **Tom** *reaches her,* **Maggie** *stops resisting. Their hands clasp. Brother and sister die together.*

A strange calm descends. It grows light. There is the sound of the river running gently by.

On the upper platform, **Stephen** *and* **Phillip** *enter and look down sadly at* **Maggie** *and* **Tom**.

Second *and* **Third Maggie**s *enter.* **Second Maggie** *goes to* **Phillip**, **Third Maggie** *to* **Stephen**. *They take their hands.*

End.

Helen Edmundson was born in Liverpool in 1964 and
spent her childhood in the Wirral and in Chester. After
studying drama at Manchester University, she gained wide
acting, directing and devising experience with the female
agit-prop company, Red Stockings. Her first solo writing
attempt, *Ladies in the Lift*, a musical comedy, was created
specifically for the company in 1988. On leaving, she worked
as an actress in various north-west theatres and on television.
Her first play, *Flying*, was presented at the Royal National
Theatre Studio in 1990. Other work includes: two short
television films, *One Day* (BBC, 1991) and *Stella* (Channel 4,
1992); *Anna Karenina*, which won a Time Out Award and
Theatre Managers' Association Award for Best Touring
Production (adapted for Shared Experience Theatre, 1992);
The Clearing, joint winner of the John Whiting Award (Bush
Theatre, London, 1993); *The Mill on the Floss* (adapted for
Shared Experience Theatre, 1994); *War and Peace* (adapted
for a Royal National Theatre and Shared Experience co-
production, 1996). She lives in west London with her
husband, actor Jonathan Oliver, and son, Edwin.

Methuen Modern Plays

include work by

Jean Anouilh
John Arden
Margaretta D'Arcy
Peter Barnes
Sebastian Barry
Brendan Behan
Edward Bond
Bertolt Brecht
Howard Brenton
Simon Burke
Jim Cartwright
Caryl Churchill
Noël Coward
Sarah Daniels
Nick Dear
Shelagh Delaney
David Edgar
Dario Fo
Michael Frayn
John Godber
Paul Godfrey
John Guare
Peter Handke
Jonathan Harvey
Iain Heggie
Declan Hughes
Terry Johnson
Barrie Keeffe
Stephen Lowe
Doug Lucie

John McGrath
David Mamet
Patrick Marber
Arthur Miller
Mtwa, Ngema & Simon
Tom Murphy
Phyllis Nagy
Peter Nichols
Joseph O'Connor
Joe Orton
Louise Page
Joe Penhall
Luigi Pirandello
Stephen Poliakoff
Franca Rame
Philip Ridley
Reginald Rose
David Rudkin
Willy Russell
Jean-Paul Sartre
Sam Shepard
Wole Soyinka
C. P. Taylor
Theatre de Complicite
Theatre Workshop
Sue Townsend
Judy Upton
Timberlake Wertenbaker
Victoria Wood

Methuen World Classics

Aeschylus (two volumes)
Jean Anouilh
John Arden (two volumes)
Arden & D'Arcy
Aristophanes (two volumes)
Aristophanes & Menander
Brendan Behan
Aphra Behn
Edward Bond (four volumes)
Bertolt Brecht
  (five volumes)
Büchner
Bulgakov
Calderón
Anton Chekhov
Noël Coward (five volumes)
Sarah Daniels (two volumes)
Eduardo De Filippo
David Edgar (three volumes)
Euripides (three volumes)
Dario Fo (two volumes)
Michael Frayn (two volumes)
Max Frisch
Gorky
Harley Granville Barker
  (two volumes)
Henrik Ibsen (six volumes)
Terry Johnson
Lorca (three volumes)

Marivaux
Mustapha Matura
David Mercer (two volumes)
Arthur Miller
  (five volumes)
Anthony Minghella
Molière
Tom Murphy
  (three volumes)
Musset
Peter Nichols (two volumes)
Clifford Odets
Joe Orton
Louise Page
A. W. Pinero
Luigi Pirandello
Stephen Poliakoff
  (two volumes)
Terence Rattigan
Ntozake Shange
Sophocles (two volumes)
Wole Soyinka
David Storey (two volumes)
August Strindberg
  (three volumes)
J. M. Synge
Ramón del Valle-Inclán
Frank Wedekind
Oscar Wilde

Methuen Student Editions